The Fractured Church

Denominations and the will of God

By Bill Sizemore

Dedication and Acknowledgments

*T*hanks, first of all, to Andy, who prompted me to begin this project and continued to encourage me and urge me on throughout. Thanks to Randy, Courtney, Jay, Marc, Bob, Jan and Terry for enabling me to keep my focus on the work at hand. Thanks to Kathy, Joni, Michaela, Daniel, Mike, Steven, and Pastor Dick for helping so much with the editing of the manuscript.

Thanks to my beautiful, intelligent, and faithful wife Cindy, who has stood beside me for more than two decades now, through thick and thin (make that "lots of thin") and for the past year and a half headed off to work every day, so we could eat and stay warm while I concentrated on this book.

Most of all, I offer my most humble thanks to the Lord Jesus Christ for whose sake I did my best to convey the harm and grief which stem from church division and the hope, the blessing, and the spiritual power which will someday be the fruits of true Christian unity. Let any shortcomings exhibited herein fall upon me and my limited abilities, and let all glory for the good stuff be to His name only! May your followers all be one, Lord Jesus, just as You asked.

The Fractured Church

Table of Contents

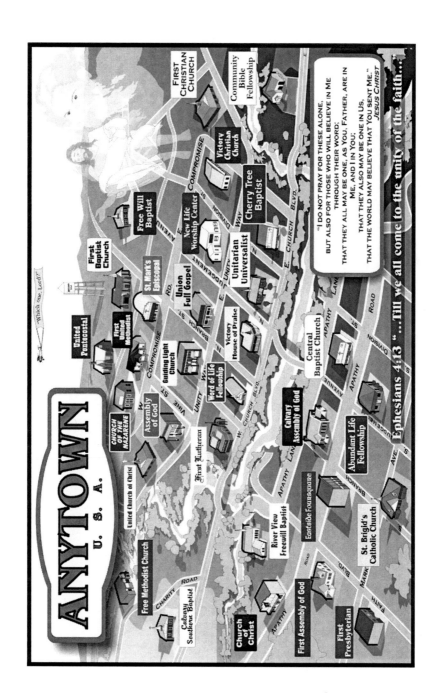

ANYTOWN U. S. A.

"Which one, Lord?"

"I DO NOT PRAY FOR THESE ALONE,
BUT ALSO FOR THOSE WHO WILL BELIEVE IN ME
THROUGH THEIR WORD;
THAT THEY ALL MAY BE ONE, AS YOU, FATHER, ARE IN
ME, AND I IN YOU;
THAT THEY ALSO MAY BE ONE IN US,
THAT THE WORLD MAY BELIEVE THAT YOU SENT ME."
JESUS CHRIST

Ephesians 4:13 "...Till we all come to the unity of the faith..."

Out of the mouths of babes...

It was Easter morning, crisp but sunny, and the Peterson family was loaded into the family van, heading down the driveway, and on their way to church, fifteen minutes away.

The Petersons didn't tend to dress up much for Sunday services. It wasn't expected where they attended, which was one of the reasons they had settled on Grace Assembly.

But today was Easter Sunday, and mother Karen knew from experience that most of the folks would be dressed a little nicer than usual, so she made sure her family looked at least good enough for the occasion. She'd even tried talking husband Richard into wearing a tie. That didn't happen, but he had run the van through the car wash. Tie or no tie, Richard Peterson was not about to have the dirtiest car in the church parking lot on Easter Sunday.

The three teenage girls were busy in the middle seat, texting away on their cell phones. Richard and Karen were occupying the captains' chairs up front, both caught up in their own thoughts, not saying much.

Suddenly, eight year old Eric yelled, "Look!" from the far back seat, as though he had made an exciting discovery. Karen turned quickly and saw young Eric tapping his fingers hard against the rear window.

"Hey, Dad!" he yelled.

"Look at all those people going into that church over there. The sign says First *Babdist* Church. Why don't we go there? It's lots closer. Why drive clear cross town when there's a church right by our house?"

The girls continued texting. They never bothered to look up; Eric was just excited and asking questions as usual.

Richard glanced over at the throngs of neatly dressed people pouring into the 1st Baptist Church. Men in suits and ties and women in flowery hats were filing through the door with fresh scrubbed kids in tow.

Richard knew the church was there, close to their house. He had passed it countless times, but never really paid much attention to it. Under his breath he wondered if he would be the only one in church this morning not sporting a tie.

The church was a one story brick building. In the middle of the roof was a shiny white steeple with a cross high atop it. The sign out front said "1st Baptist," sure enough, but the building reminded Richard of a Mormon church. The design and architecture were almost identical to many of the Mormon churches he had seen.

Truth be told, Richard had never even noticed the sign out front. He had always just assumed that the church was LDS, because it looked like one.

"Humph," Richard mumbled under his breath. "That is a Baptist church.

"We're not Baptists, Son," Richard yelled back at his son. His tone had sounded just a little harder than he had intended.

"What's a *Babdist*, Dad? Are they bad or somethin'? Are *Babdists* Christians, like us?" Eric continued. "Or do they believe in John the *Babdist* instead of Jesus?"

Eric's questions came rapid fire, the last one raising Karen's eyebrows.

"Well, yeah. I guess they're Christians alright. They believe in Jesus just like we do, but they don't believe the same as we do regarding some other things."

"What kind of things?" Eric persisted. "I would like to know. Hey, there's Timmy Clark. He must be a *Babdist*. I didn't know he went to church. He's in my class at school."

"It's complicated, Eric," Richard replied. "Baptists believe the same things we do about things like Jesus dying on the cross for our sins and being raised from the dead and all that, but they don't believe in the baptism of the Holy Spirit. Well, at least not like we do."

"Is that why we don't like 'em, Dad, 'cause they don't believe in the baptism of the Holy Spirit?"

Karen glanced over at her husband.

"I didn't say we didn't like 'em, Eric. I just said we don't believe everything the same as they do."

Richard was a little surprised at the nature of the conversation his eight year old son had initiated.

"If we like 'em and if they're Christians, then why do we drive right by 'em on the way to church and not even stop and talk?" Eric asked.

But before his dad could reply...

"Hey, look Dad, there's another church. It says, 'Our Savior's *Luthern*.' That's a cool looking church. Why don't we go there? Do we like *Lutherns*?"

"Sure, we like Lutherans. Well, some of them anyway. Maybe we could talk about this some other time, Eric, when we have more time."

Karen chuckled. "You might have your hands full with this topic, hon. There are probably five or six more churches on our way to Grace Assembly. He's going to ask you about every one, you know."

Richard nodded as Karen continued.

"I am a little troubled by Eric's impression that we don't like the people who go to those other churches. I wonder where he got that idea."

The family had driven this same route to church every Sunday for more than a year now, but for some reason today was the day eight-year old Eric Peterson chose to start asking questions about things even grownups rarely discuss.

As a matter of fact, that Easter morning the Peterson family passed seven additional churches on their way to Grace Assembly. Each one prompted a new question from the eight year old riding alone in the back seat.

"What do United *Methodusts* believe, Dad? Are they Christians?"

"Good question, Eric," was all Dad Peterson said.

Sixteen year old Chris looked up from her texting. "You know," she said, "we have a boy in youth group who just came here from Africa. I think he said it was a United Methodist Church he went to there, but it was a lot different from the one here, which is why he started coming to our youth group." Chris went back to her texting.

"Hey, there's another one," It was like Eric was on an Easter egg hunt. Every church he spotted was an exciting new prize.

"Dad, do we like Jesus Christ of *Ladder* Day Saints? Boy, they are really dressed up."

There was no reply from the driver's seat. Chris, oldest of the three girls, started to say something, but when her phone vibrated, she went back to her social life.

"Hey, Dad, that church over on Mom's side looks closed. Why doesn't anyone go to the Seventh Day *Advenust* church? The parking lot is completely empty! Don't they know it's Easter?"

There were a lot of churches close together on this stretch, so Eric's questions were hardly out of his mouth before he'd spot another one.

"Hey Dad, there's another *Luthern* Church. The sign says something about Missouri. This isn't Missouri. How come there's two *Luthern* churches so close together anyway? That's kind of weird, isn't it?

"Look at that one. It's has pretty fancy windows. Who is 'Our Lady of Sorrows?' That's a weird name for a church. Why is the lady sad anyway?"

The Peterson family was almost to Grace Assembly. Only a few more blocks to go. For some reason, the drive had seemed longer than usual.

"Hey, look at that one. It's called the 'Church of God.' And, there's one right beside it that's called the Church of Christ. How would somebody know which one to go to? If you like God more than Jesus, I guess you would go to the Church of God, huh Dad?"

Karen smiled as Richard ignored the last series of questions.

Finally, the Peterson van pulled into the parking lot of Grace Assembly.

"You sure have a lot of questions this morning, Eric," Karen said, as she unbuckled her seatbelt. Richard was carefully maneuvering the van into a parking space that was just a little narrower than he preferred.

"What brought all that on, Eric? We drive the same way to church every Sunday."

"I dunno," Eric replied. "I never noticed that there were so many other churches."

Eric had always been a rather inquisitive child, but for some reason this morning's topic seemed a little heavier than normal. Maybe it was just a curiosity thing with young Eric; be that as it may, the topic had made Richard Peterson think about some things he had not pondered before - at least, not for a long time.

Who were all those people going to all those other churches, he asked himself? Some were probably every bit as Christian as the folks he and Karen knew and loved here at Grace Assembly.

Somehow, merely by driving by all those churches Sunday after Sunday, often without so much as a glance in their direction, he and Karen had given their young son the impression that *we don't like 'em*.

The Petersons quickly made their way up the walk and into Grace Assembly. Judging by how full the parking lot was, it might be hard to find six seats together in the main sanctuary and no one wanted to sit in the overflow room and watch the Easter service on closed circuit television.

The song service was just beginning as they squeezed in front of the people already seated in the very back row. No time to look for better seats closer to the front, not this morning. The whole church was filling rapidly.

Richard made a mental note that about half the men were not wearing ties. He felt just a little relieved.

The music started just as they sat down, so they immediately stood back up. The song leader led in his deep baritone voice, "We serve a risen Savior. He's in the world today…" The whole congregation sang out loudly, most without looking at the words on the overhead screen.

Maybe it was a coincidence or maybe it was a *God thing*, but after the song service ended, the Scripture reading was out of Paul's first Epistle to the Corinthians. The passage was an admonition from the apostle Paul not to allow any divisions amongst believers. It didn't really seem like an Easter verse to Richard.

When the reading was over, the elder who had read the passage remarked briefly that it was important that members love one another and make sure, if one has any grievances with any brothers and sisters, to go to them and make things right, "so we can all maintain a spirit of unity in the church."

His remarks referred to the brothers and sisters at Grace Assembly, but this morning Richard Peterson was for the first time thinking larger than that. His son's words, on the way to church that morning, were still haunting him a bit.

Richard knew he didn't have any cause for division with other members at Grace Assembly, at least not at the moment. But what if the passage was talking about a bigger picture? He wasn't sure what to think about that. He had never thought of division as something to be avoided outside the walls of their own local church.

But what if God did? Richard thought to himself. *What if God really doesn't like the fact that the Baptists and the Pentecostals were barely on speaking terms? What if God didn't like the fact that they both used the same Bible, but disagreed strongly on what it means? What if God was displeased that many churches in town were not on speaking terms with each other?*

As usual, the Peterson's went out to eat after church. That afternoon, the route home from the restaurant took them down different streets and through different neighborhoods than those they had traversed earlier.

Young Eric never said a word about the eleven churches they passed as they rode home. Evidently, his curious mind had moved on and his attention was elsewhere.

But Richard noticed every one of them. There was a Presbyterian church, a Freewill Baptist, a Kingdom Hall, a Saint Mark's Episcopal, a Pentecostal Church of God, a Church of the Nazarene, a Free Methodist church, a Calvary Chapel, and three others with more local sounding names that did not seem to be affiliated with any particular denomination.

Richard knew from memory that there were many other churches in town besides the ones they passed that day. There was the big Foursquare Church on the west side of town and City Church, which was also quite large. There were at least two other Baptist churches that he knew of, and he was pretty sure there were lots of other churches he had never even noticed.

There they were, scattered all over town, never talking to one another, never worshipping together, and probably disagreeing over what likely were some fairly substantive issues. But were the people in those other churches Christians? Did they worship the same God? Were they saved by the same blood of Christ? Were they brothers and sisters in the Lord?

Richard found himself thinking about these things the entire way home.

Just for curiosity's sake, after the van was squared away in the garage back home, he went to the kitchen counter and looked up *churches* in the yellow pages of the local phone book. He was at sixty-three when he stopped counting. Obviously, there were a lot more churches in town than he had realized!

"And this town isn't even that big," he mumbled to himself as he laid the phonebook back on the counter.

"If I was thinking about God for the first time and wanting to go to church, but had never gone to one before, how would I choose which one to go to? They all have different names. They all believe a little or even a lot differently than the others," he whispered. "And some of these churches probably, in spite of their names, aren't even Christian, not really.

This can't be a good thing, can it, Lord? Richard thought to himself, staring at the phone book. *Your church is fractured into a thousand pieces and I can't help but wonder how displeased you must be.*

Richard was surprised by the sudden wave of uneasiness he felt. He had never paid serious attention to all of those other churches before, but here he was standing in the kitchen in his own home feeling guilty about something, and he wasn't quite sure why.

Karen walked into the room and reached into one of the cupboards beside the sink for a glass.

"What're ya doin'?" she said softly. "Is something wrong?"

"Yeah, maybe," was all Richard could say. "Yeah, maybe."

Before he went to bed that night, Richard Peterson went on line and Googled the word "denomination." He didn't always trust Wikipedia, but that site was close to the top of the page, so he clicked on it. Thirty-eight thousand! That's what the site said. There are reported to be approximately 38,000 Christian denominations, large and small.

Richard logged off the computer and changed into his pajamas. He eventually drifted off to sleep, asking God, *Is that possible, Lord? Is your church really broken into that many pieces?*

Tossed to and fro like children

The deeper one delves into the topic of church unity, the more humbling the subject becomes; not humbling in a good way, but more in an embarrassing way. This is especially true when we examine the primary reason for our divisions; disagreements regarding doctrine. Doctrinally, we Christians are a confused lot.

With all of our twenty-first century sophistication and scholarly understanding of linguistics; with two thousand years of theological study and commentary at our disposal; and with an abundance of seminaries taught by learned professors with PhDs after their names, when it comes to the issue of church doctrine, we are but children.

This may be a difficult pill to swallow and some may resent such a blunt assessment, but the indictment is not really mine; it's the apostle Paul's. To put it plainly, it is hard to imagine us handling doctrine with less spiritual maturity than the church does today. Let's consider the evidence.

In one of the passages we will explore in greater depth later on, the apostle Paul informs the Church at Ephesus that the purpose for which Jesus Christ gave the church apostles, prophets, evangelists, pastors, and teachers was to equip believers for the work of the ministry…*so that we would no longer be children tossed to and fro and carried about with every wind of doctrine.*

It is apparent from this passage that it is a defining characteristic of an immature church that it is tossed to and fro and blown about by winds of doctrine. Paul is not talking here about individual people or individual churches, but the church collectively – for he uses broad language. He says, "till we <u>all</u> come to the unity of the faith..." and are no longer tossed to and fro and blown about like children. (Ephesians 4:13)

Now step back and ask yourself this question: Is it not fair to state that the primary reason the Christian church today has thousands of denominations and countless independent churches is because we do not agree with one another regarding what is right doctrine?

Oh sure, many of us as individuals are confident in what we believe and are not easily swayed by what others say. But is that a sign of church maturity? Is it even a sign of personal maturity? It might be, if the doctrines about which we are certain are essential ones, matters about which Christians everywhere are in agreement. There are, of course, matters of faith that we should all hold confidently. We should all be certain, for example, that Jesus Christ is the only begotten Son of God, that He died on the cross for our sin, and that He literally rose from the dead and ascended back to the Father in heaven. Mature Christians should be unmovable in their convictions regarding these essential beliefs and so should every local church. Such things are not really debatable among Christians.

However, we do not have churches scattered all over our towns, all with different names and all worshipping separately, because we agree with one another. We worship separately because we disagree. We disagree because we have been blown about and tossed to and fro all over the theological map, primarily by one thing, the winds of doctrine. Can anyone deny this? No matter how certain we are as individuals, it is a defining characteristic of contemporary Christianity that Christian churches do not agree with one another.

We do not worship separately so that we can better win the lost, as some suggest. We meet in separate buildings and bear separate names because we do not believe the same things. Doctrinal disagreements are, without a doubt, the primary reason the church of Jesus Christ is fractured into thousands of pieces.

How the world sees us

As you read these words, your mind may be putting up defenses, but perhaps your perspective is too narrow. It is easy for us to gauge the condition of the body of Christ solely by the condition of the local church we attend. We do this reflexively because most of us have little comprehension of how many other churches there are in town and how separated we are from the believers who attend them. Most of us have no idea what those other churches believe or how they came to conclusions so different from ours.

We shall see later in this study that we are meant to be in fellowship with all of the believers in our geographical area. We are meant to be joined with them and vitally connected to them because, in truth, we cannot succeed in our mission and cannot grow to maturity apart from them. We shall see that it is the will of God that we value believers from other churches, that we esteem them and serve them as if our lives depended on our connection to them.

This is not a pipe dream. Jesus wanted this and prayed specifically for it. The apostles admonished us in the New Testament to make this our goal, but we have ignored the words of Jesus and his apostles. We sit in our separate churches, walled in from all those other believers, somehow fully content and comfortable in our seclusion.

We may be blind to our divisions, but I assure you, others are not. The world sees us much differently than we see ourselves. We go about life as if we have it all together, confident that what we believe is right, confident that we are mature and knowledgeable regarding matters of faith. We are impressed with ourselves and our spiritual condition, because we are, after all, the people of God, right?

This is not how the world sees us. The world sees Christians as a bunch of religious people who don't like each other very much, and in fact, are so much at odds with one another that they won't even worship under the same roof. The world sees the church as pretty messed up. The world judges our God by what it sees in us, and frankly, the picture we show them by our divisions and dissension is a gross distortion of reality. In fact, the God we show them by our actions is not all that impressive.

Remember what Richard Peterson did in the opening chapter after he had noticed all those other churches for the first time? Maybe you should try that. Open up your local yellow pages and look up "churches." What you will see on display there is a snapshot of how the world sees us. They see lots of strange and sometimes meaningless names for dozens or maybe even hundreds of "Christian" churches, all of which, for some reason, refuse to be called by the same name and want to make it clear to everyone that they are not alike.

An interested newcomer or searching soul would not have the foggiest idea how to pick one of those churches to attend. If you stop and think about it, how could they? How could they even begin to know which one was right? In some cities, it would take a person five to ten years to visit all the churches in town, if he was so dedicated in his search that he attended a different church every week!

This fact is much more debilitating than many of us realize. Our state of disunity is a serious stumbling block for those on the outside looking in. Our divisions literally keep them from believing. More specifically, our disunity prevents the world from knowing that Jesus Christ really is the Son of God, sent to us by the Father in heaven. Jesus said some powerful things about this principle in a passage we shall explore later on.

All in all, if someone was attempting to indict the modern day church for being children, in the negative sense of the word, the evidence at their disposal would be plentiful; all it would take is a phone book or a computer search engine.

Of course, it is hard for us to think of ourselves as children, as immature; especially if we have been believers for several decades. The apostle Paul, however, is writing of the body of Christ, and in that context it is apparent that you and I cannot reach maturity alone. Let that sink in for a moment. You will never truly be mature on your own, not in the sense the apostle Paul described in Ephesians 4. You can't do it and your church can't do it, at least not apart from other believers in your area. It is simply not possible.

Sure, we can grow. We can increase in our understanding of spiritual things. However, none of us, by ourselves, can attain to the measure that the apostle Paul described. It is simply too great for us. It is, by its very nature, a corporate project that we can only accomplish together.

God has placed the bar much higher than many realize

For a moment, let's consider how high the bar has been placed. Paul says in Ephesians 4 that together we are to reach the *measure of the stature of the fullness of Christ*. Don't pass over those words quickly. Consider their literal meaning. *The stature of the fullness of Christ*. Is that even possible? How could the church ever reach such a level of maturity? The very thought is mindboggling. We cannot wrap our minds around it. Our first reaction is to assume that this passage must mean something else.

But it doesn't mean something else. It means what it says and the fact that it sounds impossible should only suggest that *we* cannot do it. *The measure of the stature of the fullness of Christ* is a standard so high that only the Holy Spirit can get us there.

This level of maturity is more than the Baptists or the Methodists or the Pentecostals can pull off by themselves. The Presbyterians and the Lutherans can't do it. Neither can the charismatics. It will require all hands on deck, humbly on deck. It will require that all parts of the body of Christ be properly connected, not scattered to the four winds by divisive doctrinal differences. It will require Baptists learning from and receiving from Pentecostals and vice versa. It will require Lutherans, Methodists, Presbyterians and charismatics all sharing freely what they uniquely have and each receiving humbly from the others those things which only they can supply.

The notion that denominational churches would someday acknowledge that they desperately need one another may seem entirely foreign to us. We are so accustomed to thinking and speaking in our echo chambers, in our own ecclesiastical worlds where almost everyone agrees with us, that we hear no discord - not because there is none, but because we have moved it away from us. We have learned to do this routinely and as a matter of course.

It is generally recognized that if someone disagrees strongly with what we say and do at our church, they should be wise enough, classy enough, and gracious enough to go find another church, one where their views will be welcomed. If they are gone, they can't violate our *pretend* sense of unity, the unity we maintain by isolating ourselves from believers with different opinions.

Pretend unity; that's where we are today. Our pet doctrines and varying opinions have blown us about and tossed us to and fro until we have eventually landed in hundreds of different ports, comfortable places where we need not have contact with all those other Christians with their "inferior beliefs" and confusing practices.

We don't realize that in living in isolation from one another we are being children. Our churches have become our sandboxes. They are places where we can meet with our friends, play only with the people we want to play with, and ignore all the other children. Sure, we welcome God to come and be with us in our sandboxes, and because we are His kids, the Holy Spirit comes and visits us - and because He is there, we assume that we must be okay.

But we are not okay. The fact that God loves us just as we are today, should not lead us to believe that it is okay with Him that we live in a perpetual state of discord with His other kids, other believers for whom Christ also died. If we thought long and hard about it, we would recognize that our divisions, which we excuse so easily, are actually contrary to the very nature of God. They displease Him because they are so unlike Him, and because they hinder His highest purposes for us.

It may take a while for all this to sink in. It may take some time for the scales to fall from our eyes, but that is what must happen. We must begin to see divisions as God sees them. That is what this book is about.

What this book is not about

Over the past few decades, several books have been written on the subject of ecumenicalism, or church unity. Most have been written *by* scholars and *for* scholars. This is not that kind of book. I will not try to impress you with clever phrases or high sounding intellectualism. My goal is simply to impart to you a vision for something that at the moment you probably do not believe is possible.

Hopefully, this study will stir your heart and help you recognize the damage that denominationalism and other forms of church division are doing to the body of Christ. This must be our starting point. Before we can move forward, we must first become deeply dissatisfied with the current condition of the Christian church.

Mere dissatisfaction is, of course, not the end goal, but the first step. As the Scripture says, "Godly sorrow leads to repentance." The process of change goes like this: First, we see the sin of division for what it is. Next, we become grieved by what we see, and finally, we turn away from the thing that now repulses us and walk in the opposite direction. The first step, however, must be to have our eyes opened - for it is our blindness to our condition which keeps us ensnared.

Most who have written on the topic of church unity appear to have had as their goal to encourage Christians from all "faith traditions," to learn to get along better and recognize that we are all part of the same body of Christ. Of course, not all "faith traditions" are truly what they say; some are more *non-faith* traditions than faith traditions. Perhaps getting along better with these churches is neither realistic nor advisable. We will address this issue at length in a later chapter.

Be that as it may, it goes without saying that getting along better and being more respectful to other genuinely Christian churches would be progress, but this book is not about getting along better. This book is not about being more polite to one another or learning to *disagree more agreeably*, though those are obviously good things.

This study is about more than that. It is about bringing the church of Jesus Christ to a place of true, lasting unity, a biblical unity wherein we are all of the *same mind and judgment and all speak the same thing*. It is about coming to the place where Christians are known to one another and to the world only by the name of Christ, not as Baptists, Methodists, Episcopalians, Presbyterians, Pentecostals, Lutherans, and so on.

Tolerating one another and acting civilly toward one another is evidence of good manners, not unity. Civil behavior alone will not set us apart from the world. Unbelievers living in a polite society are perfectly capable of disagreeing agreeably. That does not make them one.

So, make no mistake about it, we are aiming higher than something mere men can do. It is genuine Christian unity that we are after. I am convinced that this is the kind of unity *the Lord is after*.

As we shall see in a later chapter, the kind of unity the Lord intends for us is so powerful that it is akin to a nuclear weapon. This is not an overstatement. Genuine unity is the most powerful force known to man. And yet, for all the power unity will bring, we must not seek unity for that reason or come in the self-serving spirit of Simon the Magician.[1] We must seek unity for the Lord's sake and none other's.

We must come to desire unity simply because Jesus desired it and prayed earnestly for it. We must desire unity because it is the will of God that we become like Him and that we reflect His true image to the world rather than the warped image we are now portraying.

The walls that divide us are of our own making

It is the underlying premise of this study that the Lord wants the church of Jesus Christ to become one, perfectly one, and that He hates the divisions which have left His church fractured into countless pieces. For that reason, we will adopt a "take no prisoners" approach to church unity. Our aim will be to end all forms of denominationalism and to rid the church of the spirit that led us into this confusing labyrinth of 38,000 disparate denominations.

This book is about breaking down the barriers that keep us divided, whether they are blatant sectarianism, denominational names, doctrinal differences, or merely unhealthy emphases on certain teachings and practices. Whatever divides Christian brother from Christian brother and Christian church from Christian church must be given up and placed on the block.

One thoughtful author, writing about the subject of church unity, described the divided condition of the church today as *an egg that had been scrambled*. The author logically concluded that a scrambled egg cannot be unscrambled. In the natural, he was, of course, correct. But never mind what cannot be done in the natural. This book is about unscrambling the egg.

Having made that clear, let's not underestimate the challenge before us. Looking around us at the condition of the Christian church today, with dozens or even hundreds of different churches in each metropolitan area, it may be hard to imagine them ever coming together in any real and lasting sense, but that indeed is where we are headed.

The curse of spiritual blindness

Our differences, however, are not our first problem. The bigger challenge is the fact that we do not seem to be aware that we are not okay as we are. Here and there we find believers who are grieved by our disunity, but there is little evidence that most Christians are even aware of our divisions, much less bothered by them. There is a valid reason for this. To most Christians, a divided church is as natural as water is to a fish. Division is the environment we live in. It's the way things are. A world full of denominations and church dissension seems entirely natural to us - for we have known no other way.

Have you ever been around a family that fights and argues all the time? Sometimes, they are not even aware that they are doing it. It is simply the way they have learned to interact. They might even miss the fighting, if it ceased, and have no idea how else to act. Our condition is the same. We are terribly divided and yet rarely think about it. We were born into it. We do not feel badly about our condition, because it is all we have ever known. How can we be aware of something that is all around us...like the air?

This blindness to our condition must come to an end. If a unified body of Christ is the will of God, if genuine Christian unity is something for which Jesus specifically prayed; how can we pretend that our disunity is unimportant? How can we think that disunity does not hurt us or keep us from accomplishing the will of God and enjoying His full blessing? Surely, it must.

If divisions within the church are expressly prohibited by Scripture, how can we continue to ignore them as if they were acceptable or unimportant? How can we defend our divisions or even justify them, as some attempt to do?

There comes a time when each of us must ask ourselves this question: Do I believe the Word of God, or do I not? Do I believe that God can do all things or do I believe that there are some things simply too hard, even for Him? Perhaps the notion that the Lord will bring the body of Christ to a place of perfect unity and unto *the measure of the stature of the fullness of Christ* challenges your faith. If so, then let it. Let it stretch you and expand your vision.

Sometimes, we have to step forward and say, "Let the Word of God be true and every man a liar." If the Lord has spoken in his Word of a body of Christ that lives and functions in perfect unity, then it will come to pass. If one generation will not embrace the promise and believe for it, the Lord will raise up a generation that will.

In a couple of chapters, we shall go with the apostle Paul on a fictional visit to a city of Corinth that is much like us. In that chapter, we will get a sense of how Paul would have responded if churches in ancient Corinth had behaved the way Christian churches behave today. Hopefully, we shall be as shaken by what we see there as the apostle Paul would have been.

As difficult as it may be to grasp the idea that all of the denominational barriers are going to come down and that all true followers of the Lord Jesus Christ will be of the same mind and judgment and will all speak the same thing, if that is what the Lord intends for His body, then we must embrace that vision. We have no choice. If He desires it, we must desire it and pray for it to come to pass.

Are the giants simply too big?

Undoubtedly, some will say that I am speaking of an impossibility. Some readers have pondered church unity before and have concluded that it is simply too hard and can't be done. In a sense, they are like the children of Israel in the wilderness. They too were afraid to enter the Promised Land because of the giants that stood between them and their inheritance. The giants were too tall and the cities too fortified, so the people of God trembled in fear. They were so overwhelmed by their fear of the Canaanites that they begged to return to the slavery of Egypt. Ten of the twelve men who had been sent to spy out the land returned with what the Bible calls an evil report. They convinced the people that Israel could not take the Promised Land, even if their God had promised to deliver it into their hands.

That is where the church stands today. It is every bit as difficult for us to believe for church unity as it was for that tiny nation of former slaves to believe they could conquer seven powerful Canaanite nations dwelling in walled cities. Well, we know how that story ended. The generation which refused to believe the promise perished in the wilderness, and forty years later the next generation went in and possessed the land.

It is likely that some readers won't want to go where this book leads. They have embraced denominationalism as a natural thing, seeing denominations, not so much as prohibited divisions, but more like separate tribes. They have concluded that as Israel was divided into twelve tribes, so is the church. To them, divisions are a natural thing, a sign of healthy diversity.

Denominations are not like the 12 tribes of Israel

The problem with this "tribe" analogy is that it breaks down all too quickly in the light of Scripture. True, there were twelve distinct tribes in Old Testament Israel, but that's where the comparison ends. There was only one religion and one belief system in Israel. No tribe was free to set up its own religious hierarchy. No tribe was free to create or adopt its own doctrines or practices. No tribe in Israel was free to create its own articles of faith or ordain its own priests. All twelve tribes had to do things according to the precise pattern God had revealed to Moses on the mount. In other words, in Israel tribal diversities ended at the tabernacle gate.

Unlike today's denominations, the twelve tribes of Israel were established by God. Their beginnings are laid out clearly in Scripture. When the nation of Israel traveled and when it camped, it was ordered in a manner commanded by the Lord himself, with the various tribes appointed to specific locations surrounding the Tabernacle. Denominations on the other hand were not established by God. The opposite is true. Denominations are divisions and God expressly prohibits divisions within the Christian church. Denominations believe different things, something entirely forbidden in ancient Israel. Denominations do not move together as one. In fact, some do not move at all, but have remained camped where they were decades or even centuries ago. Finally, denominations waste God's resources, both of money and manpower, a fact which will become increasingly clear as we proceed.

Then there is what I call the "rose colored glasses" view of denominationalism. Those espousing this view claim that denominational divisions have served to further spread the gospel. According to this view, as each denomination works to extend its own reach and influence, it spreads the gospel of Christ everywhere it goes. This view is so troublesome that an entire chapter has been devoted to refuting it. If you subscribe to this view, please place it on a back burner and continue reading. Decide for yourself later whether it has withstood the scrutiny to which we will subject it.

The more closely one studies denominational divisions and how they came about, the more one realizes how high the walls between many churches are - and how tall the giants which stand in our way. When we come to that point, we have two choices. We can either throw up our hands and shout, "Not even God could fix this mess," or we can say as Joshua and Caleb said when the ten doubting spies returned with their evil report: "Sure, there are giants in the land, *but they will be bread for us.*" These two men of faith did not stagger in unbelief; they simply believed what God had said.

The giants that stand in the way of the body of Christ coming together will be bread for us. The contrary doctrines, the crippling traditions, the pride and self interest, the sectarian spirit, the propensity for kingdom building, and the belief that my church is the right one; all of these giants must fall. Unless we are going to ignore all of the passages of Scripture that condemn church division, we must come to believe that God will root it out of His church and free us from its debilitating effects.

Later on, in two separate chapters, we will consider the various obstacles which must be overcome for unity to occur. Some of these might be challenging for some readers. For example, a misguided or incomplete doctrine regarding the end times will be a major challenge for those believers who have been expecting a hasty exit out of this world before the tribulation and the antichrist system and all that comes with that particular view of eschatology. It just may be possible that your end times doctrine does not include all of what God says must occur at the end of the age. I hope you will be open to at least considering that possibility.

Once we come to understand that church unity must come to pass, the only question remaining is: How? Will unity come by means of widespread repentance and revival or will it come by way of persecution? This is a serious matter and we will talk more about it later on, towards the end of the book.

I do not pretend to know the time table for all this to occur. Considering our current condition, it might take some time. It is my goal here simply to persuade you, from the Word of God, that unity will occur, that it must, and to suggest some things you and I can do right now to further the cause of unity within the body of Christ. Not unity for unity's sake; but unity for our Lord's sake; unity because the Lord desires it, commands it, and promises to bless us in it.

We must, however, keep one thing in the forefront of our thinking as we proceed. It was Jesus who said, "*I will build my church* and the gates of hell shall not prevail against it."[2] We must not lose sight of this fact. The Lord Jesus Christ is the one building His church; not us. What we could never do, He can and will do. No matter how impossible church unity might seem to us, He can bring it to pass. Our job is to decide whether we are going to believe Him.

As I look around me, I am fully persuaded that the fractured church we see today is not what Jesus had in mind when He prayed the following prayer just before going to the cross:

"I do not ask for these only, but also for those who will believe in me through their word, that they may all be one, just as you, Father, are in me, and I in you, that they also may be in us, so that the world may believe that you have sent me." (John 17)

These are powerful words. The last clause of this passage suggests that the way to ensure that the world will know that Jesus was indeed sent by God is not merely by preaching the gospel to them, though we surely must, but *by being one* before their eyes. If this is true, as we fail at unity, we fail at evangelism. If we take these words at face value, our witness to the truth is diminished to the extent to which we fail at church unity. Thankfully, by His grace we have seen a measure of success and souls have been won, even in our divided condition, but surely we have not succeeded as we could have had our divisions not been working against us every step of the way, contradicting everything we say.

This book may make you uncomfortable, but it is my prayer that what you read here will impart to you a vision, and that this vision will cause you both to believe and to pray earnestly that the Lord will do what only He can do.

As the walls that separate Christians begin to fall, we will find that a wealth of treasures lie on the other side. Each and every believer holds unique gifts and treasures that God has imparted to them. Outside the walls of your church are many other believers, true believers with valuable things that you and your church need to receive, just as they need to receive the gifts and treasures you hold.

34

Until we are all connected to one another, we will all be lacking. We are lacking now; we simply do not know how much.

What the Bible says about unity and division

Psalm 133 - A Psalm of David.

¹Behold, how good and pleasant it is when brothers dwell in unity.
²It is like the precious oil on the head, running down on the beard, on the beard of Aaron, (the high priest), running down on the collar of his robes! *³It is like the dew of Hermon, which falls on the mountains of Zion!* **For there the LORD has commanded the blessing, life forevermore.**

(What a beautiful picture David paints for us in this Psalm. Unity is like the refreshing dew of Mount Hermon. It is like the precious oil of anointing that ran down over the head and beard of the high priest as he prepared to minister before the Lord. It is the place where the Lord has commanded the blessing, even life evermore. Unity is a goodly place, a place to be desired, and a place of blessing. It is a place none of us has fully experienced, though some of us have had a taste.)

John 17 (A prayer of Jesus)
²⁰"I do not ask for these only (the twelve), but also for those who will believe in me through their word, *²¹* **that they may all be**

one, just as you, Father, are in me, and I in you, that they also may be in us, so that the world may believe that you have sent me. [22] *The glory that you have given me I have given to them, that they may be one even as we are one,* [23] *I in them and you in me, that they may become perfectly one, so that the world may know that you sent me and loved them even as you loved me.*

(This passage is part of the great high priestly prayer of Jesus just before He went to the cross. No word our Lord spoke may be taken lightly by those who love Him. Jesus prayed for a oneness among His followers that was perfect, like the perfect oneness the Father and Son enjoy. When Jesus asked for this oneness, He explained what the fruit of perfect unity would be. He said that when we are perfectly one, the world will know two things: First, *that He was sent by the Father*, and second, that *the Father loves us even as He loves the Son*. We will discuss the ramifications of this prayer in a later chapter.)

I Corinthians 1:10-13 (Divisions in the Church)
[10]*I appeal to you, brothers, by the name of our Lord Jesus Christ, that all of you agree, and that there be no divisions among you, but that you be united in the same mind and the same judgment.* [11]*For it has been reported to me by Chloe's people that there is quarreling among you, my brothers.* [12]*What I mean is that each one of you says, "I follow Paul," or "I follow Apollos," or "I follow Cephas," or "I follow Christ."* [13] *Is Christ divided? Was Paul crucified for you? Or were you baptized in the name of Paul?*

(Lest any think that the oneness for which Jesus prayed was some kind of mystical or intangible thing that cannot be seen or experienced, here the apostle Paul spells it out. He says we are all to be of the same mind and judgment and that there are to be no divisions among us. The Father and the Son are not divided and never disagree and in fact cannot. If we are one as they are one, then this will be true of us.)

I Corinthians 3:1-4 And I, brethren, could not speak to you as to spiritual *people* but as to carnal, as to babes in Christ. ² I fed you with milk and not with solid food; for until now you were not able *to receive it,* and even now you are still not able; ³ for you are still carnal. **For where *there are* envy, strife, and divisions among you, are you not carnal and behaving like *mere* men?** ⁴ For when one says, "I am of Paul," and another, "I *am* of Apollos," are you not carnal?

(Here, the apostle Paul delivers his indictment of the Corinthian church, which, by the way, was much less divided than churches are today. The apostle says we are divided because we are carnal. We are *not* divided because we are so committed to the truth that we refuse to compromise. That sounds great, but Paul tears away that disguise and reveals the truth. He says that our envy, strife, and divisions reveal that we are not behaving like Christians, but as mere men.)

Romans 16:17 Now I urge you, brethren, **note those who cause divisions and offenses,** contrary to the doctrine which you learned, and avoid them.

(There are those among us who cause divisions by pushing their own doctrines and teachings. They may use Bibles and quote verses, but they lead us to quarrel and squabble about useless things. We are to make note of who these teachers are and we are to avoid them, even if they are some of the most popular teachers on television and radio. See also Proverbs 6:16-19)

*Titus 3:9-11 But avoid foolish controversies, genealogies, dissensions, and quarrels about the law, for they are unprofitable and worthless. ¹⁰ **As for a person who stirs up division, after warning him once and then twice, have nothing more to do with him,** ¹¹ knowing that such a person is warped and sinful; he is self-condemned.*

(This is a tough passage and one the church has not taken seriously. The gist of the passage appears to be that we are to avoid quarreling over things that are not worth fighting over, i.e. *unprofitable or worthless* matters; and any person who insists on causing dissension and division is to be warned twice and then we are to have nothing to do with him. This is strong language, but shows how serious we are to take division and those who cause it. Are we willing to heed such strong words?)

Philippians 2:1-30 Fulfill ye my joy, that ye be **like-minded**, having the same love, **being of one accord, of one mind.** (Phil. 2:2)

(Paul says his joy is full when believers are like-minded, when they are of one mind and one accord. This is a question that we must ponder: Is it sufficient to get along with the believers in our own church while we ignore the believers in all the other churches in town?)

Ephesians 4 – (Unity in the Body of Christ) [1]I therefore, a prisoner for the Lord, urge you to walk in a manner worthy of the calling to which you have been called, [2]with all humility and gentleness, with patience, bearing with one another in love, [3]eager to maintain the unity of the Spirit in the bond of peace.

[4]There is one body and one Spirit—just as you were called to the one hope that belongs to your call— [5] one Lord, one faith, one baptism, [6] one God and Father of all, who is over all and through all and in all. ...[11]And he gave the apostles, the prophets, the evangelists, the shepherds and teachers, [12] to equip the saints for the work of ministry, for building up the body of Christ, [13]until **we all attain to the unity of the faith and of the knowledge of the Son of God, to mature manhood, to the measure of the stature of the fullness of Christ,**

[14]so that we may no longer be children, tossed to and fro by the waves and carried about by every wind of doctrine, *by human* *cunning, by craftiness in deceitful schemes. [15]Rather, speaking the truth in love, we are to grow up in every way into him who is the head, into Christ, [16] from whom the whole body, joined and held together by every joint with which it is equipped, when each part is working properly, makes the body grow so that it builds itself up in love.*

(This may be the most important passage on unity in the entire Bible. Paul speaks of unity from the very beginning of this chapter. He speaks of the things that we must all share in common. He tells us of the ultimate goal, to bring the body of Christ to the *measure of the stature of the fullness of Christ*. Paul speaks of the church as a living body, an organism in which all of the parts are connected and working properly. Only then does the body grow and build itself up in love. *The measure of the stature of the fullness of Christ* - this is where we are headed. This is the goal. This is the destiny of the church of Jesus Christ. That may seem too lofty for us, but frankly, it is hard to imagine the Lord waiting 2,000 years and settling for less.)

Genesis 11 - The Tower of Babel
[1]Now the whole earth had one language and the same words. [2]And as people migrated from the east, they found a plain in the land of Shinar and settled there. [3]And they said to one another, "Come, let us make bricks, and burn them thoroughly." And they had brick for stone, and bitumen for mortar. [4]Then they said, "Come, let us build ourselves a city and a tower with its top in the heavens, and let us make a name for ourselves, lest we be dispersed over the face of the whole earth." [5]And the LORD came down to see the city and the tower, which the children of man had built.

[6]And the LORD said, "Behold, they are one people, and they have all one language, and this is only the beginning of what they will do. And nothing that they propose to do will now be impossible for them.[7]Come, let us go down and there confuse

their language, so that they may not understand one another's speech."

[8]So the LORD dispersed them from there over the face of all the earth, and they left off building the city. [9]Therefore its name was called Babel, because there the LORD confused the language of all the earth. And from there the LORD dispersed them over the face of all the earth.

(This is one of the most sweeping statements in Scripture. We devote an entire chapter to this topic, because few of us have truly pondered the unparalleled power of oneness. If God is to be taken at His word, and He must be, there is nothing a unified people cannot accomplish. This is why Jesus prayed for His followers to be one. It is also why Satan works, on the one hand, to prevent Christian unity, and on the other hand, to unite the world in unity against the Lord and his Christ. Unity of unbelievers - in rebellion against the Lord - is the enemy's end game. Unity of believers, on the other hand, is the Lord's ultimate intention for us.)

Mark 9:38, 39 *Now John answered Him (Jesus), saying, "Teacher, we saw someone who does not follow us casting out demons in Your name, and we forbade him because he does not follow us." But Jesus said,* **"Do not forbid him, for no one who works a miracle in My name can soon afterward speak evil of Me.** [40] **For he who is not against us is on our side.**

(Many Bibles print the following heading over this passage: "Jesus forbids sectarianism." The report the disciples gave to Jesus indicates that they were upset because some guy was doing the same kinds of miraculous things they were doing, but he wasn't officially ordained or sent out like they had been. Put simply, this man was not part of their group. In reply, Jesus did not deliver a lengthy discourse. He simply said, and I paraphrase. "Guys, people who are doing miraculous things in my name are on our side; don't try to stop them." I have often wondered who this mysterious fellow was. There is no indication that he was merely *trying* to cast our demons.

It appears that he was really doing it. Apparently, this unknown man understood the authority that was inherent in the name of Jesus.

It is also apparent that this man knew Jesus and that the demons he exorcised knew that he did. Contrast his story with the seven sons of Sceva, who tried to cast out demons "*in the name of Jesus, whom Paul preaches,*" and were sent running out of the place minus some clothing. We read their embarrassing account in Acts 19:13-17)

> *Then some of the itinerant Jewish exorcists took it upon them-*
> *selves to call the name of the Lord Jesus over those who had*
> *evil spirits, saying, "We exorcise you by the Jesus whom Paul*
> *preaches." [14] Also there were seven sons of Sceva, a Jewish chief*
> *priest, who did so. [15]* **And the evil spirit answered and said,**
> **"Jesus I know, and Paul I know; but who are you?" [16] Then**
> **the man in whom the evil spirit was leaped on them, overpow-**
> **ered them, and prevailed against them, so that they fled out of**
> **that house naked and wounded.** *[17] This became known both to*
> *all Jews and Greeks dwelling in Ephesus; and fear fell on them*
> *all,* **and the name of the Lord Jesus was magnified.**

(In comparing the two accounts, it seems apparent that the first man, the one the disciples forbade, knew the Lord and had genuine faith in Him. Their problem with him was simply that he was not part of the disciples' group. If he had not known the Lord, his experience casting out demons would have been more like the experience of the sons of Sceva, who tried to use the name of Jesus like it was a magic formula. Interestingly, the fact that demons did not obey the sons of Sceva, who invoked the name of Jesus *but did not know Him*, caused the name of the Lord Jesus *to be magnified*.

We dwell on the Mark 9 passage (the same account is described in Luke 9, as well), because it is the one place in the Gospels where Jesus makes it clear to the disciples that people did not have to be part of their group to be on "*our side*". It is especially noteworthy that Jesus said "our side," and not "my side." It is as if He wanted to stress to the twelve that there are only two sides, not three and most certainly not many. The disciples did not have a side of their own, apart from Jesus. So, if someone was on Jesus' side, he was also on the disciples' side.

Should this fact not be the basis for unity? Someone is either on our side or they are not. If they name the same name of Jesus Christ and have placed their faith in Him alone, then they are not against us and we should never treat them as if they are.)

Matthew 12:22-30 Then one was brought to Him who was demon-possessed, blind and mute; and He healed him, so that the blind and mute man both spoke and saw. [23] And all the multitudes were amazed and said, "Could this be the Son of David?" [24] Now when the Pharisees heard it they said, "This fellow does not cast out demons except by Beelzebub, the ruler of the demons."

*[25] But Jesus knew their thoughts, and said to them: **"Every kingdom divided against itself is brought to desolation, and every city or house divided against itself will not stand.** [26] If Satan casts out Satan, he is divided against himself. How then will his kingdom stand? [27] And if I cast out demons by Beelzebub, by whom do your sons cast them out? Therefore they shall be your judges. [28] But if I cast out demons by the Spirit of God, surely the kingdom of God has come upon you. [29] Or how can one enter a strong man's house and plunder his goods, unless he first binds the strong man? And then he will plunder his house. [30] **He who is not with Me is against Me, and he who does not gather with Me scatters abroad.***

In the Mark 9 passage that we discussed previously, Jesus said, "He who is not against us is on our side." Here, Jesus tackles sectarianism from the other angle. Here he says, "He who is not with me is against me." There are two messages to be drawn from these two passages.

First, there is no neutral or middle ground. You are on one side or you are on the other. Second, every kingdom, city, or house that is divided will either be desolate or it will not stand. In other words, a divided church will be a losing church.

The church today is divided, fractured, and tossed to and fro. As long as it remains in this condition, it cannot succeed. The Scriptures are clear: Every kingdom, city, and house will suffer if it is divided. Do we suppose that we are somehow an exception to this?

Let us now go with the apostle Paul as he drops in on the church he had pioneered years earlier in the Grecian city of Corinth. Let's observe Paul's reaction when he discovers that the church at Corinth has turned into *us*.

The Fractured Church – chapter 5

Paul returns to Corinth

L et us imagine that we are a band of missionaries accompanying Apostle Paul on a journey back to the Grecian city of Corinth, years following his letters to that church. We are going to check on the spiritual well-being of the brethren. Exercising a bit of literary tom-foolery, let's throw in elements that the apostle would encounter in one of our modern cities...and watch. Before we begin, let's review a little relevant background:

> Corinth was a bustling metropolis. With three harbors on a rugged coastline where good seaports are rare, the city was a major hub of commerce. At one time, Corinth had been four times the size of Athens, but the city had been all but leveled in 146 BC by the Roman general, Lucius Mummius.
>
> Julius Caesar rebuilt Corinth as a Roman colony in 44 BC, employing the services of a widely diverse population of veteran legions, freed slaves and conscripted foreigners from throughout the Empire. The new city grew rapidly, and earned a reputation for ungodliness, especially of the sensual type.
>
> The rebuilt city was less than a hundred years old when Paul established the church there. It was this rebuilt Corinth that our band approached on the morning of our imaginary visit.

There had been a great harvest of souls upon Paul's visit to Corinth with many new converts added to the Kingdom of God. Many of those new believers had come from the city's lower social classes. The apostle had spent a considerable amount of time in Corinth establishing the church, so he was aware of the nature of its many challenges.

Even though the move of the Holy Spirit had been mighty in Corinth, the church had a tendency towards spiritual immaturity. Believers quarreled with one another and tended towards excess, even in spiritual matters. The Corinthian church was blessed by spiritual gifts, but at the same time was overly tolerant of moral proclivities among its members. The issue that troubled Paul the most about this church, however, was its strong tendency towards division and sectarianism. Believers in Corinth were always breaking into factions and cliques.

Subsequently, Paul had written two long letters to the Corinthians, explaining sorrowfully that he could not speak to them as he would to spiritual or mature believers; instead he was forced to speak to them as *babes in Christ*. Because they were acting like children, the apostle spoke to them as children. He was, frankly speaking, calling them a bunch of babies,

> *"I fed you with milk and not with solid food; for until now you were not able to receive it, and even now you are still not able for you are still carnal. For where there are envy, strife, and divisions among you, are you not carnal and behaving like mere men? For when one says 'I am of Paul,' and another, 'I am of Apollos,' are you not carnal?"*

It is important to recognize that the Christians Paul addressed in his letters were members of the same local church. After all, there was only one church in the city. But, they were not behaving in a spirit of unity, and for that they were soundly rebuked. Consider the opening words of Paul's first letter,

"To the church of God, which is at Corinth, to those who are sanctified in Christ Jesus, called to be saints, with all who in every place call on the name of Jesus Christ our Lord."

Admittedly, this is the kind of passage readers usually skim over. After all, it's just a greeting. However, Paul's greeting to the Corinthians reveals at least two truths pertinent to this study. First, the apostle acknowledged that there was but one church in the city of Corinth, a church comprised of all the believers in that area who were sanctified in Christ Jesus. He did not recognize multiple Corinthian churches, just one.

Second, he declared with certainty that the believers in Corinth were called to be saints *along with all of the other believers everywhere "in every place,"* who also call upon the name of the Lord Jesus Christ. In other words, there was both a "church of God," which consisted of all believers everywhere, and a local church in Corinth, a church which was comprised of all believers in and around that city.

Now, with that background in mind, let's get on with our journey:

Our small band spent the night at a country inn just outside of town. We awoke early Friday as Paul wanted to travel before the heat of the day. After a quick meal of local fruits and breads, we set off.

It was barely daylight when we began, but the dirt road leading into the city was already crowded with travelers. The carts and animals moved at such a brisk pace that a thick cloud of dust hovered above the road, quickly dirtying our robes and feet.

Before and behind us, the line of small carts were two and three abreast, each pulled by a donkey laden with baskets overflowing with bolts of colorful cloth, ripe produce and other goods and wares. Farmers and merchants were making their way toward the city for another day of business.

We'd traveled a short time when we noticed a large wooden sign, situated off to the side of the road. *Welcome to Corinth* was carved deeply into the dark wood and painted a bright yellow.

Surrounding the sign was a knee-high wall of mortared bricks with bright flowers planted in the moist ground around the posts.

"That's new," Paul nodded toward the display.

The large Greek letters were easy to read, even from a distance. Beneath the *Welcome to Corinth* sign was another long, narrow sign, which was suspended from the sign above by shiny, brass chains. This lower sign read *Population 756,816*. As we drew nearer, we saw that below the population sign hung still another. It was long and narrow like the one above, but smaller. In orange letters, it read, *Corinth's churches and synagogues welcome you*.

Below that sign, and hanging from it, were dozens and dozens of still smaller signs, all hanging in neat rows, connected by chains, forming three long columns stretching all the way down to the tops of the flowers. Altogether, the sign arrangement, the brick wall, and the bed of brightly colored flowers, made for an impressive display of civic pride.

As we drew close enough to read the rows of smaller signs, Paul stopped and simply stared. With furrowed brow, he slowly scanned the list, his head turning from side to side, lips moving in a low whisper as he read. About midway down the columns of names, Paul turned and looked at each of us; on his face was an expression of shock and dismay. There was a hint of something else too, but it was hard to read.

Finally he spoke, his low voice carrying a firmness that made the rest of us shrink back a bit, "What does this mean?" he asked. "How can there be so many churches?"

We were silent, unable to answer. We all read some more. There were a lot of names on that sign, and except for one or two, none of us had ever heard of them. Some of the words sounded familiar, but we had never seen them used in the context of a church name. Familiar sounding words like *Baptist, Pentecostal, Episcopalian, Congregationalist*, and *Presbyterian* were used more than once, but were joined with other words like "First" or "Free" or "United," as if to ensure that those reading the sign would recognize that they were somehow not the same as other churches with similar names. Other names, such as *Lutheran, Wesleyan,* and *Methodist* were entirely foreign to us.

Some signs used words like *Catholic, Orthodox, Reformed, Latter Day Saints*, and *Jehovah.* We were familiar with the words, of course, but not in the way in which they were used.

Altogether, there were more than sixty little signs, each one different from the others, each indicating that it was the name of a different church in the city of Corinth.

The apostle glanced towards the city gates, still a quarter of a mile away. Then he turned and looked behind at those approaching where we stood, as if looking for his answer among them. An older man dressed in a fine purple robe and a white turban was passing by on our side of the road. He was leading a small gray donkey, heavily laden with baskets filled with beautiful ceramic pots on one side and various sized copper kettles on the other.

Abruptly, Paul stepped towards the man, his hand raised, politely gesturing for the merchant to stop. "Excuse me, sir."

The man, startled by the sudden interruption, led his donkey to the side of the road. He whispered something in the animal's ear which caused it to halt abruptly, making its load lurch suddenly forward. Darting a furtive glance toward the city, the man steadied the donkey's load and then turned and looked down at the apostle. His hair, at least what could be seen protruding from under his turban, was mostly gray, as was his neatly trimmed beard; his eyes were a light gray and appeared clear and honest.

"Please," the apostle began, gesturing toward the sign, "can you tell me, what is the meaning of this list of churches? When I was in Corinth last, there was only one church in the city, and now there are scores, all with different names. How did this happen?"

The merchant shook his head, "I have no idea, friend. I don't go to any of them. I have a business to run and a family to look after. Frankly, I am not a very religious man."

Paul's shoulders slumped.

The man continued, gesturing towards the sign, "Listen, even if I wanted to go to a church, I don't know which one I'd choose. The Christians in this city say they are *the people of the way*; it appears there is not just one way, but many, because these churches all disagree with one another and believe different things. How would a simple merchant like me know which one is right?

"Besides, I don't think church people like each other. They argue and fight over things that I don't understand and don't care about. They all have their own buildings and meet separately. Each thinks that theirs is the right church and all of the others are wrong. It's confusing and unappealing to an outsider like me.

"So, I run my business, live my life, and ignore them all. Like I said, if I ever wanted to start going to a church, how would I ever choose?"

The merchant darted another glance toward the city and then looked intently down at Paul, as if expecting an answer.

"You say these churches all own their own buildings?" Paul asked the merchant. "Why would they do that? Where did they get the money to buy so many buildings?"

The merchant shrugged, "Churches are famous for taking offerings. I assume that's where they get the money. It has always puzzled me that they'd build these large ornate structures, some of them obviously very expensive, only to use them one or two days a week, and then only for a few hours. As a businessman, it is hard to see the sense in that."

The man began to pull lightly on the donkey's reins, suggesting that he was ready to be on his way. "I'm sorry, stranger, but I need to get my wares to the marketplace. The breeze is from the east this morning, so it will be a hot one. Most buyers finish before noon, so I must go.

"Maybe you should ask someone who belongs to a church," the merchant offered, again gesturing towards the sign. "There are quite a few who do. They'll know more than I do."

The man pulled more firmly on the reins, nodded courteously toward our party, and continued on his way.

Paul turned to puzzle over the small signs once more, at times tilting one to examine each yellow letter, as though that might help him decipher the meaning of the name carved there. Paul was, of course, a well-traveled, well-educated man, especially in regard to religious matters. Still, what he read appeared foreign to him.

The traffic into the city was thinning. Coming toward us from the direction of the gates were three women, laughing and talking and swinging large empty reed baskets. Paul waved to get their attention, and they walked over. One was older and gray-haired, another was probably the older woman's daughter, and the last, a teenager.

"My name is Paul and these are my friends," Paul began. "Most of us are from Tarsus. We're confused about this sign. Can you tell us why there are so many churches in the city, and why they all have different names?"

As one, the three ladies glanced at the display and then back at Paul. The oldest stepped forward, as if to take the lead. There was an air of dignity about the woman, but she hesitated for a moment before speaking. Gradually the warm smile was replaced by a serious expression. Then she spoke. Her voice was quiet at first.

"Well, it's hard to explain," she began. "First, there are a lot more churches in Corinth than the ones listed there. Many new ones were established after the sign was built and their names haven't been added yet.

"Second, most major denominations have started churches in Corinth. Plus, many existing congregations have split and divided over various doctrines, or over arguments about who is going to be in charge."

Paul seemed perplexed. "But, how...I mean *what* doctrines do they disagree over? Why don't they stay together and work things out? Who gives them permission to start their own church where there already is one...or in this case many?"

The lady appeared baffled by Paul's questions, as if he was suggesting something entirely new or strange. At that moment, the younger woman stepped forward and gently touched the older one on the arm, as if to signal that she wanted to speak.

"Most of the churches in Corinth agree on lots of issues," she began, "but they disagree on plenty, too. For example, some believe in baptizing babies, but others say you should wait until children are old enough to understand what it's all about. Also, there's disagreement over the method of baptism: sprinkling, pouring, or dunking, as well as various conflicts over *why* one should be baptized and how important it is."

"They break fellowship with other believers and worship separately over baptism?" Paul asked dryly. "What else?"

The first lady chimed in, "Lydia is right. There are other areas of disagreements. Baptism is only one. Some believe in miracles and praying for the sick and speaking in tongues, and others say spiritual gifts and miracles are not for today. Because they disagree about spiritual gifts, one group has almost nothing to do with the other."

Paul asked, "Why don't they just resolve these matters? Regarding the gifts of the Spirit, there are only two possibilities, aren't there? The gifts of the Holy Spirit are either real or they are not. It's not really a matter of opinion."

"Well, they haven't been able to figure that out," the woman replied. "In fact, some of those who don't believe in speaking in tongues and miracles say such things are false signs from the devil."

"That's a pretty strong conclusion," Paul muttered. "No wonder they don't worship together."

The older woman continued, "Sometimes the two sides accept that both sides are believers, only they're believers who disagree with each other on an important issue. They choose to worship separately because their differences are irreconcilable. They get along better if they avoid each other.

"And, sometimes people start new churches over other things. My husband is an elder in our church. Our denomination broke off from the main group, because we believe our local church should own our buildings and the other group insists that only the parent denomination should own church property."

"Often," Lydia interjected, "someone from some other town wants to pastor their own church, maybe because they just graduated from seminary, so they look for a town that doesn't have a church that's affiliated with their denomination; then they move there and start a new branch. Eventually there will be a church affiliated with their denomination everywhere. At least, that is the goal."

Paul appeared stunned. "Let's back up a bit. You have used the term 'denomination'. What is a denomination, and why would someone go start a new church in a town already full of churches, just because they don't have one with their name on it?"

Lydia, laughing politely, turned to the older woman for help.

The older woman set her empty basket on the ground and crossed her arms. "A denomination is an organization that consists of all of the churches in all of the towns around the world who believe the things that the denomination says their people should believe and who carry the same name. They have a headquarters which governs the individual churches. The denomination usually owns the church buildings, and can hire and fire the senior pastor at any of the churches."

"Senior pastor?" Paul asked.

At this the youngest of the three spoke up. Apparently, this was a question that she believed she could answer. "The senior pastor is the man who runs the church," she said. "You know, it's like his job. He does all the preaching and stuff."

"That's interesting," Paul replied to the youngster. "Please go on. I'd like to know more about what these churches teach."

The young girl continued, "A friend of mine at school told me his church doesn't believe that Jesus is the Son of God, but was just a good man or a good teacher. His minister says Jesus never really performed miracles and never really rose from the dead. I told him that churches like his are not Christian, but just say they are.

"One church down the street from my house teaches that if you say Jesus is God, then you have more than one God, so they say Jesus isn't really God.

"Then there are the Mormons. See their name there on the sign? Actually, the sign says, ***Church of Jesus Christ of Latter Day Saints***. We have lots of Mormons at our school. They believe so many things that are different from other churches that most churches say Mormons are not really Christians. I think some of them might be...But, I think their church believes that Jesus and Satan were brothers up in Heaven, or something like that."

Paul glanced quickly at the two ladies, as if to affirm what the younger girl said. They nodded. He kicked at the dust with his sandal. He was beginning to get the picture, and it was all a bit much to take in, even for an apostle. He looked up, "What do the names Lutheran and Wesleyan mean?"

The older woman spoke, "Lutherans were the first Protestants who broke away from the Catholic Church. They call themselves after Martin Luther, who rebelled against the Catholics because back then the Catholics were selling forgiveness for money..."

"What?!" Paul exclaimed. "Selling forgiveness? God doesn't require money... Why would anyone...

"Ok," Paul sighed, shaking his head. "Please go on. This Luther fellow rebelled against the Catholics and started the Lutherans. How did the Catholics get the power to sell salvation for money? Why were they not excommunicated from the church for doing such a thing?"

The woman replied, "the Catholics *were* the church. They said they could do anything they wanted. They made the rules, and if they said you had to pay money for forgiveness, then you paid money, or you would be condemned to hell for eternity. They don't do that anymore. But, they still believe many things that Protestants don't."

The young girl spoke up. "Catholics think Christians should pray to Mary, the mother of Jesus. They think that she was perfect and never sinned. They even call her the 'Mother of God'. Most Christians do not agree with Catholics about Mary."

The older lady took a step closer and spoke to Paul in a low voice. "Most of us believe that a lot of folks who go to the other churches in town are probably Christians, even though we disagree with one another regarding some things. Catholics insist that they are the only church, because they are the oldest and were started by Peter."

Few scholars knew more about religion than Paul; yet what we had stumbled upon that day outside of Corinth was obviously bewildering to him.

"Listen, sir," the older woman said. "If you want to know more about these matters, you and your friends can come to our home tonight for supper. My husband knows a lot more about such things. I'm sure he would be happy to answer your questions. If you like, I will ask him to invite the other elders to meet with you after our meal. You sound like you know the Lord. Do you?"

"Yes, I know Him," Paul replied. "I met Him on the road between Jerusalem and Damascus."

The ladies glanced at one another, as if puzzled by Paul's reply.

Paul continued, "We would be pleased to accept your invitation, and to be able to speak with your husband and the elders. So, thank you. I would also like to see some of those buildings. A merchant I spoke to earlier this morning told me some of them are expensive and ornate."

"Our house is not far from the center of the city and there are many churches in the area," the lady said, adjusting her blue scarf over her hair. "I will have someone meet you at the fountain in front of the Temple of Aphrodite at the tenth hour and lead you to our home. I suggest that you stay clear of the temple itself, as there are many prostitutes there. Corinth is infamous for its temple prostitutes.

"Meanwhile, if you want to see some of the churches of Corinth, just walk around the city. You will have no problem finding them. As you can see, there are many and they are clearly marked. Most will be locked, it being a week-day. Some are staffed during the weekdays, however, and may let you look around."

With that, the lady picked up her basket, and nodded politely, "We will see you all at supper. I will serve lamb."

Paul bowed his head in acknowledgment.

As they turned to leave, Paul said, "I have one more question, if you don't mind."

The women paused.

Paul asked, "Do you think divisions would end if someone could answer the churches' questions and try to resolve the matters that separate them?"

Lydia answered slowly, "I don't see how...Who could do it? Theologians have debated the issues and still disagree. We disagree about the meaning of communion, whether women should be allowed to preach, whether everyone is a priest. We disagree about whether you have to be baptized to be saved, whether

Christians should tithe, whether to keep the Sabbath. We will never come to agreement on these matters, I fear.

She hesitated for a moment before continuing, "There is probably no one person who all of the churches would recognize as having the authority to answer their questions. Who would that person be?

"The Catholics listen to their Pope, but his answers are only respected by Catholics. The denominations have boards, but their authority doesn't reach beyond their own denomination. I can't imagine there is any one person with enough stature that everyone would listen to him, except the Lord himself."

After we bid the ladies farewell for the second time, we turned again toward the city. We were almost to the gates when Paul spoke, a grim look on his face. "I am reminded of the Book of Judges," he said. "In those days, there was no king in Israel, so every man did that which was right in his own eyes. After the death of Moses, the people followed Joshua, and God gave great signs to show that Joshua was indeed God's chosen leader. The people followed him, and the tribes began to conquer their enemies and possess the land allotted to them. However, after Joshua and his generation died, the people of God had no leader, so once again they began to slide into sin and worship other gods.

"There were judges from various tribes who rose up from time to time and some of the people followed them. Judges like Gideon and Jephthah brought peace and prosperity for a period of time. Overall, however, the tribes remained separate and scattered; each would fight its own battles.

"Sometimes, tribes would even war against one another. It was a dark time for God's people.

"It appears that Israel's history has repeated itself in Corinth. As long as I was here, or Peter or James was available to answer the heretics and stop the divisions, the Corinthian believers grew in the Lord and stayed together. I thought they had come to understand that the body of Christ must not be divided.

"But, judging by what we've learned today, the Corinthian church has fractured into many pieces. There are many churches in this city, churches which do not believe the same things and will not worship together. And, it appears that some have abandoned the truth altogether.

"And, if the attitudes of other believers in the city are similar to those of these women, they aren't troubled by their divisions. They are guilty of a grievous sin and do not know it.

"No wonder the merchant had no idea how he would pick a church. I don't know how I would either. I must see these churches and talk to their leaders. We must stop what has happened in Corinth, before it can spread to other cities. In fact, it sounds as if these *denominations* are already at work spreading divisions everywhere they go.

"I will continue to hope. There was a day when believers in Corinth heeded the words I wrote them. Maybe that day is gone, but maybe they have simply lost my letters, which warned them of such things. I will ask the elders about that, and other issues, when we meet tonight after supper. Perhaps this evening will be a beginning."

Paul passed through the gates and we fell in behind him. The sun was higher in the sky and already hot on our foreheads as we entered the city and began to look around us for church buildings.

We wondered if, when Paul met with the leaders of the church the three ladies attended, would he choose to answer their questions and settle their disputes, or would he teach them how to maintain a spirit of perfect unity with the other churches - in spite of their differences?

We thought our question would likely be answered that night over supper. One thing was certain, before the apostle left Corinth, the believers there would know the gravity of their divisions. Paul would most certainly see to that...

It is time for us to leave Paul there in "Corinth" and return to our study. But before we do, ponder this thought for a moment: If Paul really would have discovered in ancient Corinth what you and I know he would find today if he visited almost any city in the western world, would he not have considered the situation a full blown crisis, a threat of monumental proportions? Would he have not taken whatever steps were necessary to prevent the spread of such rank division and dissension?

We may ignore our divisions. We may go on with our denominational lives as if our terribly fractured condition is of little consequence, but I assure you, the man who wrote more of the New Testament than any other, would not. The Corinthians' divisions were but a shadow of ours and the apostle delivered them a stinging rebuke. I tremble to think of what the man of God would say if he saw what we have done to the body of Christ today.

Will God answer the prayer of Jesus?

et's stop for a minute and try to put into perspective what the
apostle Paul discovered in our imaginary trip to Corinth in the
last chapter. Did Paul not find in Corinth precisely what he would
find if he visited any of our cities today? If he came to your town,
would he not find churches scattered all over the city, all with different brand names and different doctrines and virtually no connection to one another? Would he not see in our countless divisions
the fruit of the very root he was trying to kill 2,000 years ago in the
church at Corinth?

Given that the answer to this question is rather obvious, there are
two issues which we must now address. First, how does our grossly
divided condition affect our ability as a church to fulfill our mission
here on earth, and second, will God answer, in any literal or visible
sense, the prayer of Jesus for His disciples to be one?

What Paul saw in the real Corinth, the church to which he wrote
two epistles, were divisions within the city's one church. Paul was
alarmed because even though there was only one church in Corinth,
there were dissensions in its midst. If Paul had not intervened and
soundly rebuked the Corinthians for their carnality and divisive
spirit, before long, the people who favored Apollos or Cephas or
Paul over the others would have stirred up enough dissension and
strife that believers in the church would have separated from one

another. They would have argued and debated until their contentions tore them apart.

Paul was not about to let that happen. When he heard of their discord, he asked them pointedly, "Is Christ divided?" Presumably, this outrageous question was meant to be rhetorical. The very suggestion of such a preposterous thing was meant to end all dissension.

However, if Paul was here today and asked us the same question, I wonder if he would ask it rhetorically. Before we answer too quickly, perhaps we should stop and think more deeply about the issue Paul was raising. Paul was suggesting to the Corinthians, in rather unambiguous language, that the factions which were developing in their church were threatening to do an unthinkable thing; i.e. divide the body of Christ in their city.

Have we divided Christ?

Now, let's fast forward to modern times. Is what we see in our cities today not the very thing Paul was trying to prevent in Corinth; i.e. the dividing body of Christ? It is difficult to say what I am going to suggest now, but if the body of Christ, the church, is truly divided, as it appears to be, is Christ not divided? Have we not done the unthinkable thing? Have we and our forefathers not divided Christ's body into pieces? I realize that I am using common language here, but if we have done this terrible thing, do we dare minimize or trivialize our deed?

Christians tend to think of Christ's body as something that exists apart from Him, because He is in heaven and His body is on earth. But the Head and the body are connected. In the Spirit, the two are not separate, which is why Paul would exclaim, "Is Christ divided?" to the contentious Corinthians. Looking around us at the condition of the modern church, it appears that we indeed have divided Christ. We have broken His body into pieces and scattered them all over town. Even in our smaller cities, we see the body of Christ divided into dozens of separate and distinct pieces that rarely, if ever, touch one another.

It is self-evident that we cannot function as a body if we are not connected to one another. A foot cannot function unless it is connected to a leg. It is impossible that it could. A hand or a heart or a kidney is of no value sitting somewhere alone and dismembered. If one part of the body is to provide service to the rest of the body and in return be nourished by all the other parts, they must all be connected; otherwise the body cannot do what the body was designed to do.

This is why unity is indispensible to the church's mission; we simply cannot function as the body of Christ when we are not joined to one another. Jesus knew this. He prayed that we would all be one, so that the world would know that He was sent by the Father. We ignore this prayer and pretend that the world somehow will know that Jesus was sent by the Father simply because we say so, no matter how disconnected and divided we remain. There is, however, little basis for such a conclusion. We may see thousands or even millions saved and assume that this level of success proves that unity is unessential. While we may be content with the level of harvest we have enjoyed, we should remain painfully aware that billions remain lost in darkness and unbelief, not knowing that the Son of God was sent by the Father in heaven to save mankind.

Jesus said to His followers, "They (the world) will know that you are my disciples by your love for one another." These words are not obscure or mysterious. They are clear and precise. But they beg this question: Are we showing the world how much we love one another, when we wall ourselves off from one another and worship separately? Or, do we show them the opposite? Arguing with one another, calling ourselves by different names, and refusing to worship under the same roof are hardly what one would consider "expressions of love."

The purpose of this chapter is to demonstrate that our divisions undermine our ability to reach the lost. They rob us of the key element that Jesus said we needed to persuade the world of His divinity. The message that must be carried to the unbelieving world is this: Jesus was not just a man and not just a good teacher; He was and is the only begotten Son of God, sent to the earth by the Father in heaven to save mankind. It is not enough to say these words, we must demonstrate their veracity by our oneness. This is clearly the essence of Jesus' prayer.

Many of us have wondered: What can we do to persuade the world that Jesus was not just some noteworthy, historic figure who lived an extraordinary life, like Buddha or Confucius, and then passed away and went to his grave, as is the destiny of all mere mortals? How can we persuade the world that Jesus is the Son of God, God in the flesh; sent here by the Father in Heaven? What scientific proof can we offer? What message would persuade them? These may sound like tough questions, but in reality Jesus has already answered them. He has told us what would make them know, but we have ignored His unambiguous words.

Jesus' prayer in John 17, which we shall examine in a moment, was between Him and the Father. Nonetheless, John was inspired to inform us in his Gospel what Jesus said in that prayer. There is a reason we were allowed to listen in. We were made privy to this "Son to Father" communication so we could learn something of the utmost importance, something that is, in fact, the *key* to our success in reaching the world.

Before we look at this prayer more closely, let's consider further the possibility that we ought not to be satisfied with the degree of evangelistic success we have enjoyed thus far. Yes, we are making converts and leading souls to Christ and this is clearly a good thing. But what if we are enjoying our current level of success with both of our hands tied behind our backs? What if we are preaching the truth with our lips, but with our divided condition so contradicting our message that we are rendering our words largely ineffective, and thus leaving much of the crop un-harvested? What if, while we are preaching, we are simultaneously doing the one thing that can neutralize what we say? (Author's note: *Some readers have discounted the possibility of a great harvest because they have been told that the church was never meant to succeed to that extent and that things are only going to get worse here on earth. I ask those readers to put such preconceptions on hold until we address them in the chapter, "God's Big Picture.")*

What exactly did Jesus ask for?

Let's look closely at what Jesus prayed in the seventeenth chapter of the Gospel of John. In this prayer, the eternal Son asked the eternal Father to accomplish something really big, something that without His intercession would not be possible, something that only the Son of God would have the faith to request.

It is reasonable to assume that a prayer offered by God's own Son, above all other prayers, will be answered. If the Father would deny a request from His own Son, then the rest of us might as well not pray another prayer. Given Jesus' perfect oneness with the Father, we must assume that He will indeed receive that for which He asked.

With that admittedly lengthy introduction in mind, let's examine what Jesus asked the Father to do - and then look around us and ask ourselves honestly whether that prayer is being answered in the church today. Jesus prayed these words:

*"I do not ask for these only (the twelve), but also for those who will believe in me through their word, [21] that they may all be one, just as you, Father, are in me, and I in you, that they also may be in us, **so that the world may believe that you have sent me**. [22] The glory that you have given me I have given to them, that they may be one even as we are one, [23] I in them and you in me, that they may become perfectly one, **so that the world may know that you sent me and loved them even as you loved me."** (NKJV)*

You might have noticed that Jesus used different words when He provided in His prayer the *reason* unity or oneness is so important. The first time, He said we were to be one, "...**that the world may believe that you have sent me**." The second time, He said, "... **that the world may know that you sent me**..." The word *"know"* conveys something new: In addition to *believing* that the Father sent Him, the world would *"recognize mentally"* that the Father had sent Him. This appears to strengthen the proposition that Christian oneness or unity is intended to be persuasive or even inescapable evidence of the Son's authenticity.

Two powerful messages in this one prayer

This is a powerful prayer and we can glean several facts from it. Jesus proclaimed that the Father and the Son are one. He informed us that the Father and Son are, in fact, *perfectly one,* and that this is the level of "oneness" that Christ's followers are to experience and exhibit before the world. We can also glean from this passage that if we become one, as the Father and the Son are one, then the world will know two things: That Jesus was sent by the Father and that the Father loves us just as He loves the Son. Both of these are staggering statements.

Taken at face value, this is a world-altering prayer. Jesus' words assure us that believers really can be one, just as the Father and the Son are one, as incomprehensible to the human mind as that may be. Then add to that notion the thought that the Father could love us *just as* He loves his own Son. I have to tell you, I almost cannot conceive of such a thing, but still I must accept that it is real.

I know how much I love my 22-year old son, who is currently serving in the United States Marine Corp, and yet the love I have for him can be but a mere shadow of the perfect love the Father has for his Son. Nonetheless, according to the passage we just read, this is the kind of love Jesus is asking for us. Could Jesus have meant this literally? Could God really love us as He loves his own Son? The answer is, "Yes."

He can love us as He loves his Son because He has joined us to his Son and made it so that we are Him and in his Son and share in their oneness. That may seem too much, but that is what the prayer says.

What did Jesus mean by oneness?

Let's focus for a bit on the oneness part of this prayer and keep in mind that this prayer is still hanging out there in eternity, unanswered, though it was made as a request from the Eternal Son 2,000 years ago.

If we examine Jesus' words in light of the most time honored, orthodox doctrine of Christianity, i.e. the doctrine of the Eternal Godhead, we must recognize that the oneness for which Jesus prayed is the most complete and perfect kind. To understand what is meant by the kind of oneness Jesus requested on our behalf, we must consider the kind of oneness the Father and Son enjoy. We must ask: How are the Father and the Son *one*?

Theologians agree that the Father and the Son are so *one* that in theological terms, they literally cannot be separated. While their Persons may be distinguished, they are forever inseparable and eternally one.

But their oneness is more than that. The three Persons of the Eternal Godhead are perfectly and unalterably of the same mind and judgment in all things. The Father, Son, and Holy Spirit have not and indeed cannot disagree. They are forever in one accord. This is basic Christian theology.

For Jesus to ask the Father to make us *one*, as He and the Father are *one,* is to ask that we be so joined to one another that we are entirely of the same mind and judgment and are thus inseparable. Joined in this kind of oneness, Christians won't believe things that are different from one other. We won't say things that contradict one another. We will not be robots. We will have our own unique personalities, but we will be entirely of the same mind regarding the things of the Spirit. We will all have the mind of Christ.

So, how does this indisputable theological fact relate to the issue at hand? We are, after all, mere humans and thus incapable of acting in the same kind of unity as the Eternal Godhead. Or are we? We offer this defense, perhaps with a certain sense of humility, but in reality it may be no defense at all.

When the apostle Paul rebuked the Corinthians for their carnality and their divisions (I Cor. 3:1-4), he used some peculiar language. Paul did not address the Corinthians as "mere" men but in fact rebuked them for acting like they were. Think about that. Paul rebuked the Corinthians for acting like ordinary humans. (Instead of "mere men," some translations use words like "acting in a human way" or "being merely human.") So, what does this terminology mean? Why would Paul rebuke Corinthian believers for acting like "mere humans?" Is that not what they were?

Apparently, Paul believed that once we are born again we are no longer mere humans and thus are not supposed to act as if that is all we are. We are sons of God and joint heirs with Christ. and we are supposed to behave as if we know that. We are not to behave as if we are merely human beings. We are to rise above that. This is not a far-fetched concept, nor is this exclusively a Pauline doctrine. The apostle John wrote, **"Beloved, *now* are we the sons of God and it does not yet appear what we shall be."** We might think we are merely humans, but neither Paul nor John allows us this excuse. John makes it clear that *now* we are sons of God. Not someday up in heaven, but *now*.

So, two apostles refuse to let us off as easily as we might have hoped. This "merely humanly" issue is an important point, so let's reinforce it further. Consider II Peter 1:3-4.

[3] as His divine power has given to us all things that *pertain* to life and godliness, through the knowledge of Him who called us by glory and virtue, [4] by which have been given to us exceedingly great and precious promises, **that through these you may be partakers of the divine nature, having escaped the corruption *that is* in the world through lust**.

So the apostle Peter is in agreement. He tells us of *exceedingly great and precious promises*, that we would be partakers of the divine nature. These are powerful words. We may choose to live as mere men, but we are not expected to, not given the fact that we are sons of God and are made partakers of His divine nature. Don't get me wrong, I am not trying to make us gods or imply some kind of sinless perfection in the here and now. I am just saying that we are not mere men. As born again believers who have been empowered by the Holy Spirit and made partakers of His divine nature, we may still act carnally and behave as "mere men," but we stand rebuked for doing so. When believers strive with other believers and churches divide from other churches, *we are not acting like what we are; we are acting like what* we *once were*.

This is likely the reason Jesus prayed the way He did in John 17. He knew that his followers would have the tendency to forget who they really were and begin to act like mere men. He knew that his prayer would be necessary to sustain us, and that we would never be one unless He prayed it into being!

Genuine unity would not be possible without this prayer

In Luke 22, we are told that Jesus prayed specifically for Peter, a man Jesus knew was going to endure trials that he was not prepared to face. Afterward, Jesus told Peter, *"Simon, Simon! Indeed, Satan has asked for you, that he may sift you as wheat.* [32] *But I have prayed for you, that your faith should not fail..."* The prayer of Jesus in John 17 is this kind of prayer, but this time He did not pray just for Peter. He prayed for all of us. Knowing our propensity for division, He prayed that all who believe on Him would be *one*.

For this prayer to be answered, all of us must be transformed by it, just as Peter was transformed by the prayer Jesus prayed for him. Fifty days after denying that he even knew Jesus, Peter stood up and preached boldly to thousands of Jews, saying "This Jesus, whom you have crucified, God has made both Lord and Christ." Three thousand souls came to Christ that day! Such was the power of Jesus' prayer for Peter. It literally transformed the man. So must the prayer of John 17 transform us. We are a carnal, contentious bunch and would never be capable of unity without the power of that prayer.

It is likely that most of us have skipped our way through John 17 many times, never considering the ramifications of the words Jesus prayed. Whatever He meant, genuine unity and Christian churches all being of the same mind and judgment could not be part of the package, right? That is simply not fathomable.

One might be tempted to think that Jesus' prayer perhaps meant something other than the seemingly far-fetched, literal interpretation laid out here. Would it not be easier to assign some other meaning to the words, and make them less daunting? Here's the problem: What I have suggested here appears to be precisely what the apostles understood this prayer to mean. The inspired men who wrote the New Testament took the words of Jesus' prayer at face value. They really believed Him. They expected Christians to act in accordance with the prayer of Jesus, no matter how contrary to their old nature that might be.

The apostle Paul, who wrote a larger share of the New Testament than any other apostle, believed that it was not only possible for believers to be one and to behave as one, but that it was in fact our responsibility to do so. Paul wrote to the Corinthians,

> *"Now I plead with you, brethren, by the name of our Lord Jesus Christ, that you **all speak the same thing**, and that there be no divisions among you, but that you **be perfectly joined together in the same mind and in the same judgment.**"* (I Corinthians 1:10 NKJV)

Is this not the very thing Jesus was speaking of? Jesus prayed that believers would be "perfectly one" and Paul said we were to be "perfectly joined together." Paul makes it clear that he is speaking of the same thing Jesus prayed for when he goes on to say that believers were to *all speak the same thing and be of the same mind and judgment.*

By employing such language, is Paul not describing the same kind of unity that Jesus prayed for, the kind of unity that the Father and Son share? Isn't this the same kind of unity in which the Eternal Godhead is *"perfectly joined together in the same mind and in the same judgment?"* Are the words of Paul to the Corinthians not a clear echo of the words of Jesus in John 17?

Again, let us fast forward to our times. Is it not fair to say that the church today is known to the world more for our disagreements and disunity than for our oneness? Do our local yellow pages not proclaim to the world that Christians are not one? Do all those church buildings with their different names not betray our true condition? Do our contradicting doctrines not testify against? Do not all of these things shout to the world that Christians are a terribly fractured bunch and not one at all?

Let that sink in for a moment. Jesus prayed that we would all be one, and that in this way, the world would know that the Father sent Him. Yet here we are, doing our best, in every way possible, to show the whole world that we are not one. We preach the gospel and then instead of showing the world what Jesus is really like, we show it the opposite. It is a wonder of grace that we have borne any fruit at all.

Our divisions are indeed a grave thing. We must come to see this. Our divisions do immeasurable damage to the body of Christ and we must begin to acknowledge this fact. It must grieve our Lord to see His church so terribly divided, yet somehow it does not grieve us. How is it that we are so oblivious to our condition and feel no shame? We drive down the street on the way to church like the Peterson family in the first chapter; we pass five or ten other churches before we finally come to the one that is of the "brand name" with which we associate, and we think nothing of it. We pass by all those signs of our division, blatant signs, and we simply ignore them.

Who do we think those people are, the ones in those other churches? Are they strangers to us? Are they distant relatives? Are they spiritual siblings with whom we are not on speaking terms? Perhaps we think they are lesser Christians because they are not our brand of Christian? Perhaps we think, deep down inside, that God loves us more than He does them, even though they confess the same Lord Jesus Christ, as we do.

Paul was angry with the Corinthian believers and all they were guilty of was tolerating divisions or cliques within the one church in Corinth. Is our divisiveness not many times worse than theirs? Paul asked the Corinthians who were part of his fan club: "Was Paul crucified for you? Were you baptized in the name of Paul?"

Perhaps we cannot relate to these words, so let's put them into a context we can better understand. Perhaps the apostle might say to us, "Was Luther crucified for you? Was Calvin or Wesley? Were you baptized in the name of Billy Graham, Chuck Swindoll, Joel Olsteen, Pat Robertson, or J. Vernon McGee?"

Would Paul not look at us today and ask pointedly, "Are you a Christian or are you more a Presbyterian, Baptist, Methodist, Anglican, Catholic, or Pentecostal?" The Corinthian church drew a strong rebuke for its four factions, but we have more than we can count and sometimes they are all present in the same city!

Have we simply ignored this prayer?

As we close this chapter, I ask you to ponder this: Just hours before the Son of God and Savior of mankind, went to the cross to suffer the wrath of God for the sins of every man, woman, and child who would ever live, including you and me, He knelt before the Father and made His last recorded request. What did the One who gave his life for us desire; what did He who was about to make the greatest sacrifice of all time want the Father to do for Him? He asked that those who believed on Him would all be one. It is painful to consider how little value we have placed on those words.

How can we say we serve the risen Savior and ignore this prayer? How can those of us who have been redeemed by His blood so calmly and routinely dismiss the thing our Lord so earnestly desired for us? If unity of believers was so important to Jesus, should it not be important to us?

Perhaps we would show more interest in unity if we realized how powerful it really is. That is what we shall do next.

The Tower of Babel
Unity, a power greater than the atom

ℒℛ

The Book of Genesis records in a very small space some of the most important events in the history of the world. The entire Old and New Testaments record approximately 4,100 years of human history, and yet a full 1,600 years of that is described in just the first nine chapters of the Book of Genesis.

Sometimes, God says a lot in very little space. In the first couple of chapters of the Bible, we learn that God created the sun, the moon, and the stars; and that He created the earth and all of the plants and animals on it. In the third chapter, we discover the immeasurable impact the disobedience of one man could have on the entire human race, as we see the first humans and all their offspring banished from the garden and cut off from free access to the presence of God.

A few short chapters after Adam's fall, we learn that God is both willing and able to judge the entire planet and every person on it when He sent a worldwide flood, a terrible judgment that wiped out almost every living creature that moved about on the face of the earth, a judgment that was but a harbinger of a final and even greater judgment that is yet to come.

Sandwiched between the flood of Noah, which occurred approximately 1,655 years after creation, and our first introduction to Abraham, who lived approximately 2,000 years after creation, we find the rather odd story of the Tower of Babel. This story takes less than a chapter to tell, but it is a powerful one. And it is an especially important one to us, because of the rather astounding thing it reveals about the power of unity.

What occurred at Babel, there on the Plain of Shinar, is of great significance and changed the course of human history. It was at Babel that the nations of the earth were originally divided. It was at Babel that the one language, which until then all the people of the earth had shared, was divided into something in the neighborhood of seventy-two different languages, bringing about an unprecedented confusion among the human race.

What happened at Babel is also of enormous *spiritual* significance. In the story of the Tower of Babel, God revealed something extraordinary, i.e. that there is a force, a power so great that He had to divinely intervene to prevent the human race from ever using it.

That force, that source of unstoppable power, is unity. This is such a powerful revelation that I am surprised that God let the secret out. Nowhere else in the Bible does God speak of the human race as He did at Babel. What God said at Babel explains why Satan is so afraid of church unity and why he has spent centuries doing everything in his power to ensure that the church of Jesus Christ is as fractured and divided as possible.

With that thought in mind, let's look at what happened at Babel. The story is recorded in the eleventh chapter of Genesis. Pieces of the story you are about to read are gleaned from ancient Hebrew tradition rather than Scripture, but those parts only help us tell the story and are not critical to our thesis.

The location, we are told, was the Plain of Shinar, located in the country we now call Iraq, the seat of ancient Babylon. Shinar was a wide, flat place and many men had gathered there. Shinar was a long journey westward from the spot where the ark of Noah had come to rest several centuries earlier.

After the waters of the Great Flood had sufficiently subsided, a mere eight souls had stepped forth into the new world, a world containing no animal life except the animals that had ridden out the deluge with Noah's family in the ark. The millions of humans who had lived before the flood were all dead. Except for those creatures preserved within the ark, there were no other air-breathing land animals or men anywhere on the face of the earth.

Noah and his three sons had been fruitful after the flood and had multiplied. Just as the planet had been populated in the beginning with the offspring of Adam and Eve, so would the earth again be populated by the offspring of Noah's three sons and their wives.

There was a problem, however. Even though mankind had multiplied quickly after the flood, they had not scattered and filled the whole earth as the Lord had intended. Some had other plans, plans that were carried out in defiance of God.

Up until this time, everyone on the face of the earth had spoken the same language, the language which Noah and his sons and their wives had spoken. Anywhere on earth that men traveled, they could communicate with anyone they met. There was no language barrier whatsoever.

After all, languages divide people. They separate nations. Languages make people suspicious of one another. They make commerce more difficult.

Also, as people live separately, they gradually develop different customs, making them even more unlike those people who are more distant from them. People separated geographically because of language barriers tend to breed primarily with people of their own kind. Over time, the genetic make-up of people living at a distance from others tends to give them physical characteristics unique to them. These differences foster even further division.

None of this was known to the men at Shinar. They all looked similar and spoke the same language and thus were able to act in concert - as one people. They had no comprehension of the advantages they possessed.

It appears from the biblical text that it was the descendants of Ham, Noah's middle son, who did not wish to scatter. Ham was the son on whom Noah had placed a curse. It was Ham's descendants, who purposed in their hearts to defy the Lord by building a great city at the Plain of Shinar.

In the middle of the city, they wanted to build a tower so high that it could be seen from many miles around. The tower would keep

Ham's descendants from being lost out there in the vast, unmapped terrain, which seemed to stretch on forever.

The Scriptures say the people who gathered at Shinar wanted to make a name for themselves. It was a proud reason, but it was their expressed purpose for building the city.

In that day, there was a man who saw himself as one born to rule over other men. The man's name was Nimrod. Some translators say he was called Nimrod "the great hunter." Other translators say he was called Nimrod, "the man who hunted in defiance of the Lord."

Nimrod was Ham's great grandson. Hebrew tradition says he set out to build the Tower of Babel for the express purpose of defying God. He had become a powerful ruler and wished to establish his own kingdom and rule over as many people as possible. Nimrod saw God as a competitor. Nimrod wanted men to fear and obey him, not God.

The memory of the great flood was not so distant for the people of that day. They had heard the story in great detail from their grandparents or great grandparents. And who would not fear a God so powerful that He could send a flood great enough to cover the entire earth and drown every man, animal, and bird?

According to legend, it was Nimrod's plan to place at the top of this great tower a giant statue, a likeness of himself. The statue would be an image of him as a hunter with his bow outstretched and an arrow pointed up towards the heavens – aimed right at God himself.

Stories had been spread among the people that Nimrod and some of his fiercest warriors had fired arrows up into the sky and that the arrows had come back bloody, proving that the gods who had destroyed the earth centuries earlier could be killed. If the gods bled, Nimrod said, then they could be killed.

Nimrod told the people that it was weakness, a sign of cowardice to fear a god. He told the people that he was willing to lead them in rebellion against the gods and ensure that those cruel gods never again would destroy the earth like they had with the flood of Noah's day. He rallied the people to his "great" cause.

There are legends and traditions which suggest that there were also other reasons for building so great a tower.

Some say the tower was meant to be a high place from which men could better observe the sun, moon, and stars and worship the hosts of heaven rather than the God who had made them. Idolatry of this nature was common when mankind was new upon the earth.

Some commentators suggest that the top of the tower was to be outfitted with stone engravings of the signs of the zodiac. They say that the passage in Genesis 11 should not say that the tower was to be built "to the heavens" but rather that the top was to be "with the heavens," or a high tower with the top ornate with the signs of the zodiac.

Whatever their reasons were, the descendants of Ham commenced to build a great tower there on the Plain of Shinar. The undertaking was an immense one, even by modern standards, but it could be done. There was no shortage of earth for making bricks and there was plenty of sun for baking them hard. According to the account in Genesis 11, there was even a local form of asphalt or slime to mortar the bricks together.

The people had all of the makings of an ancient Middle Eastern city. All they needed was a man with the ambition to drive the people and make it all happen. Nimrod was such a man, a prototype, if you will, of a last day antichrist. Nimrod could have pulled it off, too, but something went catastrophically wrong with his plan. Perhaps the day it happened went something like this:

The day started like every other day

The hot afternoon sun was beating down on the desert floor. From horizon to horizon, the sky was a pale blue with never so much as a wisp of a cloud to provide shade for the parched ground below. In that regard, this day was just like every other day there on the plain.

Although the sky above was calm and peaceful, the scene there on the desert floor was quite the opposite. Like ants, men and women were scurrying back and forth, working tirelessly from sunrise to sunset. They were busy baking and stacking bricks, lots of bricks.

Nimrod pushed the people hard. His plans were ambitious and far too immense to allow the people to rest. The men worked. The women worked. Children barely old enough to labor worked all day long in the hot sun. It is said that the pregnant women were not even allowed a day off to bear their children. They gave birth right there on the job and then carried the child with them for the rest of the day, while the work continued.

Back and forth the workers moved, ever in the same dull routine. Some were making the bricks, mixing water with the dry earth, squaring off each brick before it hardened and ensuring that each brick was the size and shape the planners on the tower above them required.

The bricks were large. They had to be. The tower had to reach up to the sky. That was the plan. The tower had to be high enough to be seen from afar off. It had to be the greatest building ever built, the tallest in the world. Nothing would stop it. There would be no rest until it was finished.

While some workers were making bricks, others stumbled back and forth hour after endless hour, bringing earth and water and then more earth and more water to the brick makers. It was mindless, exhausting work, but conscripted workers have no choice. They work until they are told they can stop. Nimrod had a plan and the people were going to do as he demanded. He told them they would be proud, that they would be the greatest people on the face of the earth when the job was completed.

All around the base of the tower, assembly lines had been set up to supply the bricks for those whose job it was to move the loads of bricks up the ramp that circled the entire outer wall of the tower. As the tower grew, the distance from the desert floor to the new level became even greater and so the task became increasingly more difficult.

Up on the tower, the more skilled workers set the bricks in place and mortared each one with buckets of slime that other workers continually packed up the ramp. It was an enormous undertaking, but it was all part of one man's master plan.

The base of the tower was very wide. Somehow, the architects who had designed it knew that for the top to be as high as Nimrod wanted and for the tower to serve its purpose, the base would have to be wide.

From a distance the structure looked more like a mountain than a tower, an ever growing mountain swarming with human ants. Hour after hour, day after day, the workers brought load after load of hardened bricks and bucket after bucket of wet slime up the sides of the tower. The tower grew higher and higher, as if reaching up to touch the pale blue sky.

You might ask, how high could these ancient people really have built a tower made only of mud bricks? You might be surprised by the answer. Modern architects have calculated that the hardened bricks baked there on the desert floor could have been stacked a full seven hundred feet high before the weight of the structure would begin crush the bricks on the bottom. This calculation, however, was based on a structure with outside walls running parallel to each other and straight up and down.

If on the other hand, the base itself was larger than the top and the structure narrowed as it ascended, architects today theorize that the bricks could have been stacked high enough that it would be difficult for the workers to breath the thin air at so high an altitude.

With this design, the outside wall of the tower could be angled up from the desert floor and serve as a construction ramp, a makeshift or temporary road up which new bricks could be more easily moved from level to level.

If you think about it, what was there to stop the people from doing what they set out to do? They had a workable design, plenty of earth and water and a natural source of mortar. They had an ambitious taskmaster and the workforce necessary to get the job done.

They also had one other thing working in their favor. The Bible says that the people building the Tower of Babel "were all one." Whether they worked willingly, out of devotion to the project, or whether they labored at a whip's end, there was a singleness of mind and unity of purpose. According to the Lord himself, it was this *oneness that* made their goal possible. Because of their unity, they could have succeeded, *even if the thing they purposed to do was displeasing to the Lord.* Such is the power of unity. Let's say that again. Because of their unity, they could have succeeded, *even if the thing they purposed to do was displeasing to the Lord.*

Whether the project involves an ancient tower, a modern sky-scraper, or a fabulously ornate cathedral, it can be built if people set their minds to it and work as one, whether or not the project is the will of God. This is but one of the lessons we can glean from the goings on at Shinar.

It was for this reason that the Lord himself put a stop to the Tower of Babel.

The division of language

In the eleventh chapter of Genesis, we are told that the Lord saw the city and the tower that the "sons of men" had built. Looking over the project, the Lord said,

> *"Indeed **the people are one** and they all have one language and this is what they begin to do; **now nothing that they propose to do will be withheld from them.***
> *"Come, let Us go down and there confuse their language, that they may not understand one another's speech." (NKJV)*

And that is exactly what happened. It must have been the strangest thing. One minute the people were talking and jabbering with those working next to them, and then suddenly they could no longer understand each other.

Suddenly, the sounds that came out of their mouths were gibberish to the ones working next to them. The brick makers could no longer call for more water. Those setting the stones in place could no longer communicate that they needed more slime to mortar the bricks into place. The architects could no longer tell the workers where to place the bricks.

Of course, what happened at that moment had a more far-reaching impact than simply losing the ability to communicate. As much as anything, it was the shock of it all. No one had ever met anyone who spoke a different language. Such a thing was totally unknown. Everyone had always understood everyone else's speech.

The strangeness of the phenomenon must have contributed greatly to the chaos. One minute the people were all one and the next they were all strangers jabbering unintelligible sounds at one another. The scene must have been the epitome of confusion. No one knew what to think.

What could have caused such a thing? Was it the work of the gods or some devil? Had the people suddenly caught some form of madness? Everyone must have thought, "I'm speaking normally. Why is everyone else making these crazy, senseless sounds?"

It was too much. No one could work in such conditions. Instead of working, people ran around looking for someone who wasn't crazy. Eventually, everyone found others whose speech made sense to them. These were their new friends. People gathered into groups based on their common language and separated themselves accordingly.

The Bible says that the work on the project ceased and the people were scattered over the face of all of the earth. They ceased work on the tower and they stopped working on the city that they had been building *"to make a name for themselves."* Just like that, it was over. Nimrod's plan was thwarted. The Tower of Babel was never finished.

Why? Because the people were no longer one. They could not finish because they were divided.

The power of unity

Looking back at what happened at Shinar, it is difficult to miss the assessment the Lord made of that situation. The words God uttered as He observed what the people were doing indicate with some certainty that we humans, when acting in unity with our fellow men, can do anything we set our collective mind to do.

Obviously, God did not wish for *mere men* to have such power. Unity was too dangerous a weapon for rebellious men to possess.

To prevent such ambitious and defiant undertakings in the future, languages were so divinely confused that it is estimated by Hebrew scholars that as many as seventy-two different languages were brought into existence on that one day. The chaos and confusion resulting from the sudden introduction of so many new languages is the reason why the tower was called the Tower of Babel or *tower of confusion.*

As a direct consequence of their language barriers, mankind broke up into clans, joining with those who spoke their same language. Together these groups set off in different directions, scattering across the face of the earth as God had intended.

The consequences of what happened then are still with us today, only magnified. In modern times, when the nations of the world come together at the United Nations to discuss matters, which are ostensibly of world importance, hundreds of translators are required just to hold the meetings. Hundreds! Not only are there so many different languages, but within those languages are local dialects, often so diverse as to be almost unintelligible, even to those speaking the same root language.

Mankind is still divided today because of what God did in the eleventh chapter of Genesis. God has done nothing to reverse the effects of Babel. It is not the will of God for ungodly men to be of one accord. He would rather that they remain divided in their rebellion.

Even if division was sown in the earth by God himself, specifically to prevent the sons of men from being one and acting in unity, it is not His divine will for the same to be true of His church. The division the Lord used to divide the nations is not His plan for the body of Christ. Churches today are not divided from one another because of an act of God. We are divided because the enemy has sowed discord among us. We are divided because of sin and carnality, i.e. our pride, our greed, our lust for power and influence.

It should be obvious from the scriptures we have discussed already that there are to be no divisions amongst believers. Divisions are strictly prohibited. Nonetheless, here we sit, divided into countless fractures and sects; and all the while acting as if there was nothing wrong with us. We are so confident that our church is the best church in town and that our denomination, if any, is the right one, that we almost take pride in our divisions.

The original title I chose for this book was not "The Fractured Church," but "Babel Reversed." I initially chose that title because it is apparent from Scripture that God wishes to reverse in the body of Christ what He did to sinful men at Babel. He wants the world divided, but He wants believers to be perfectly united and perfectly joined together, speaking the same thing and being of the same mind and judgment.

We have missed that target. We have allowed the enemy to use our carnality, our pride, our ambition, our selfishness, and our desire to build our own kingdoms to do to us what God did to the defiant ones at Babel.

Satan loves our divisions. He delights in them. He knows that a divided church cannot truly defeat him. He knows that the gates of hell are safe from any serious assault by a church that is divided. He knows a kingdom divided cannot stand, so he does his best to break us up. And we let him. We even help him.

Admittedly, even in our small bands, Bible-believing Christians are a force to be reckoned with and cannot be ignored. Even small bands of united believers can cause damage to the kingdom of darkness. But Satan will rue the day that the people of God come at him with one accord, so perfectly joined in unity that they are indeed one body, one warrior with every part functioning perfectly in its proper place, rising to the stature of the fullness of Christ.

A popular television series recently featured an episode where the drama's heroine, a successful lawyer, was confronted by her teenage daughter, who had decided she wanted to be a follower of Jesus and wanted her mother to take her to church the following Sunday. The hesitant mother finally acquiesced, but then stopped and asked her daughter, "Which one?" It was one of those telltale moments. Neither mother nor daughter had any idea how to pick a church to go to. There were just too many.

Like the Corinthian businessman the apostle Paul confronted in our imaginary trip to Corinth, this TV mom had no idea which church was "the right one." From her perspective, what were the odds of her blindly picking a church out of the yellow pages or online, and it being the right one, or even a good one?

Babel reversed

Unity is a powerful thing. It is a weapon of unlimited power. It's also a place, a place where the Lord has commanded a blessing. It's a condition, a condition of being one with not only each other but also with the Creator of heaven and earth.

It is no wonder that we have not been able to obtain easily this thing, this weapon, this place or this condition called unity. It is, after all, the greatest prize. It is the end game, so to speak.

The rewards of real unity will be immeasurable. When Babel is reversed in the body of Christ, souls will come into the Kingdom of God in unprecedented numbers and eventually the kingdoms of this world will become the kingdoms of our God and his Christ.

Unity is a force so powerful that it may only be entrusted to the Body of Christ and none other. When there is genuine unity in the Body of Christ, the will of our Father will be done on earth as it is in Heaven, as our Lord taught us to pray.

In writing this book, I am not trying to build anything or tear anything down. To the extent such things are necessary, it must be the Lord's job to do it. The church is, after all, the Lord's house and He is the one who must build it.

Let us begin to pray that the Lord will accomplish His purpose; that He will bring about by His Spirit not just the end of denominationalism and sectarianism, but the building of a glorious house for all the world to behold. A house wherein all who are called by His name will be one, as He and the Father are one, so that finally the world will know that Jesus Christ really was sent by the Father.

How the early church was structured

ᔕᔦᔧᔧ

To understand the way churches are structured today as compared to the ways things were done in the days of the early apostles, it might be helpful to forget what we think we know, wipe the slate clean in our minds, and take a fresh look. The reason for this will become apparent as we proceed.

In the early days of the Christian church, there was only one church per city. That church consisted of all of the Christians who lived in or around a particular metropolitan area. Some of these churches were actually quite large, consisting of thousands of believers. Although it is the norm today, nowhere in the New Testament is there any suggestion of multiple, separate churches coexisting in a single metropolitan area.

There were no church buildings, so it was common in the early church for believers in a particular city or town to meet in smaller groups from house to house – in the homes of believers. All we can glean from Scripture regarding early church meeting places is that there was only one church per city and those churches met in houses.

Romans 16:5 *"Likewise greet the church that is in their house…"*
II Corinthians 16:19 *"The churches of Asia greet you. Aquila and Priscilla greet you heartily in the Lord, with the church that is in their house."*

Colossians 4:15 *"Greet the brethren who are in Laodicea, and Nymphas and the church that is in his house."*
Philemon 1:2 *"to the beloved Apphia, Archippus our fellow soldier, and to the church in your house…"*

Because of the limited space in a residential setting, it is possible or even likely that several such meetings were going on in a city at the same time, though all were under the auspices of the city's one church eldership. Sometimes the believers in a city may have congregated in larger meetings for special occasions, like the one where Paul preached so long that one of the congregants dozed off and fell from the third loft and was taken up dead. (Acts 20:9) But there is no evidence anywhere in Scripture of church-owned buildings.

It is important to recognize that in the beginning, geography was the only basis for church separation. Doctrine was never a basis for having multiple churches in a single city. This is evident from the Book of Acts all the way through to the end of the New Testament. In the Book of Revelation, when the ascended Christ uttered seven separate messages to the seven churches of Asia Minor, His messages were addressed to specific churches, churches identified only by the names of the cities in which they were located. The Lord spoke to the church at Ephesus, the church at Smyrna, the church at Philadelphia, and so on.

There were, of course, no denominations or "brand" names for Christians. There were no Baptists, Methodists, Presbyterians, or Pentecostals. There were no Orthodox, Anglican, or Catholic churches. They were just plain ole Christians and they were all referred to as "saints."[3] To put it plainly, the kind of sectarianism such as is common today, would not have been tolerated by the apostles, who strove to maintain unity within the church at all times.

Also, there were no popes, metropolitans, or cardinals. There were no regional superintendents and no denominational headquarters. Men would invent these things much later on.

Although some of the apostles lived in Jerusalem and held council there with the elders of the Jerusalem church, the real authority rested with the apostles and not the Jerusalem church itself. For a while, there was simply no other established church.

When other churches were added, the church at Jerusalem did not rule over them. It was not their headquarters, and neither was Rome, at least not until several centuries later.

Church government was local and each church was autonomous and self-governing. Churches were governed by a group of godly men called *elders, presbyters, or bishops*. An apostle could step in and speak to a local church with the authority inherent in his office, but there was no other outside authority. The authority of an apostle was a spiritual one rather than a political one. His authority was vested in his gifting rather than his official position. A man could claim to be an apostle, but he had to also be able to demonstrate the signs of an apostle, a point we will discuss in greater detail later on.

Appointing a board of elders was an integral part of establishing a new church. In Titus 1:5 the apostle Paul reminds Titus that he had been left in Crete to *"set in order the things that are lacking and appoint elders in every city..."* This was the pattern the apostles followed. They preached the gospel in a city, and then before leaving the area, they made sure that elders were appointed to govern the new church.

Governance by elders was entirely the norm for the early church. Even after the twelve apostles and Paul had passed on, Clement of Rome, who was a disciple of the apostle Peter (and incidentally was referred to as an apostle himself), wrote in 96 A.D. of only two offices in the church, namely bishops and deacons. He wrote that the church was to be governed by the *"elders that are set over it."*[4] There were no denominational headquarters to intervene. Local elders governed local churches. Period. That was the design in the early church.

In those times, even the position which we call senior pastor did not exist, at least not officially. It is possible, and even likely, that some men's gifting made them "first among equals" as they worked with the other elders of their local church, but there is no mention in Scripture of an official "senior pastor" or head pastor position. This position sort of evolved over time and it is not difficult to understand why.

Church government changed as revival diminished

Eventually, some churches found that leadership or governance by committee was unworkable, especially over an extended period of time, though there is no mention of this in Scripture. Possibly, this came about as the dynamic of the Holy Spirit gradually began to diminish. Charles Schmitt in "Floods Upon the Dry Ground" writes,

> *"A college of men can only be induced to be of the same mind, maintaining the same love, united in spirit, intent on one purpose, as long as Christ's manifest presence and dynamic activity is strong among them."[5]*

This seems to be a reasonable explanation as to why there is no historical record, until the middle of the second century, of single bishops ruling over local churches, although by the end of that century the practice was "well-nigh universal."[6] As the Holy Spirit dynamic of the early church began to wane, it became less workable to govern by committee or a board of elders.

Lutheran historian, Lars P. Qualben, said of this phenomenon, "*...a new generation had grown up that had not been won directly for the church from heathenism, but had been born and educated in Christian homes. Instead of the immediate gifts of the Spirit, Christians rather relied on organizations and outward religious authority.*"[7] (This is a rather natural development and seemed to accompany the ebb and flow of revival throughout church history.)

This is the pattern that was repeated many times throughout history: Revival came. While the Spirit was moving, men held positions in the church by reason of their obvious gifts. Over time, the revival waned and men gradually began to hold positions more because of natural abilities, political connections, or because someone gave them the authority.

Charles Schmitt aptly describes this process as the church becoming less an organism and more an organization. Instead of a living thing, the church became more of an organized structure.[8]

It is likely that leadership by a single pastor was not encouraged at first, because of the tendency of the original apostles to downplay personalities. As was evident in the church in Corinth, men have a tendency to gravitate to certain personalities like they do movie stars and professional athletes. For some reason, we like our stars and celebrities. Christians are in no way immune to this kind of idolatry.

The apostles played down individual personalities

The apostles went out of their way to avoid personality cults. They wanted Christ to have the preeminence in all things. When some of the Corinthians said they were *of Paul*, he responded sternly, "Did Paul die for you?" In other words, don't ascribe to me some place that no man can hold, some place where only Christ can sit. The apostles went out of their way to avoid doing things that would cause people to gather around them as individuals.

In one case, Peter and John performed a notable miracle (recorded in Acts 3) and the people were greatly impressed with what they had done. The humble response from the apostles went something like this, "Why are you looking at us as if we did this miracle by our own power and godliness? God did this; we didn't."

The apostles consistently pointed people to Christ, not the "Paul and Silas Evangelistic Association." They carried great power as apostles, but they did not dare accept glory in their own names. They knew better than to do so. Luke records, in the book of Acts, a story of King Herod giving a speech that so impressed the people that they said, "It is the voice of a god." Herod accepted the praise and was struck with worms in his insides and died.[9] Many preachers today have forgotten what happened to Herod and would be well advised to adhere more meticulously to a "To God alone be the glory" media strategy and platform style.

Avoiding personality cults was a big deal to the early apostles. Paul said he intentionally did not baptize people lest they take pride in the fact that they had been baptized by him and conclude that this somehow made them part of a special company. Too many church leaders today seem to relish the attention their fame affords them. Much more could be said about this, but it is apparent to the whole world that in our day of big time radio and television ministries, some have strayed far from this principle.

In summarizing this section, it is possible, if not likely, that the end of the age is upon us, though no one has been able to make that case with any degree of certainty. But if it is, in the days ahead, things may begin to change rapidly. It might be helpful as we move forward to recognize that pretty much the entire ecclesiastical hierarchy that exists today was nonexistent in the early days of the church. The overarching church offices, such as popes and cardinals and denominational boards and superintendents simply did not exist and are not found in the Bible. For that reason, we might be well advised to cling to such structures less tightly.

There are only two local church offices named in the New Testament: Deacon and elder. Deacons were godly men (and perhaps women) who handled the practical affairs of the church, while the elders or bishops were godly men who provided the spiritual oversight. Within a couple of centuries, the church would abandon this simplicity and create a system far more structured than the apostles intended, but in the beginning it was all very simple.

The controversy regarding prophets and apostles

In the early church, there were specific ministry gifts in operation, including the ministry of apostles, prophets, evangelists, pastors and teachers. It is likely that some of the deacons and elders in the early church also functioned as prophets, evangelists, pastors, or teachers – as Phillip and Stephen did.

Few doubt the existence of evangelists, pastors, and teachers in the modern day church, but whether there are still apostles and prophets is a somewhat controversial issue, at least in some circles. This is primarily due to the fact that the original twelve are given a special status in Scripture, even by Christ. It is not necessary to make a case here for whether there are prophets and apostles today. However, the question may prove in time to be relevant to our topic.

The word "apostle" simply means a *sent one* or *one sent with a message or sent on a mission*. Twelve men were uniquely chosen for this role, though not all survived to fulfill their calling. One of the original twelve, Judas, killed himself after betraying Jesus. Judas was replaced shortly thereafter (Acts 1) by a vote of the remaining eleven, who had reason to believe there were supposed to be twelve apostles and that all twelve had to have been witnesses of Jesus' ministry. The eleven chose Mathias, a man who had been with them from the beginning, but previously had not been named as one of the twelve.

Twelve is a significant number in Scripture. For example, there were twelve tribes of Israel and there were twelve apostles in the early church. There is some special or prophetic significance to this. Jesus promised the twelve apostles that they would sit on twelve thrones and judge the twelve tribes of Israel[10] and in the Book of the Revelation we are told of the heavenly city: *"And the wall of the city had twelve foundations, and in them the names of the twelve apostles of the Lamb."*[11] So, apparently it was important that there be twelve apostles of the Lamb.

However, after recognizing the unique role of the twelve, the ministry and role of apostles becomes less certain, because the twelve are not the only apostles named in the New Testament. As you probably know, Paul was called by Jesus to be an apostle. Paul was never one of the twelve and had not been with Jesus throughout his ministry. So apparently, having been with Jesus and witnessing His entire three-and-a-half year ministry was only a qualification for being named among "the twelve." You could be an apostle without having witnessed Jesus' ministry, but you couldn't be one of the twelve.

Paul, however, wasn't the only additional apostle. There are several other men who also are called apostles in the New Testament, though it is not always clear in the text that they were apostles in the same sense that Paul or the twelve were. There are several passages where the same Greek word, *apostolos,* is used, but it is not translated *apostle.* An arbitrary decision was made by some translators not to translate the same word in certain passages as they did elsewhere. Even if we accept the translators' decisions, still there are others who are called apostles in the New Testament.

Barnabas is called an apostle in Acts 14:14. James and Jude, the brothers of Jesus, are called apostles, (James in Galatians 1:19). The seventy men that Jesus sent out in the Gospels are all called apostles (Luke 10:17). Silas, who ministered with Paul, was called an apostle. We may not think of all of these men (and there are several others) as apostles, but the same Greek word is used to describe them.

Those who claim that the office of apostle ended with the death of the last of the twelve, presumably John, usually claim that miracles, spiritual gifts, and the ministry of the prophet also ended with the passing of the early apostles. This position cannot be proved or disproved with absolute certainty from Scriptures, because the theory is based on inference and "circumstantial evidence."

The issue is further complicated by the fact that several of the apostolic or early church fathers, men who lived well after the twelve had passed on, were openly referred to as apostles. This historical reality suggests that the early church may not have viewed the office of apostle as limited only to the first century, though it is not wise to assume that everything the second and third century church believed and practiced was correct.

I speak with some trepidation here, because it is part and parcel of some dispensationalist and cessationalist teachings that there was no further need for apostles, prophets, or the gifts of the Spirit after the New Testament was completed. But what if those who teach this theory are mistaken? What if these ministries and gifts are needed in *our time* as much as in the early church? What if the church cannot come to maturity without them? This is an important question and the answer should be determined by the church as a whole, and not by any one group.

There are websites which claim that all Pentecostals and charismatics are lost and on their way to hell, even though they profess the name of Christ and believe the same essential doctrines as those condemning them. While it is with difficulty that I refrain from responding to claims like this, I must. What I hope to do instead is demonstrate that extremely divisive claims like this should not be left unsettled, but should be addressed by the Christian church as a whole and not some faction or subset of it. With churches condemning to hell the tens of millions who believe in prophecy and speaking in tongues, there is an obvious and perhaps urgent need to resolve this matter. As serious as this issue is, let's lay it aside for now and get back to the issue of apostles.

There are missionaries today, who go into the far reaches of the earth and preach the gospel with signs following[12] and build churches from the ground up, just like the early apostles did. They go where there are no churches and they start churches. They set elders over them and father them until they are established and strong. The ministries of some modern day missionaries appear to be indistinguishable from the apostles of the New Testament. Are these missionaries really apostles by another name or are they simply missionaries, a term not found in the Bible?

The church is instructed by Christ to prove those who claim to be apostles, but are not.[13] Is the church following up on this instruction or ignoring it? I submit that the church cannot rightly fulfill this responsibility as a divided entity. If different churches come to different conclusions, the result will be division. If a man goes forth today and preaches the gospel with genuine signs[14] following, and starts new churches, how does he differ from say Paul or Barnabas? This is an especially important question, because apostles are described in Scripture as part of the foundation of the church. Paul said in Ephesians 2:

> [19] Now, therefore, you are no longer strangers and foreigners, but fellow citizens with the saints and members of the household of God, **20 having been built on the foundation of the apostles and prophets**, Jesus Christ Himself being the chief corner*stone,* [21] in whom the whole building, being fitted together, grows into a holy temple in the Lord…"

And there is this passage in I Corinthians 12:

> [28] And God has appointed these in the church: **first apostles, second prophets**, third teachers, after that miracles, then gifts of healings, helps, administrations, varieties of tongues. [29] *Are* all apostles? *Are* all prophets? *Are* all teachers? *Are* all workers of miracles? [30] Do all have gifts of healings? Do all speak with tongues? Do all interpret?

If the ministries of apostle and prophet are part of the foundation of the church, perhaps the church as a whole should have a serious discussion regarding whether these offices ceased to exist 1900 years ago, or on the other hand, should exist and be functioning in the church today.

Let's briefly address the issue of prophets, which was a common ministry in the early church. Some make the same claim regarding prophets as they do apostles; i.e. that there was no further need for prophets once the New Testament was completed. That side claims that the Bible contains everything the modern day church needs to know, and therefore, there is no further need for supernatural revelation in our time. Most who promulgate this view argue that all modern day "prophets" are imposters or false prophets.

The other side generally agrees that the New Testament is the only authoritative basis for doctrine, but argues that the New Testament does not provide the kind of revelation the early church experienced through the gift of prophecy and that such revelation is still needed. They point to the ministry of Agabus, the early church prophet mentioned in the 11th and 21st chapters of the Book of Acts. In one case, Agabus prophesied of a great famine that was coming and in another he warned Paul prophetically that the Jews were going to put him in bonds and deliver him over to the Gentiles. Apparently, this kind of predictive prophecy was common in the early church, because Paul reported, "*the Holy Spirit testifies to me in every city that imprisonment and afflictions await me.*"[15] In other words, everywhere Paul went, local prophets[16] were confirming or foretelling what was about to happen to him.

It appears from other passages that the debate over the gift of prophecy is not an entirely new one. For example, Paul told the Thessalonican church not to despise prophesying, but rather to prove all things.[17] Why would Paul give such an exhortation? Why did he think it was important to tell a church not to despise prophesying? Were there believers in Paul's day who were afraid of this gift and wanted it stopped? Is that what we are dealing with today, or were such gifts designed to cease at the end of the first century?

In summary, there were apostles and prophets in the early church and their ministries were considered foundational. The question of whether they exist today is an important one and should be answered one way or the other, but not by any one group or by any one school of thought. The body of Christ must find the answer together. It is at least possible that there are weaknesses in the church today which might stem directly from the lack of these offices, or perhaps the failure to recognize or acknowledge them.[18] The same argument can be made in reverse. If the side that argues against manifestations of the gifts of the Spirit in modern times is right, then there are a lot of false prophets afflicting a lot of Pentecostal and charismatic churches today.

But here is the bottom line: Both sides of this debate cannot be right. One side is wrong and as a church, we must find the correct answer and no longer be divided by it. We cannot continue to believe differently regarding such fundamental issues. The Word of God does not give us that choice.

A "cults" class visits a charismatic church

Before we move on to the issue of church buildings in the early days of the church, I want to share a story involving the controversy over the modern day manifestations of the gifts of the Spirit:

Some years ago, there were two Bible Colleges situated only a few blocks apart in a certain city. One was charismatic and the other was cessationist (believes the gifts of the spirit ceased 1900 years ago). The charismatic college was located in and was part of a large charismatic church.

Every year, the professor of the cults class at the cessationist school would take students on a field trip to the charismatic church – to view a "cult" in action. The visiting class had no respect for the church it was visiting and after it had "seen enough," would get up as a group and walk out in the middle of the service, rudely disturbing the church it was visiting.

Over time, it happened that the presidents of the two colleges had occasion to meet in a setting that afforded them the opportunity to get to know one another and work together on certain projects. Eventually, the two became trusted friends and recognized one another as valued brothers in Christ. The two men also discovered that, other than the charismatic issue, their essential doctrines were almost identical and that they both served the same Christ. The mutual respect became evident when the president of the charismatic college invited his counterpart to come and speak at the charismatic school's chapel services and the invitation was accepted.

Out of that relationship, it came about that the two schools even held a joint chapel service and worshipped together. Imagine that; the student body of a Bible college, which at one time had studied the other as a cult, met and worshipped the Lord with the students of the other school. But that is not the end of the story. Eventually, the two men organized a joint, citywide "praise gathering." Between ten and twelve thousand Christians, charismatic and non-charismatic alike, met in a large stadium/arena setting and worshipped the Lord together. The evangelical side agreed to allow clapping and lifting of the hands and the charismatic side agreed that there would be no outburst of speaking in tongues. It was an historic occasion. It is my prayer that such gatherings will spring up all over the world and that eventually there will be no need for unique ground rules when they do.

The early church owned no buildings

One major difference between the early church and the church today is the early church's lack of property ownership. It may seem a bit odd to those of us living in towns where there are dozens or even hundreds of church buildings, but historically it was 250 years or so *after* Jesus ascended back to Heaven that there is any reference to a church owning any kind of building that was designated specifically as a meeting place for believers.

To early Christians, the term "church" had nothing to do with physical buildings. The church was simply a body of believers dwelling in or around a certain town or city. Churches were people, not physical structures. This is an important distinction, one to which the New Testament speaks clearly.

The apostle Peter describes early church believers as "living stones" being built together into a spiritual house. (I Peter 2:5) A physical building was simply not part of the equation. The house

God was building in the New Testament church was entirely a spiritual one.

This concept, of a *spiritual* house of God rather than a *physical* one, in all likelihood did not come easily to Jewish Christians in the early church. The Old Testament spoke much of manmade structures, namely the Tabernacle of Moses and the Temple of Solomon. To the Jewish mind, this was where God dwelled, in the Holy Temple or in the Ark of the Covenant.

The New Testament concept of God dwelling in the hearts of men rather than a building that men had constructed, was entirely new, but embracing it made consecrated church buildings literally a nonissue for the early church.

Summarizing what we have seen thus far

Let's summarize these two points before we move on. The highly structured forms of church government we see today, whether denominational or otherwise, and the sometimes vast real estate holdings, which are now common to churches and denominations, were entirely unknown to the local church as the apostles left it. Whether men intentionally created what we see today or whether the current systems simply evolved over time, matters little. Suffice it to say that much of what we call "church" today is not "based on the Bible." The point I am trying to make is: For better or for worse, we are not required to do things the way we do them. We just do.

In the days that lie ahead, it might be prudent to cling less tightly to those church offices and organizational structures that are extra-biblical. The things which exist today may serve the purposes of God, and they may not. But know this: *It is at least possible that we have organized and structured the church far more than the Lord ever intended and far more than is helpful.* If that is the case, we may have wasted a lot of God's money and resources on things that were never His will.

With this basic framework in mind, let's talk now about church history and acquire a basic understanding of how all of these denominations came about and how the church came to be so terribly divided. Church history is a huge topic and requires thousands of hours of study to construct a scholarly sense of it. We obviously are not going to do that here. It will be useful, however, to understand the basics and get a cursory sense of the way things fell apart, before we talk about how divisions might be mended.

Church history, a long record of division

As we discussed in the previous chapter, the early church was not divided into denominations or sects. Even though there are tens of thousands of "Christian" denominations in existence today, that didn't happen right away. In fact, it took 1,500 years for the first ones to form. For many centuries, there was only one church in every town.

Because there were no denominations, there were, of course, no official church headquarters. Each local church was autonomous and self-governing, as we have discussed. Eventually, as we shall see later on, a few of the larger churches, such as the ones in Rome, Jerusalem, Antioch, Alexandria, and Constantinople, became more influential in determining matters of church government and doctrinal orthodoxy.[19]

After the original apostles passed on, men we now refer to as the "early church fathers," led the church, especially in areas of doctrine. These "apostolic fathers" were men who had known or served directly under the original apostles and possessed a certain authority based on that connection. They wrote and spoke extensively and many of their writings are with us still today.

Notwithstanding the presence of these respected second and third generation disciples, disputes arose from time to time over matters of doctrine and church policy and sometimes these fathers did not entirely agree regarding the solution. However, rather than divide over their differences, the churches found ways to work them out.

Using church councils to clarify essential doctrines

Several times over the first 500 years of church history, church leaders and scholars from across Christendom met in organized councils to sort out major doctrinal disputes. Church councils addressed such weighty matters as the nature of Christ. They addressed the issue of whether Jesus was God or man, or both, or perhaps a mixture of the two and thus not fully God or man. This was pretty serious stuff and the future of Christianity hung in the balance. Literally.

The conclusions of these councils determined what was heresy (false doctrine) and what was deemed right and true doctrine for centuries to follow, even up to this day. Discussions at these church councils were at times heated, and final decisions sometimes came by a simple majority vote, because a perfect consensus could not be reached. Nonetheless, the vast majority of Bible believing Christians today agree that these councils, at least the earlier ones, got it right, particularly *in regard to the essential doctrines.*

For example, in the fourth century A.D., church councils determined from among the many gospels and epistles in circulation, which books should be canonized into what we know today as the New Testament. This undertaking was launched pursuant to an order from a Roman emperor, who was trying to quell widespread dissension regarding which gospels and epistles should be considered inspired. In spite of any political motivations which may have existed, a decision was made, the New Testament that we have today was canonized, and the dissension was largely put to rest.

There remains some disagreement over the decision that was made, but overall there is widespread agreement that the 27 canonized books of the New Testament were indeed the correct ones. Once again, we see that the entire future of Christianity, including the makeup of the Bible itself, was determined by church councils.

This is important that we recognize this and consider the ramifications. Long after the original apostles left the scene, the church found ways to settle disputes without dividing because of them. The early church worked its way through some pretty serious controversies without splitting, and even though decisions were not always unanimous, the conclusions they reached were good ones and are generally accepted today.

The nature of Christ and the Triune God

It was during this period (the first 500 years of church history), that official statements of faith, such as the Athanasian Creed, were developed to distinguish between right doctrine and heresy concerning the nature of the triune Godhead. The creed the council drafted to address one of the greatest mysteries in the Bible is a little difficult to follow, but still today it is generally recognized as being largely correct and consistent with the things the Bible says about the Godhead.

In 351, the Council of Nicea hashed out the doctrine of Christ, clarifying that Jesus Christ was fully man and fully God and not a mixture of the two or a created being. Nicea made it clear that Jesus had a real body and was not some phantom who merely appeared as a man, as the Gnostic heretics were claiming. This doctrine was of the utmost importance to the purity of the Christian faith. The apostle John had written that *antichrist* was anyone who preached that Jesus Christ did not come in the flesh.[20] This placed the subject of the nature of Christ in a unique position among doctrines, a position right at the top of the theological heap. This was one doctrine believers had to get right, because their souls depended on it.

Dealing with false doctrine was a major challenge for the early church, but faithful men proved that, by the grace of God and the aid of the Holy Spirit, the church was up to the task of sorting out even the most weighty matters. The early church found a way to sort things out with a clarity that prevented divisions within the body of Christ. This was largely possible because there was only one church in each city and no denominational authority. All of the city churches were anxious to come to agreement regarding all of the essential doctrines and had the authority to sign on to whatever conclusion the councils reached. It apparently did not occur to local churches that they could simply believe whatever they wanted and then casually part ways if they disagreed with the rest of the body of Christ. The unity of the faith was universally recognized as expedient, and churches everywhere went to great lengths to maintain it.

The gradual rise of Rome's supremacy

Unfortunately, the vibrancy and genuine spirituality of the early church did not endure. Over the centuries, less spiritual men gradually seized the reins of ecclesiastical power and the church became increasingly more structured. As revival diminished, men attempted to maintain by organization what had been naturally present in better times. Rather than gifted believers doing what they were called to do, church offices began to resemble political appointments.

Eventually, the bishop of Rome came to be seen as the most influential bishop in the Christian church and Rome became the dominant center of Christendom, but this did not happen quickly, as some suppose. For several hundred years prior to Rome's ascendancy, there was no formal or authoritative church center and what leadership did exist was shared, as we said earlier, with the churches at Antioch, Jerusalem, Alexandria, and Constantinople.

There are several reasons the church in Rome eventually became dominant. It was an exceptionally large church, having grown to something in the neighborhood of 30,000 believers. The Roman church was widely known and respected for its generosity to needy believers in other cities. Additionally, some traditions claim that the apostle Peter served at one time as the chief bishop in Rome, and of course, the apostle Paul spent two or more years there, teaching believers the truths of the faith.

To give readers an idea as to the size of the Roman church, by the middle of the third century, the church in Rome had one Bishop, 46 elders or presbyters, seven deacons, seven sub-deacons, 42 acolytes (people who assist in performing liturgies), and 52 exorcists, readers, and janitors.[21] Even by modern standards, the believers in Rome had become a "mega-church."

As the power of the church at Rome grew, its influence over other churches became more formal. New ecclesiastical titles and positions were added, creating a hierarchy not mentioned anywhere in Scripture. Instead of a loosely organized network of autonomous local churches, the church gradually began to resemble what we might call today, a multinational corporation, ruled from the top. Keep in mind that this took several centuries to develop.

The Empire changes its policy regarding Christianity

While Rome was in the process of gradually establishing itself as the center of Christendom, the Roman Empire took a turn that would alter the course of western civilization for centuries to come. At first glance, the paradigm shift that occurred might seem like a good thing, but its effect on the church was destined to be quite the opposite. Almost out of nowhere, the Empire changed its attitude towards Christianity. Early in the fourth century, the intense persecution the church had endured for the first three centuries of its existence began to dissipate. By the end of that century, the pendulum had swung all the way to the opposite extreme.

Here's how it happened, well, at least according to Roman Emperor Constantine. In the year 313, the emperor claimed that he saw a vision of a flaming cross in the sky along with the words, *"By this sign conquer."* The vision so impressed Constantine that he allegedly embraced Christianity. He issued the Edict of Milan, ordering that Christianity be tolerated. Suddenly, it was okay to be a Christian. Later, just prior to the end of the fourth century, Emperor Theodosius went even further and declared Christianity the official religion of the Roman Empire. During the course of one century, an empire, which for 300 years had persecuted and killed Christians, shifted to a policy of tolerating them and eventually to requiring that everyone become one.

At first glance, this may have seemed like real progress. A religion that had started with a mere 120 disciples praying in an upper room in Jerusalem had become, in a period of 350 years, the official religion of the vast Roman Empire! Looking back, however, it is readily apparent that the church had grown and flourished in its purest form while it was enduring Roman persecution. There was nothing like knowing that your faith could cost you your life to weed out the fakes. In the early days of the church, persecution was accepted as part of the package when a new believer came to Christ. Early Christians knew from harsh, real-life experience that *"all who live godly in Christ Jesus shall suffer persecution."*

Religious mixture undermines the foundation of the church

For better or for worse, the time of intense persecution had come to an end. The ramifications of what came next are easily overlooked, but making Christianity the official religion of the empire brought with it certain challenges the church had not encountered previously. First, there was a demographic problem. The Roman Empire was immense. It encompassed many diverse cultures and pagan religions. Non-Christians, who were forced into the church by imperial decree rather than by genuine conversion, simply blended their local superstitions and pagan practices with this new *state sponsored* Christianity. The result was religious mixture and a vast array of local hybrids of Christianity. The simple Gospel of Christ and the apostles became Christianity plus fertility gods, Christianity plus superstition and witchcraft, Christianity plus Roman and Greek mythology. If it existed, it was mixed with Christianity.

Many of the strange beliefs and hitherto unknown practices which were added to Christianity during this era exist still today, and they continue to dilute and weaken the faith of millions who have no idea that their religion is substantively different from the faith once delivered by Christ and the apostles.

As a result of all of this religious mixture and increasingly formal structure, the revival flavor of the church continued to dissipate and the move of the Holy Spirit further declined. Over time, some of the most basic and essential doctrines of the faith were replaced by manmade policies. Like a loathsome disease, spiritual darkness began to envelope the organized church. Salvation by faith in Jesus Christ was replaced by a doctrine of works and such obscene practices as paying money to the church for the forgiveness of sin. Men were taught to pray to Mary and deceased saints. Religious relics[22] were venerated (treated with reverence) and used in worship.

These practices were heavily laden with superstition. If a person had enough money or influence, he could even be buried close to where the apostle Peter allegedly was buried, with the understanding, of course, that there was some eternal advantage to this.

Absent any widespread move of the Holy Spirit, ritual and ceremony eventually replaced inspired worship and preaching. Church services became highly symbolic affairs, laden with mystery. Instead of participating in the worship, members of the congregation became mere observers while the clergy performed.

The Holy Spirit continued to move here and there

It is important to recognize that this decline did not occur rapidly. It clearly did not follow immediately after the passing of the original apostles, as some claim. The true gospel was preached and spiritual gifts were still operating in local churches for quite some time after the twelve apostles were gone. In fact, revival fires continued to burn in small pockets outside the organized church all through the Middle Ages.

Following are a few references from, "Floods Upon the Dry Ground," a history of Christian revivals that chronicles moves of the Holy Spirit through the centuries. Author Charles P. Schmitt makes it abundantly clear that the gifts of the Spirit continued to operate in the church for hundreds of years after the death of the twelve apostles. Here are four of the many examples he offers:

Justin Martyr, who lived from 100 A.D. to 165 A.D. and is recognized as the greatest of the early defenders of the faith, wrote of the gifts of the Spirit, *"the prophetic gifts remain with us even to the present time...it is possible to see among us women and men who possess gifts of the Spirit of God."*[23] Justin Martyr was not even born until after the twelve apostles had passed from the scene.

Irenaeus (130-200 A.D.) was a disciple of Polycarp, who was a disciple of the apostle John. Irenaeus testified regarding the spiritual gifts, *"For some do certainly and truly drive out devils, so that those who have been thus cleansed from evil spirits frequently both believe and join themselves to the Church. Others...see visions and utter prophetic expressions. Others heal the sick by laying hands upon them, and they are made whole…the dead even have been raised up, and remained among us for many years…we do also hear many brethren in the church who profess prophetic gifts and who through the Spirit speak all kinds of languages…It is not possible to name the number of gifts which the Church throughout the whole world has received from God in the name of Jesus Christ."* [24]

Tertullian of Carthage (155-255 A.D.) said in response to a heretic, *"let him produce gifts of the Spirit,"* saying that he himself produced visions and prophesies and interpretations of tongues without any difficulty. [25]

Novatian (210-280 A.D.) said, *"the Holy Spirit places prophets in the church, instructs teachers, directs tongues, gives powers and healings, does wonderful works, offers discrimination of spirits, affords powers of government, suggests counsels, and orders and arranges whatever gifts there are of charismata; and thus making the Lord's church everywhere, and in all perfected and completed.* [26]

These men lived and wrote several generations after the first apostles died, but they were hardly unique in their testimonies. Schmitt chronicles similar reports of manifestations of spiritual gifts all through the Dark Ages, though often they occurred in monasteries or home settings outside the official church, which conducted more formal and ritualistic services.

It's easy to understand why those operating in the spiritual gifts would not have been welcome to do so in the context of the organized church. There is nothing more threatening to a pretend "man of God" than a real one. A spiritually gifted leader exposes the emptiness of the counterfeit. It has always been so. The reaction of the priests and Pharisees to Jesus and John the Baptist proved this beyond all doubt. The religious rulers of the Sanhedrin had all of the trappings of religion, but they lacked the authority that comes only by knowing God.

The first major church division

Eventually, the organized church lost its way entirely. Wandering in darkness and lacking true spiritual authority, it was no longer able to preserve the society around it. As the lamp of truth faded in the church, most of the civilized world began a long slide into what is known today as the Dark Ages. During this period, the church continued to function outwardly as if all was well, but spiritually it was dead. A highly structured ecclesiastical system had replaced the living, thriving organism the church had once been.

Even though Rome had become the dominant church, a rival to its power was born, Constantinople. Named after Emperor Constantine, Constantinopolis was a thriving city located in what is now the nation of Turkey. In an effort to demonstrate that the Roman Empire ruled both the eastern and western worlds, the city of Constantinople (the English pronunciation) was established as the religious center of the more eastern reaches of the Empire.

The two cities became competing heads of the Christian church. Church leaders in Rome and Constantinople communicated with one another regarding matters of doctrine and policy; they cooperated with one another in church councils, and they even sent aid to each other on occasion, but they were nonetheless competitors.

Over time, the tension between the two centers grew. Rome was under serious military assault from the barbaric tribes from the north. Meanwhile, the Church at Constantinople was under assault from the new but very militant Muslims. A time came when the church at Constantinople faced possible annihilation at the hand of the Muslims and called on Rome for aid. The Roman Church declined to help their beleaguered eastern counterpart, and this decision brought the tension between the two to a head.

In 1054 A.D., the Eastern Orthodox Church formally broke away from the Roman Catholic Church, or was it vice versa? Either way, the heads of the two churches officially excommunicated one another and became enemies and outspoken religious competitors. The reason for the split was blamed on a doctrinal difference; i.e. whether the Holy Spirit proceeds only from the Father or from both the Father and the Son. However, it is commonly recognized that this was merely an excuse for what was really a political falling out.

The schism between the East and the West was the first real church split of consequence in history and it was far-reaching in its impact. The division between the Catholic Church in the west and the Orthodox Churches in the east continues to this day. (We will speak more about these two entities and the unique challenges to unity they pose in the chapter titled "The Catholic Challenge.")

After 1054, these two religious centers functioned as two separate churches, both with somewhat similar structures. The Eastern Orthodox eventually split into several separate entities based on the countries in which they operated; the Russian and Romanian churches being the largest. Their common center is still Constantinople, though today the city is called Istanbul. Operating largely in communist or former communist countries, Orthodox Churches are often the officially recognized church in their country. As such, they routinely work closely with the government to exclude missionaries from the west and prevent non-Orthodox churches from competing with them.

Both the Catholic and Orthodox Churches claim their leaders possess the authority inherent in apostolic succession, meaning they can trace a line of church officials going all the way back to the original twelve apostles. Both churches maintain a very formal structure with a hierarchy of clergy who go about garbed in religious vesture and conduct services with a heavy emphasis on symbol, ritual, and sacraments. Orthodox churches tend to be somewhat exclusive. A stranger walking into an Orthodox Church today should not automatically expect to be served communion with the rest of the congregation, unless they have been baptized in an Orthodox Church.

Because the focus of this study is church unity, we shall direct most of our attention toward the Roman church in the west, as that church is more relevant to our topic. It is the Roman Catholic Church from which Protestants split and it is the thousands of divisions within the Protestant churches, which have resulted in the situation we are attempting to address here, i.e. churches with different names and doctrines scattered all over our cities and towns.

The Catholic Church rules the Middle Ages

I must tell you something up front: You might get the impression, as we move forward, that I am beating up on the Roman Catholic Church. Doing so is perhaps unavoidable. The Catholic Church was the ruling church when the Protestant Reformation was birthed, and it was the fact that the Roman Church had gone so very far off course that made the first round of divisions necessary. (To be fair, we must recognize that some of the things the Catholic Church did during this era would not be approved by the Catholic Church today. Unfortunately, it is also true that in response to the Protestant Reformation, which we shall discuss shortly, some of Rome's most objectionable doctrines and practices were strongly reaffirmed by the Church at the Council of Trent and are still official Catholic doctrine today.) With that disclaimer in mind, let's get back to the Middle Ages, which by the way is roughly the period from the fifth through the fifteenth century.

One cannot grasp the complexities of church history without recognizing one undeniable fact: At some point during the Middle Ages, the "official" Christian church became as much a political entity as a religious one. Throughout the Middle Ages, the Roman Catholic Church aggressively sought political influence on every front, but especially among the monarchies of Europe. The Church was so successful at acquiring political influence that at times Catholic popes literally controlled some of the most powerful monarchies in Europe.

Even when the church didn't have outright control of a king or queen, it often exerted tremendous influence. Non-subservient kings were routinely threatened with excommunication if they declined to kiss the pope's ring and submit to his edicts. This was no hollow threat. Even non-believing monarchs were nervous about the common people believing that their king or queen had been condemned to hell by their church.

During this era, the reach of the church went far beyond matters of religion, and it was painfully clear what its real priorities were. Heretics were routinely burned at the stake for teaching any doctrine contrary to official church dogma, but those seeking money and political influence rather than true religion, were tolerated and even rewarded for their ambition. A preacher had to be very careful what he said, but moral and financial corruption among church officials was openly tolerated.

Selling forgiveness of sin

It is an axiom of human nature that politics and money breed corruption, whether inside or outside the church. During the Middle Ages, church offices often were meted out to unsavory types, men who were scoundrels in every sense of the word yet desired the political power that came with holding a high ranking position within the church.

Obviously, when money is more important than truth, bad things will happen. Doctrines with no basis in Scripture were adopted and made official church policy, because they were financially profitable. One such policy, the selling of indulgences, almost singularly launched the Protestant Reformation. The doctrine of indulgences was created and made acceptable by famed Catholic theologian Thomas Aquinas.[27]

Indulgences are based on the theory that the collective good deeds of Christ and past saints form a great pool of good works, out of which a sinner could extract what he needed, *but for a price*. A person could receive indulgence, not by repenting, praying or asking in faith, but rather by paying for it. If a person paid money to the church, the money or other material asset would mitigate the consequences of his sinful deeds here on earth or shorten his time in purgatory. In other words, if you had the money and were willing to pay up, your sins were less of a problem.

Indulgences were great money makers for the church. The way the system was designed, indulgence could even be purchased in advance - for sins not yet committed. The corruption inherent in such a system is blatantly obvious, but the financial windfall indulgences brought to the Catholic Church was too enticing to resist. The sale of indulgences financed the construction of some of the most ornate Catholic cathedrals in all of Europe, such as St. Peters Basilica in Rome[28] (which technically is not a cathedral). Indulgences were sold openly and unashamedly as a means of constructing new cathedrals and restoring older ones.

In "Floods Upon the Dry Ground," Church historian Charles P. Schmitt recounts the following, real or legendary, exchange between Thomas Aquinas and Pope Innocent IV:

Bags of treasure, garnered by selling indulgences, were pouring into the church's coffers. Innocent IV and Aquinas were standing together watching load after load of indulgence loot being carried into the church. The pope turned to Aquinas and remarked with a smile, "You see, the day is past when the church could say, 'Silver and gold have I none.'" Aquinas's reply to the pope was, "Yes, Holy Father, and the day is past when the church could say to the lame, 'Rise and walk.'"[29]

This story, truth or legend, illustrates just how far the Roman Church had strayed from its original mission. Rather than reaching the lost for Christ and maintaining a vibrant spiritual life, the priorities of the church had become money and political power. The more the church's wealth and political power increased, the more its spiritual power and doctrinal purity suffered - at least within the organized church.

Purgatory, another extra-biblical doctrine

Indulgences were not the only money making scheme the church developed. Purgatory was also a real moneymaker. Purgatory is alleged by the Roman Catholic Church to be a place between earth and heaven, a sort of in-between place. Purgatory, as the Catholic Church teaches it, is not in the Bible, per se, though outside the church the theory of a stopping off place for souls, where they could be purified and prepared for the afterlife, dates back several centuries before the Christian era. The Catholic Church formally adopted the concept and made it official church policy.

Like indulgences, purgatory was a powerful weapon in the hands of the professional pardoners the church employed. If you were told by an agent of the church that the soul of your dear deceased mother was stuck in purgatory and would remain there until you paid enough money to get her out, what could you do but pay up? If you paid the money, the church prayed your beloved parent, child, or aunt out of purgatory and on up to heaven. You were relieved, your loved one got to go to heaven, *and the church got richer*. If you didn't pay, your relative would stay in purgatory, suffering and being "refined" for who knows how long.

A wealthy church with impoverished members

It is difficult to grasp the extent of the Catholic Church's wealth and power during this era, but we can at least get a general idea. During the Middle Ages, the Roman Catholic Church became the largest landowner in all of Europe. The Church owned as much as half of all the land in Germany, half the land in France, and forty percent of the land in England and Sweden. That kind of wealth is hard to imagine.

The Roman Catholic Church was rich in natural things. It was flush with money and property, but while it basked in its great wealth, it kept its adherents spiritually deprived and impoverished. The common people were not even allowed access to Bibles. Even if they could lay their hands on one, they couldn't have read it. The Bible the Roman Church used was written in Latin so the common people would not understand what it said. Likewise, the Church's religious ceremonies were intentionally shrouded in mystery. According to the doctrine of transubstantiation, communion or the "Eucharist" involved literally eating the flesh and drinking the blood of Jesus Christ, which understandably kept the people in awe.

To keep lines between the Church and the people clearly drawn, the clergy dressed in robes so everyone would understand that they were not like other people. To further maintain that separation, Mass was conducted in Latin so only trained members of the clergy could be certain what was being said.

The Church had a logical reason for not allowing the common people access to the Scriptures: Many of the doctrines and practices of the Church blatantly contradicted the Bible and the church did not want commoners second-guessing its decisions. The Church's official position was that the Catholic Church, acting as the Bride of Christ on the earth, spoke for Jesus Christ and thus could do no wrong. In the opinion of the Catholic Church, the very fact that it had done something automatically made it right, contradictions with Scripture notwithstanding.

The pope and tradition trump the Scriptures

Eventually, this led to a triumvirate or three-fold system of authority. The long standing traditions of the church and the "infallible" words of the Pope became equal in authority to the Bible itself. Instead of one source of authority, the Catholic Church had three, and two of those sources were perpetually changing. If the Catholic Church had always done something in a particular way, or if some Pope had stated that a certain thing was true, either of these had as much authority as anything the Bible said about the same matter. In essence, this doctrine allowed the church to do anything it wanted and never be "wrong."

We will speak of all this at greater detail in the chapter titled "The Catholic Challenge," but take note for the moment that very little of what the Church did during this dark period has been annulled or rescinded by the contemporary Catholic Church.

We need to stress again that it would be a mistake to conclude that during this time of great spiritual darkness, all Catholic clergy were corrupt or were people of bad faith. This was not the case. There were many powerful moves of the Holy Spirit in various monasteries and other small groups where a remnant of monks, priests, and everyday believers were seeking God with hungry hearts and faithfully studying the Scriptures. Here and there, these pockets of devout believers were in a very real sense, keeping the gospel flame alive. Great darkness had all but enveloped the known civilized world and the organized church, but there were always those who kept the faith, at least to the extent they understood it.

Efforts to reform the church from within

Even during the spiritual Dark Ages, when the official church was at its lowest ebb, not every member of the Catholic clergy accepted the strange new doctrines the church had introduced. There were always "good Catholics," who sought to change the church from within. Long before Martin Luther and the Protestant Reformation, others tried to right the wayward Roman ship.

For example, William of Occam (1280-1347), was a Franciscan who taught at the University of Paris. His writings, which would later influence Martin Luther, openly challenged the infallibility of the pope. William taught that only the Holy Scriptures were truly infallible. He also taught that the church was not superior to the state in regard to secular matters, which was an attempt to put an end to the Church's politicization of Christianity. Alas, it is not such an easy matter to persuade men to give up their power and influence, even if the Word of God is on your side. Occam's message was not well received. The powers that be were not interested in reformation.

John Wycliffe (1320-1384) also tried to reform the church from within. Long before Luther and the Reformation, Wycliffe taught justification by faith, and by faith alone. Wycliffe, himself a Roman Catholic priest, declared that the Scriptures were the only source of truth, and that the pope, if he did not rule in the spirit of the gospel, was not the vicar of Christ, as he claimed, but rather the "vicar of Antichrist." Such boldness required great courage.

Wycliffe also challenged other unscriptural Catholic doctrines, such as purgatory, transubstantiation, the worshipping of saints, and the practice of confessing sins to a priest rather than to God. Wycliffe is widely remembered for making the first English translation of the Bible available to the English people. It was an accomplishment that infuriated Catholic authorities, who continued to insist that the Bible was too dangerous for common people to handle.

The Reformation became inevitable

Looking back with 20/20 hindsight, the corruption of the Roman Catholic Church by Luther's time made the Protestant Reformation all but inevitable. Efforts to reform the church from within had not been successful and the people were hungry for the truth. Open revolt eventually became the only alternative.

All of this church history, even as abbreviated as it is here, might be a bit tedious for some readers. However, it is important to go through this, if we are going to understand how the church got into the fractured, divided condition it is in today. What we have seen thus far creates the backdrop for the period of time we will discuss next, a period during which church divisions, hitherto a rarity, would become every bit the norm.

Keep in mind that it took a thousand years for the first major church split to occur; the split between the Roman Catholic Church and the Orthodox Church in 1054. It took half that time for the next major split to occur, i.e. the split between the Lutherans and the Roman Catholics. This made for only two major church splits in fifteen hundred years. Once the Protestants got going, however, the scramble would be on.

The mindset that led to the Protestant Reformation

It would take several volumes to discuss in detail the splits and divisions that occurred once Martin Luther opened the floodgates in 1517, but that exercise is not necessary for the purposes of this book. Our goal here is not so much to study the detailed history of the Protestant era, but more to see the general nature of, and reasons for, the major splits that occurred and hopefully glean from the exercise lessons that will help us see a way out of the maze in which we find ourselves today.

While the Catholic Church ruled unchallenged, doctrinal order could be maintained simply by threats of excommunication or execution. After Luther's revolt, however, it became apparent that one could challenge the religious powers that be and live to tell about it; and eventually a lot of people did. In a sense, once the authority of the established Church had been successfully challenged, it became apparent that any believer could take his Bible in hand and preach whatever he found there, or thought he had found there. This was something the Catholic Church had long feared might occur. Once that mold was broken, it became theoretically possible for there to be as many churches as there were opinions. The long term dangers inherent in such an approach would not become obvious for another hundred years or so, and in fact, are not fully understood yet.

Think about it this way: If Martin Luther's opinion is as valid as the pope's, then maybe mine is too. If there is no authority to keep teachers and preachers in line, and no enforcement mechanism to maintain a mutually agreed orthodoxy, one man's opinion really is as good (at least to him and his followers) as the next man's, even if it is just an opinion - and even if it's wrong.

This was one of the fruits of putting the Scriptures into the hands of the common people. One Roman Catholic author had these disparaging things to say about Luther and the Bible:

"The common people concerned themselves (in Luther's time) mostly with the bible, which was translated into the mother language. It was seen in the houses and lay upon the tables. The common worker had the Bible in his work place and the women lay it upon their knees. The entire world busied itself with the reading of the Bible. The sects which were armed with these books, whenever they came upon a priest or someone from another spiritual order, immediately began an argument with these books. One demanded that he should be shown from Scripture the mass, another purgatory, another infant baptism, another the Trinity. Finally they wanted all articles of faith to be proven with express Words, and rejected the unwritten Word of God and the apostolic precepts. For the arch heretic Luther had taught: The Scripture (and he authorized everyone to explain it) is alone the judge of all arguments in religion."[30]

As right as it was, putting the Bible in the peoples' hands was not without consequence. It might not have been immediately apparent that a doctrinal "free for all" would be one of the ramifications of Luther's revolt, but looking back, it clearly was. Time has shown us that when it comes to Christian doctrine, free speech can be a double-edged sword, for when it comes to doctrine, there is no shortage of conflicting opinions. It is a wonderful thing for everyone to have a Bible and to read it often. And it is certainly proper to require church leaders to justify their doctrines and policies when those doctrines and policies do not appear to align with Scripture. There is a danger, however, in believing that everyone with a Bible has the authority to ignore centuries of established orthodoxy, of the good sort, and create their own doctrines.

As we pointed our earlier, the Book of Judges closes with this saying: ***In those days there was no king in Israel; every man did that which was right in his own eyes.*** This passage is an apt description of the last five hundred years of the Protestant Reformation. Substitute the following language, and it is easy to understand why Protestant churches divided and split thousands of times over its 500 year history: ***In those days there was no recognized authority in the church, so every teacher taught what was right in his own eyes.*** Churches divided over and over, because there was nothing to stop them from doing so. There was no recognized authority to which they could appeal to settle their doctrinal disputes.

I do not make this observation in support of the pope or the Roman Catholic Church. Those authorities ultimately proved themselves unworthy of the power they held. They feared the Bible because they were violating it, often blatantly so. Nonetheless, the problem which has led to so many church divisions within the Protestant movement does seem to be a systemic one. What I am suggesting is that there is something fundamentally wrong with the way most Protestant churches view doctrine and the entire matter of orthodoxy.

Author John H. Armstrong called this problem "the Great Evangelical Catastrophe," saying, "*We have exalted our interpretation of the Scripture by boldly proclaiming: 'My authority comes only from the Bible.' Thankfully, many are waking up to the tragedy of this false individualism and are wisely looking for help from the three classical Christian traditions and the scores of ancient writers who feed their hunger.*"[31]

Armstrong calls for a renewed respect for orthodoxy and tradition and greater familiarity with the writings of the early church fathers. (A similar view is also advocated by C.S. Lewis in "*The Incarnation of the Word of God.*") Until we address the free-flying way many evangelicals approach doctrine, divisions will continue to multiply. There is no reason to think that we are going to stop at 38,000 denominations.

Luther breaks the mold

Let's look now at how the era of church divisions, divisions on an epic scale, commenced. The first crack in the dam appeared early in the sixteenth century, when a Catholic monk in Germany decided that he could no longer hold his peace while the Church he loved ignored the Scriptures he loved even more.

In 1517, Martin Luther nailed his Ninety-five Theses to the door of the Catholic Church in Wittenburg, Germany. It was not Luther's plan to break with the Catholic Church. Like others before him, he just wanted to reform it. At first, Luther tried to avoid stirring up a revolt among the common people. He discreetly drafted his "Ninety-five Theses" in Latin, so only the clergy would be able to read them. Obviously, things did not go as Luther planned. Almost immediately, several local printers translated Luther's words into German and distributed them widely among the general population. Just like that, the cat was out of the bag and the fight was on. The common people were primed and ready to hear the truth, and once Martin Luther lit the match, there was no stopping the fire that sprang to life.

Another factor provided the Protestant Reformation the means to spread like wildfire: the invention of the printing press. The printing press allowed, for the first time in history, the mass production of books. Once the Bible began to be printed and distributed in the languages of the common people, once they began to read the Word of God for themselves, the Catholic Church was in trouble. The Church could no longer hide the fact that many of its practices and doctrines did not align with the Scriptures.

Even with all that dry tinder lying about, the Protestant Reformation likely would not have occurred if the Catholic Church had shown any sign that it was open to reform. But it didn't. The Roman Church of 1517, a church that believed it was incapable of error no matter what it did, was anything but receptive to Luther's suggestions.

The rulers of the Roman Church were accustomed to the sheep doing what they were told, but in Martin Luther they met their match. Luther may have been a Catholic priest, but his passion for what he believed and his stubborn personality drove him to stand his ground. He absolutely would not be intimidated. The Church wouldn't budge and Luther wouldn't back down; and with that the Protestant Reformation was born.

Luther's simple but revolutionary message

Distilled to its essence, Luther's message was simply one of grace as opposed to works. Luther proclaimed in no uncertain terms that men were saved solely by faith in the death and resurrection of Jesus Christ and not by their own self-righteous works (and certainly not by buying indulgences from the Roman Catholic Church.)

Luther also taught that every believer was a priest with access to God through Christ, a clear New Testament concept, but hardly one the Roman Catholic Church was eager to embrace. Luther's message would have stripped the church of much of its power and was a threat to its revenue stream. In short, Luther's gospel was a threat to the established order, an order the Roman Church was highly motivated to preserve.

As obvious as Luther's message might appear to Bible-believing Christians today, it was quite revolutionary in the 16th century. The church was very clergy oriented and had been for hundreds of years. To most of the civilized world, salvation was thought to come by doing whatever the Roman Catholic Church told you to do. In that world, the Bible was largely irrelevant. Look at it this way: Church officials claimed they possessed the power to condemn a person's soul to hell, if he or she did not swear unquestioning allegiance to the pope and the edicts of the church. The simple message that one could be saved by believing in the death and resurrection of Jesus Christ and confessing one's sins directly to Him was a major paradigm shift to all who heard it; it was an entirely new way of looking at Christianity.

Of course, it wasn't really a new message, but for those who had never heard it, it was pure and sweet. Salvation was a free gift. You didn't have to work for it and you didn't have to pay money for it; you only had to believe.[32] For those who had been living in spiritual darkness and oppression, this was good news indeed.

Another major aspect of Luther's teachings, the priesthood of all believers, was equally seismic in its impact. When the people discovered that, according to Scripture, all Christians are priests, the iron rule of the Catholic Church and its clergy was all but broken.

The first Protestant church is born

This is not really a history book, so let's skip over a lot of the back and forth between Luther and the ruling pope, and let it suffice to say that the pope condemned Luther's suggested reforms and the Lutherans permanently broke with the Roman Catholic Church. A brand new church was born.

It is important to note that some things were different in the new Lutheran church, but in other ways the new church was still very similar to the old. The Lutherans were out. They were no longer Catholics, but how far out were they? Other than the basic changes Luther had proclaimed, the Lutheran's entire understanding of Christianity and religious frame of reference was Catholic. For example, Luther and other early Protestants continued to believe in and teach the Catholic doctrine of the perpetual virginity of Mary, meaning Mary had no children other than Jesus.[33]

Luther focused primarily on two very basic New Testament truths, salvation by faith in Christ and the priesthood of all believers; all based of course on the sole authority of the Scriptures. These were vitally important steps. However, unbeknownst to Martin Luther and his followers, what Luther had launched was not the end of the reformation, but merely the beginning. The church had lost a lot more than these two truths during its long decline into the thousand years of darkness.

It only took a short time for Luther's two world-altering truths to sink in and take hold, but the reformation Luther began would take several centuries to complete. It had taken centuries for the church to lose the purity of doctrine and spiritual power it had once possessed, and it would take *at least* five centuries for the restoration to be complete.

Ana Baptists reintroduce water baptism

A decade or so after Luther's revolt, the next wave of reformation began; restoring the doctrine of water baptism; not baptism of infants, but of all new converts. Surprisingly, the Lutherans would have none of it. To Catholics and Lutherans, adults who had been baptized as infants did not need to be re-baptized simply because they had made a voluntary decision to become a Christian.

Many Protestant churches take this doctrine for granted today, but in the sixteenth century, re-baptizing people as adults could get a person killed. Ana Baptists (re-baptizers) were martyred by the Catholics and the Lutherans for teaching and practicing this new "heresy." Ana Baptists, who later became known as Mennonites, were burned at the stake or drowned in water for re-baptizing people, but like Luther a decade earlier, they would not back down.[34] (Note: There were some Ana Baptist sects which were violent and did their share of marauding and plundering, but most were nonviolent and died for their faith without resistance. Ironically, it was the nonviolent segment that eventually survived.)

Eventually the fundamental doctrines of salvation by faith and water baptism of adults became widely recognized as vital New Testament truths, but this did not occur without considerable cost to those who initially restored them. Perhaps the next time you hear a preacher invite listeners to come forward and get saved simply by placing their faith in the death and resurrection of Jesus Christ, you will remember that the original Lutherans fought to restore this doctrine at great personal risk. And the next time you see some young person or adult getting baptized in water, you might remember that Ana Baptists died at the hand of sixteenth century Catholics and Lutherans to restore that truth.

Still, there was much more restoration to come. The waves of revival were going to continue to break upon the shore as truth after truth began to be restored.

The reformers resist reform

Unfortunately, it is at this point in history that we see an alarming pattern developing. Just as the Roman Catholic Church had resisted Luther's message of salvation by faith in Jesus Christ, the Lutherans spurned the Ana Baptist's water baptism message. In turn, the Lutherans and Ana Baptists would resist the next move of the Holy Spirit, just as those new movements would in turn resist the movements following theirs.

The holiness movement led by the early Methodists was opposed by other Protestant Christians with the same intensity and vigor as the message of salvation by faith and the doctrine of water baptism had been opposed decades earlier. This reoccurring theme is one we cannot ignore, because it says something about basic human nature, and why divisions occur.

Perhaps, the restoration of each subsequent truth was rejected simply because it went beyond what the previous movement knew or understood. Perhaps, each preceding group rejected the subsequent move of the Spirit because the new message did not spring from it. After all, if God had something new to say, He would say it *to us or through us* and not through some other group, right? Whatever the cause, the pattern became an obvious one, and remains with us still today.

Jesus may have forewarned us of this phenomenon when He spoke of the problem with putting new wine in old bottles. Jesus was simply telling us something about human nature. We humans tend to become set in our ways. We know what we know, but we never know what we don't know. We miss what follows our work, because we are so intent on preserving what came before. Because this is true of humans, it is also true of the organizations that humans form.

There are those in every movement who embrace the next move of the Spirit and continue to move forward, but not all; and perhaps not even most. Often, it is the leaders of a movement, generally second or third generation leaders, who are settled in, well established, and comfortable, who focus more on preserving what God has done in the past than keeping their ears to the ground to hear what comes next.

It's like ancient Israel during its wilderness wanderings. The Israelites were allowed to camp at one spot for only so long, then without warning, the cloud (representing the presence of God) would begin to move. When the cloud moved, the people either broke camp and moved with it, or they were left behind.

In the centuries following the Lutheran and Ana Baptist movements, each newly restored truth was met with vigorous resistance from the group or groups whose revivals had preceded the new one. Rather than embrace the new thing the Lord was doing, they largely rejected it. Consider for a moment the words of the prophet Isaiah in chapter 43:

> [18] *"Do not remember the former things,*
> *Nor consider the things of old.*
> [19] *Behold, I will do a new thing,*
> *Now it shall spring forth;*
> *Shall you not know it?*
> *I will even make a road in the wilderness*
> *And rivers in the desert." (NKJV)*

Divisions within the new Protestant churches were often the consequence of one group's rejection of something new that was breaking forth. Those embracing the new move of the Holy Spirit eventually would split away from the established order so they could live in the new truth the Lord was restoring. (Please continue to keep in mind that these were not really *new* truths, but old ones, which were believed and practiced by the early church, but lost during the Dark Ages, or if you will, the great falling away.)

One teacher explained the phenomenon of new movements being persecuted by previous ones in this way: When an ocean wave breaks on the shore, the biggest obstacle it faces as it seeks to make its way up the beach is not the resistance of the beach itself, but the preceding wave, the wave that is now receding. As the previous wave recedes, it blocks the progress of the new wave that follows it. It is the receding wave that the new wave must overcome to make its way to the shore. That is the history of the Protestant Reformation.

In his book "The End-Time Revival," Paul N. Grubb said of those denominations which say they seek revival, but oppose revivals that start somewhere other than their group:

*"They have been looking for the last day revival to come to their organization, and since it has not, they look askance at those who are part of this mighty visitation. **They are sure that when God moves, He will move through them; a mistake repeatedly made all through church history.** Blind to the leading of the Holy Spirit, they fail to realize the carnality of division. Instead, they justify their position, and accuse this heaven sent visitation of causing strife while claiming to preach unity! **But who is divisive? – where is the division? Does it lie with those who follow the cloud by day and the fire by night; or with those who insist on compassing the mountain?"***

Ponder the implications of Mr. Grubb's observation for a moment. In a very real sense, many (but not all) denominations exist today as monuments to something very real that God did at some time in the past. They were once the cutting edge. The founders of the movement may have fought vigorously to birth something they believed was worth fighting for, even dying for. Then they set up camp at that spot. Unfortunately, when the next move of the Spirit broke forth in some other place, they rejected that move; they criticized it, and remained camped where they were – even though the cloud had moved on.

Keep in mind that divisions always spring from human failures. Breakups may at times be inevitable, but the blame ultimately lies with people being people. There is always a human cause for them. The apostle Paul made it clear that we have divisions because we are carnal. Of course, carnality comes in many forms, some of which are quite subtle, but it is clear that all of us are afflicted with pride and stubbornness; even the best of us. Even the apostle Peter was rebuked openly by the apostle Paul for behaving differently towards the Gentiles when fellow Jews were around. Think about that. One apostle had to confront another apostle, one of the original twelve mind you, for rank hypocrisy. (See Galatians 2:11-14) All of us are capable of missing the truth at times. None of us is exempt from the frailties of the human condition. To know that must be to guard against it.

To illustrate further; Martin Luther, for all the good he did, was but a man. He brought the Scriptures, the grace of God, and the message of salvation to many, but among other things he was an extremely stubborn man; he was strongly anti-Semitic; he vigorously persecuted the Ana Baptist reformers; and he even tried to eliminate four books from the New Testament canon (Hebrews, James, Jude, and Revelation).

Human nature has invariably wreaked havoc with moves of the Holy Spirit. What begins with Him is always pure at its source, but our tendency towards pride, exclusivity, and extremes often corrupts what the Spirit of God is doing. When the Lord moves upon us, we tend to take what He is doing and run amuck with it. We bounce back and forth between extremes and then eventually, hopefully, we get it right. Historically, it usually took at least a few decades for any kind of balance to be reached when a lost doctrine was being restored. In the meanwhile, the extreme behavior of some adherents all but ensured the hostility and criticism of those watching from the outside, including other believers.

A handful of denominations becomes many

Looking back over the past 500 years of the Protestant Reformation, we saw one Protestant church, the Lutherans, give birth to two or three Protestant churches, and then those few gave birth to a dozen more. After that, the splits and divisions increased exponentially as dozens of different denominations became hundreds and then thousands.

Thus far I have tried to explain the fracturing of the church in human terms, but let's see if we can summarize what happened historically and not get too bogged down in the details. If it all becomes too confusing or tedious, perhaps the charts on the following pages will make things a little clearer.

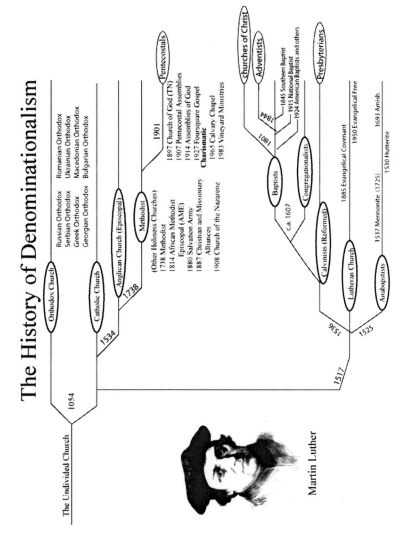

The History of Denominationalism

The Undivided Church — 1054

Orthodox Church
Russian Orthodox
Serbian Orthodox
Greek Orthodox
Georgian Orthodox
Romanian Orthodox
Ukrainian Orthodox
Macedonian Orthodox
Bulgarian Orthodox

Catholic Church — 1534

Anglican Church (Episcopal) — 1738

Methodist — 1901

(Other Holiness Churches)
1738 Methodist
1814 African Methodist Episcopal (AME)
1880 Salvation Army
1887 Christian and Missionary Alliances
1908 Church of the Nazarene

Pentecostals
1897 Church of God (TN)
1907 Pentecostal Assemblies
1914 Assemblies of God
1927 Foursquare Gospel
Charismatic
1965 Calvary Chapel
1983 Vineyard Ministries

Churches of Christ

Adventists — 1844

1845 Southern Baptist
1915 National Baptist
1924 American Baptists and others

Presbyterians — 1801

Baptists — c.a. 1607

Congregationalists

Calvinists (Reformed) — 1536

Lutheran Church — 1525

1885 Evangelical Covenant
1950 Evangelical Free

1537 Mennonite (1725)
1530 Hutterite
1693 Amish

Anabaptists

Martin Luther — 1517

These charts were prepared by Rebekah Allman using information gleaned from "Chronological & Background Charts of Church History" revised and expanded edition by Robert C. Walton, 2005, history.pcusa.org/history/denominations.cfm and other sources

127

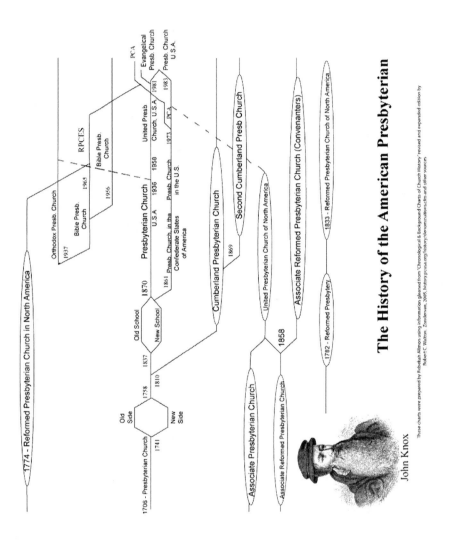

The History of the American Presbyterian

John Knox

These charts were prepared by Rebekah Allmon using information gleaned from "Chronological & Background Charts of Church History," revised and expanded edition by
Robert C. Walton. Zondervan, 2005, history-pcusa.org/history/devsum/allsum.cfm and other sources

128

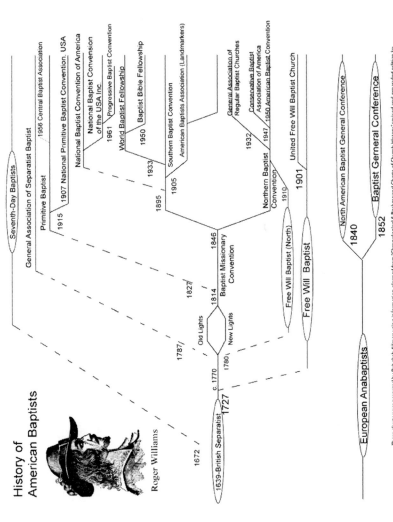

History of American Baptists

Roger Williams

1672

1639–British Separatist
1727
c. 1770
Old Lights 1787
New Lights 1780
1814
Baptist Missionary Convention
1846
1827

Seventh-Day Baptists

General Association of Separatist Baptist

Primitive Baptist
1956 Central Baptist Association
1915
1907 National Primitive Baptist Convention, USA

National Baptist Convention of America

National Baptist Convension of the USA Inc.
1961 Progressive Baptist Convention
World Baptist Fellowship
1950 Baptist Bible Fellowship
1933

Southern Baptist Convention
American Baptists Association (Landmarkers)
1895
1905

General Association of Regular Baptist Churches
1932
Conservative Baptist Association of America
1947 1950 American Baptist Convention

Northern Baptist Convention
1910

United Free Will Baptist Church
1901

Free Will Baptist (North)

Free Will Baptist

North American Baptist General Conference
1840

Baptist Gerneral Conference
1852

European Anabaptists

These charts were prepared by Rebekah Allmon using information gleaned from "Chronological & Background Charts of Church History" revised and expanded edition by Robert C. Walton, Zondervan, 2005, historynacusa.org/history/denominations.cfm and other sources

129

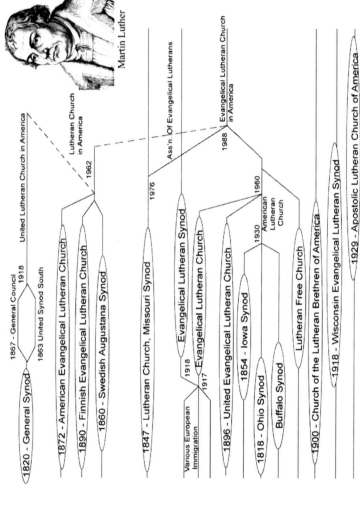

History of American Lutherans

Martin Luther

1867 - General Council
1918 — United Lutheran Church in America

1863 United Synod South

1820 - General Synod

Lutheran Church in America

1962

Ass'n. Of Evangelical Lutherans

1976

Evangelical Lutheran Church in America

1988

1872 - American Evangelical Lutheran Church

1890 - Finnish Evangelical Lutheran Church

1860 - Swedish Augustana Synod

1847 - Lutheran Church, Missouri Synod

1918 — Evangelical Lutheran Synod

1917 — Evangelical Lutheran Church

Various European Immigration

1896 - United Evangelical Lutheran Church

1854 - Iowa Synod

1818 - Ohio Synod

Buffalo Synod

1930

1960

American Lutheran Church

Lutheran Free Church

1900 - Church of the Lutheran Brethren of America

1918 - Wisconsin Evangelical Lutheran Synod

1929 - Apostolic Lutheran Church of America

These charts were prepared by Rebekah Allison using information gleaned from "Chronological & Background Charts of Church History" revised and expanded edition by Robert C. Walton, Zondervan, 2005, history.pcusa.org/history/denominations.cfm and other sources.

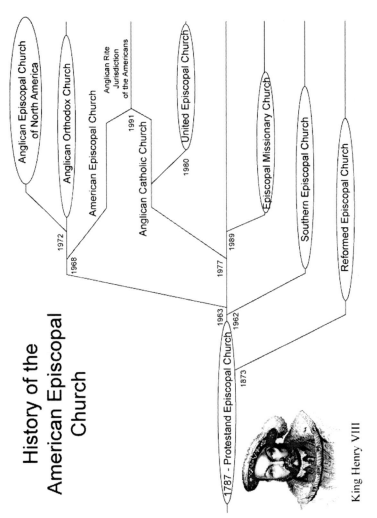

History of the American Episcopal Church

Anglican Episcopal Church of North America

Anglican Orthodox Church

American Episcopal Church

Anglican Rite Jurisdiction of the Americans

United Episcopal Church

Anglican Catholic Church

Episcopal Missionary Church

Southern Episcopal Church

Reformed Episcopal Church

1972

1968

1991

1980

1989

1977

1963

1962

1873

1787 - Protestand Episcopal Church

King Henry VIII

These charts were prepared by Rebekah Allmon using information gleaned from "Chronological & Background Charts of Church History" revised and expanded edition by Robert C. Walton, Zondervan, 2005, history.pcusa.org/history/denominations.cfm and other sources.

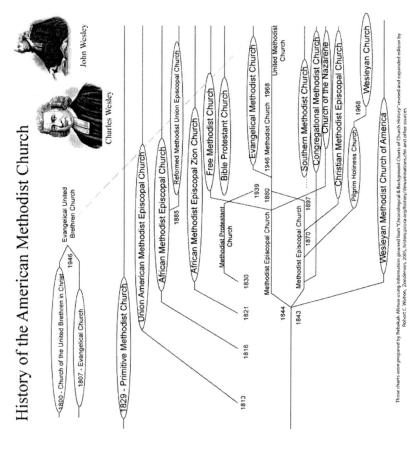

History of the American Methodist Church

John Wesley

Charles Wesley

1800 - Church of the United Brethren in Christ

1946 — Evangelical United Brethren Church

1807 - Evangelical Church

1829 - Primitive Methodist Church

Union American Methodist Episcopal Church

African Methodist Episcopal Church

1885 — Reformed Methodist Union Episcopal Church

African Methodist Episcopal Zion Church

Free Methodist Church

Bible Protestant Church

Methodist Protestant Church

1830

1821

1816

1813

Evangelical Methodist Church

1939

1860 — 1946 Methodist Church 1968

United Methodist Church

Methodist Episcopal Church

Southern Methodist Church

1870

Congregational Methodist Church

1897

Church of the Nazarene

Christian Methodist Episcopal Church

Methodist Episcopal Church

1844

1843

Pilgrim Holiness Church

1968

Wesleyan Church

Wesleyan Methodist Church of America

These charts were prepared by Rebekah Allmon using information gleaned from "Chronological & Background Charts of Church History" revised and expanded edition by Robert C. Walton, Zondervan, 2005, history.pcusa.org/history/denominations.cfm and other sources

132

History of the American Reformed and Congregationalist Churches

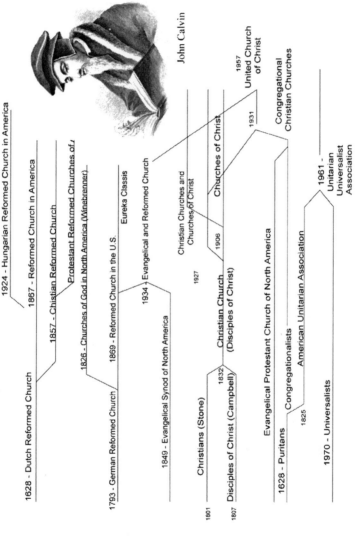

1628 - Dutch Reformed Church

1924 - Hungarian Reformed Church in America

1867 - Reformed Church in America

1857 - Christian Reformed Church

Protestant Reformed Churches of

1826 - Churches of God in North America (Winebrenner)

1793 - German Reformed Church

1869 - Reformed Church in the U.S.

Eureka Classis

1934 - Evangelical and Reformed Church

1849 - Evangelical Synod of North America

John Calvin

Christian Churches and
Churches of Christ

1927

1906

Churches of Christ

1931

1957

United Church
of Christ

Congregational
Christian Churches

Christians (Stone)

1801

1832

Christian Church
(Disciples of Christ)

1807

Disciples of Christ (Campbell)

Evangelical Protestant Church of North America

1628 - Puritans

Congregationalists

1825

American Unitarian Association

1961 -
Unitarian
Universalist
Association

1970 - Universalists

These charts were prepared by Rebekah Allmon using information gleaned from "Chronological & Background Charts of Church History" revised and expanded edition by Robert C. Walton, 2005, history.pcusa.org/history/denominations.cfm and other sources

History of the American Pentecostal Church

Aimee Semple McPherson

1943 - Church of God (Queens Village, NY)

1957 - Church of God of All Nations

1823 - Tomlinson Church of God
1953 - Church of God of Prophecy

1886 - Church of God (Cleveland, Tenn.)
1922 - Original Church of God, Inc.

1886 - Church of God

1886 - United Holy Church of America, Inc.

1944- Pentecostal Holiness Church

1953 - Emmanuel Holiness Church

1898 - Fire Baptized Holiness Church

1899 - Pentecostal Holiness Church

1918 - Pentecostal Fire-baptized Holiness Church

1901 - Pentecostal Union

1917 - Pillar of Fire

1914 - Assemblies of God, General Council

1914 - Church of God by Faith, Inc

1914 - Pentecostal Assemblies of the World, Inc.

1924 - Pentecostal Church Inc.

Pentecostal Assemblies of Jesus Christ Inc

United Pentecostal Church, Inc.

1917- Pentecostal Church of Christ

1918 - International Church of the Foursquare Gospel

1976 - International Pentecostal Church of Christ

1919 - Pentecostal Church of God of America, Inc.

1919 - International Pentecostal Assemblies

1919 - Church of our Lord Jesus Christ of the Apostolic Faith, Inc.

1957 - Bible Way Church, World-Wide

1919 - Bible Standard, Inc.

Open Bible Standard Churches, Inc

1932 - Open Bible Evangelistic Association

1932 - Calvary Pentecostal Church, Inc.

1947 - Elim Missionary Assemblies

These charts were prepared by Rebekah Allmon using information gleaned from "Chronological & Background Charts of Church History" revised and expanded edition by Robert C. Walton, Zondervan, 2005, history.pcusa.org/history/denominations.cfm and other sources

The History of the American Mennonite Church

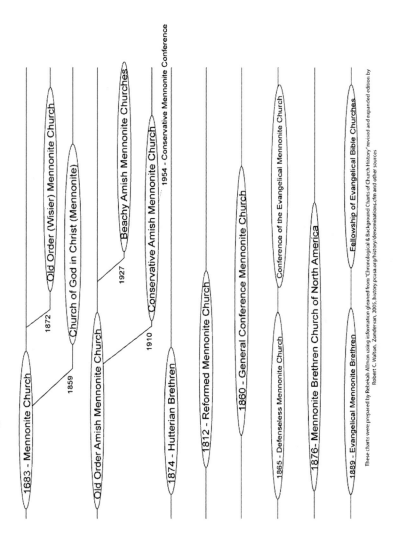

1683 - Mennonite Church

1872

Old Order (Wisler) Mennonite Church

1859

Church of God in Christ (Mennonite)

Old Order Amish Mennonite Church

1927

Beachy Amish Mennonite Churches

1910

Conservative Amish Mennonite Church

1954 - Conservative Mennonite Conference

1874 - Hutterian Brethren

1812 - Reformed Mennonite Church

1860 - General Conference Mennonite Church

Conference of the Evangelical Mennonite Church

1865 - Defenseless Mennonite Church

1876- Mennonite Brethren Church of North America

1889 - Evangelical Mennonite Brethren

Fellowship of Evangelical Bible Churches

These charts were prepared by Rebekah Alltman using information gleaned from "Chronological & Background Charts of Church History," revised and expanded edition by Robert C. Walton, Zondervan, 2005; history.pcusa.org/history/denominations.cfm and other sources

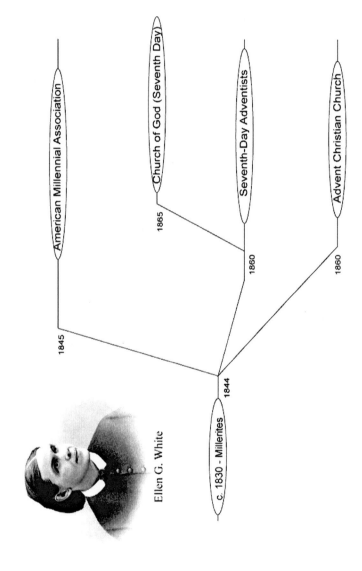

History of the American Adventist Church

American Millennial Association

Church of God (Seventh Day)

1865

Seventh-Day Adventists

1860

Advent Christian Church

1860

1845

1844

c. 1830 - Millerites

Ellen G. White

These charts were prepared by Rebekah Allmon using information gleaned from "Chronological & Background Charts of Church History," revised and expanded edition by Robert C. Walton, Zondervan, 2005, history.pcusa.org/history/denominations.cfm and other sources

Using very broad strokes, here is a quick summary of how all this played out: First, the Lutherans broke away from the Roman Catholic Church beginning in 1517, primarily over the doctrine of salvation by faith rather than by works (and the sale of indulgences by the church).

Then in 1525, the Ana Baptists broke with the Lutherans over the doctrine of water baptism.

The Calvinists broke away from the Lutherans in 1536 over what the Calvinists called covenant or reformed theology; a belief system emphasizing the sovereignty of God and such doctrines as election, predestination, and eternal security.

Around 1607, the Baptists (not to be confused with the Ana Baptists) and the Congregationalists broke away from the Calvinists. At this point, things were just beginning to heat up among the Protestants, but let's put them on hold for a moment and look back at the self-proclaimed "mother church."

While the Protestant churches were busy parting ways with one another, the Catholic Church was suffering another major division. In 1534, just 17 years after Luther broke away, Henry VIII, King of England, split with the Roman Catholic Church. The pope would not allow Henry to have his marriage annulled so he could marry another woman, one he hoped would provide him a male heir, so he effectively terminated the pope's authority over him. He started the Church of England and made himself its official head. This was one of the stranger splits in church history, but it was a significant one. The Church of England, also known as the Anglican Church, was quite similar to the Roman Catholic Church, and yet this new church would eventually be the fountainhead for even larger breakaway movements, starting with the Methodists.

It was from the Methodists that the Salvation Army, the Church of the Nazarene, and as we shall see momentarily, the Pentecostals would come. (I wonder what Henry VIII would have thought had he known that the church he launched to circumvent Catholic doctrine regarding divorce would someday give birth to the modern day Pentecostal movement.)

This might be a good time to note that the closer in chronological time a division was to the Catholic Church, the more the newly formed church resembled the Catholic Church. The Orthodox Church, the first split, has a priest class and is very liturgical; and like the Catholic Church, it rules from the top down. Other churches that split from the Catholics early on, such as the Lutherans and Episcopalian Churches tend to place a heavier emphasis on ritual and on the sacraments than those Protestant churches that formed later. The further a church is time-wise from its connection to the Catholic Church, the less it resembles it.

Now, let's briefly examine the ongoing divisions from a slightly different perspective.

The main splits, who begat whom

Again, using broad brush strokes, within a period of *roughly two decades* beginning in 1517, the Catholics had split into Catholics, Lutherans, and the Church of England, (which included the Puritans). That's three major groups.

The Lutherans in turn had split into Lutherans, Anabaptists, Mennonites, and Calvinists. In other words, in a matter of approximately twenty years, one church, the Roman Catholic Church, had become seven or eight separate churches, all with their own structure and differing doctrines.

The Church of England (Anglicans/Episcopalians) then split into the Anglicans and Methodists. Over the next century and a half, the Methodists would birth the African Methodist Episcopals, the Salvation Army, the Christian Missionary Alliance, and the Church of the Nazarene. It was from the Methodist branch of Protestantism that the Pentecostals were birthed at the beginning of the 20th century. Pentecostals in turn would split many times, as we shall see shortly.

Going back to the Calvinists – you might recall that they were one of the first groups to break away from the Lutherans. The Calvinists eventually gave birth to the Baptists and the Presbyterians, both of which split many times and today form some of the larger Protestant groups in existence. In fact, approximately twenty percent of all Americans call themselves Baptists of one stripe or another.

Presbyterians, who were started by a fiery Scottish preacher named John Knox, are known primarily for their form of church government, which consists of a board of elders or presbyters governing each local church. Many Presbyterians continue to embrace the "covenant theology" John Calvin promulgated, including a heavy emphasis on predestination. Unfortunately, the largest Presbyterian denomination in modern times is known for its liberal theology, its rejection of the inerrancy of Scripture, and more recently, its acceptance of gay and lesbian clergy, a policy that has led to still further splits among Presbyterians. (More will be said about this in the chapter titled, "Churches that are not really churches.")

As you saw on the preceding denominational charts, the Lutherans split many more times, as did the Baptists, the Methodists, the Adventists, the Reformed/Congregational churches, the Presbyterians, and the Pentecostals. Keep in mind that the charts only hit the high spots. There are several thousand smaller denominations that are not charted. If it was possible to cover them all, this book would be nothing but a book of charts. Seriously.

Churches broke away from churches which had split from other churches which had split from still others until the family trees of some denominations are all but impossible to trace.

Probably no church has split more than the Baptists. The Baptists split from the Calvinists. In 1607 the Congregationalists broke from the Baptists. Then in 1801 the Churches of Christ broke from the Baptists. In 1844, the Adventists broke away from the Baptists. After enduring all of these major splits, the Baptists divided again when the Southern Baptists broke off. Then in 1915, the National Baptists split off and in 1924 the American Baptists formed as a separate group. Since then, the Baptist movement has split into so many pieces that it is likely that no one knows who they all are.

The Great Awakening

In the next to the last chapter of our study, we will discuss more fully the Great Awakening,[35] which occurred in the mid to early 1700's and continued on into the middle to latter part of the 1800's. For the moment, suffice it to say that there was wave after wave of widespread revival that encompassed parts of Western Europe and the United States and changed the course of western civilization in countless ways. The Great Awakening took place within a highly denominational setting but seemed to ignore denominational lines. The Holy Spirit moved in small towns, major cities, and on college campuses. Dry, barren souls were reinvigorated, new ministries were birthed, and millions were converted. It is commonly held that the revivals of the Great Awakening contributed greatly to the birth of the American revolution and later to the abolition of slavery.

The revivals of the Great Awakening fell where they were needed most, in denominational churches that were all but dead. Through the revivals of such men as John and Charles Wesley, George Whitefield, Jonathan Edwards, Charles Finney, and Charles Spurgeon, the Holy Spirit moved sovereignly to breathe new life into dry churches. Many churches increased numerically at an unprecedented rate during a short period of time. Revivals during the Great Awakening were known for their fervor and a profound sense of conviction of sin. Several new denominations were formed during this period, including the Churches of Christ, Disciples of Christ, and the Seventh Day Adventists.

Pentecostals, Latter Rain Revival and the Charismatics

The most recent movements have been more Pentecostal and charismatic in nature. Pentecostals started as a movement in Los Angeles sometime around the year 1901, though there were several prior outbreaks of speaking in tongues and prophecy in the 1800's. As we have mentioned, the Pentecostals broke away from the Methodist and Nazarene Churches over the issue of the baptism of the Holy Spirit and speaking in tongues, and the manner in which those gifts would be exercised. The Pentecostals subsequently split into various denominations, most notably the Church of God (Tennessee), the Assemblies of God, the Foursquare Church, the Pentecostal Church of God, and the United Pentecostals. In addition to these, there are countless other small Pentecostal denominations and independent churches.

Then in 1948, the controversial Latter Rain movement, which initially started in a Bible college in Canada, gave birth to a new string of nondenominational Pentecostal and Restoration churches, which emphasized spiritual gifts and the laying on of hands and prophecy. This movement was soundly rejected by the larger Pentecostal denominations, most notably the Assemblies of God, primarily because the Assemblies had long taught that one "tarried," sometimes for many years, to receive the baptism of the Holy Spirit and speaking in tongues, while the Latter Rain folks taught that the baptism of the Holy Spirit could be received immediately by the laying on of hands.

Was 1948 a significant year?

A lot happened in the period immediately surrounding the year 1948. After centuries of nonexistence, the nation of Israel was formed and officially recognized in what was widely known as the ancient land of Palestine. For many, this was a prophetically significant event and marked the beginning of the end of the current age. At almost this same exact time, other far-reaching evangelical ministries were launched, such as evangelist Billy Graham, whose crusades touched the lives of millions, and Bill Bright, who launched Campus Crusade for Christ and other successful ministries. As we mentioned earlier, in and around 1948 the Latter Rain movement broke forth. This movement contributed significantly to the widespread charismatic movement which began a decade and a half later.

Latter Rain churches expressed deep dissatisfaction with the denominational nature of the church. Church historian, Richard M. Riss cites a statement made by George Hawtin, one of the leaders of the Latter Rain revivals as saying:

"A few weeks ago I was presented with a list of almost one hundred LATTER RAIN CHURCHES. I do not know where the list came from, though my own name was upon it...this is fundamentally and foundationally and scripturally WRONG. If you are a member of the Latter Rain sect you are just as separate and sectarian as if you were a member of the Pentecostal sect,

or the Apostolic, or Baptist, or Methodist sects, and so forth...
What gross hypocrisy is this to condemn others because they
are Pentecostal, Presbyterian, Baptist, Methodist, Foursquare –
and a thousand other brands, and then call yourselves LATTER
RAIN?...There shall be no sects or denominations, but the blood
washed of all kindreds and tongues shall by one Spirit be bap-
tised into one Body, and that Body shall be the Church..."[36]
(emphasis in original)

According to Riss, the Latter Rain movement established "count-less independent churches" throughout North America. Several of those churches became large "restoration churches," numbering in the thousands, and still today are fiercely nondenominational.

The charismatic movement, in turn, birthed thousands of new, nondenominational churches, which generally embraced all of the traditional orthodox doctrines held by other evangelical churches, but added to them open acceptance of speaking in tongues and the operation of the other gifts of the Spirit. The charismatic movement represented, at least for many, the balance in the exercise of spiritual gifts which was, at times, missing in the early extremes of the Pentecostal and Latter Rain movements.

The healing evangelists

Appearing on the scene in the 1940's and continuing to this day was a host of high profile healing ministries. Some of these "faith healers," as they have come to be called, hold their meetings in over-sized, portable tents while others routinely fill large metropolitan auditoriums and stadiums. Typically, full-page newspaper ads announce their meetings and invite the public to come and bring the sick, the lame, the blind, and the deaf. In the early days of these ministries, several healing evangelists became household names such as William Branham, Oral Roberts, A.A. Allen, and Kathryn Kuhlman.

Healing evangelists tend to be nondenominational, some strongly so, though they lean towards Pentecostal and charismatic. A few of them have been so flamboyant, financially free-wheeling, and morally reckless that they have given their type of ministry a bad name.

This has given critics room to paint them all with a broad brush and understate their impact, though to this day these ministries continue to reach millions with the gospel of Jesus Christ.

The success of healing evangelists has contributed majorly to making the Pentecostal and charismatic churches the fastest growing segment of Christianity today,[37] especially in African and South American nations. Occasionally, one of these evangelists teaches a suspect doctrine or strays off into some extreme emphasis, but most are theologically sound and preach the genuine message of repentance and faith in Christ; the major difference being their emphasis on preaching "with signs following."

The charismatic renewal

The charismatic movement was not restricted to Pentecostal or charismatic churches, per se, but in fact, spread to churches in most of the major denominations. With a little searching one can find charismatic Methodist, Presbyterian, Episcopalian, and Lutheran churches. There are even charismatic Catholic churches, many of which do not interpret Catholic doctrine quite the same as the Catholic Church does.

Most charismatic churches are independent and anti-denominational, but not all. Some of the newer and more organized charismatic groups include the Calvary Chapel and Vineyard Churches.

Summary and disclaimer

Finally, by way of disclosure, neither the descriptions set forth here nor the denominational charts are intended to be exhaustive. Their purpose is merely to give readers a sense of how fractured the Christian church is today. You might be well served to examine the Yellow Page listings in your area or do an online search to get a better feel for the extent of the divisions in your area. Please keep in mind that the issues raised here regarding denominations are not intended to imply that there are not millions of faithful, devoted believers worshipping and serving God within the confines of existing denominational structures. There are.

Our purpose is to make it clear that Christian churches have divided over and over again during the course of the past 500 years. Of course, it would be great if the result of this was simply lots of Christian churches spread across the world, each serving as a local expression of the love of Christ and each bringing the Gospel to its local community. Sadly, it's not that simple. There are lots of churches, alright, but they contradict one another and believe different things, and for the most part, they are not connected to one another as parts of the same body. In fact, most churches act as if the other churches, even ones just down the street, do not exist.

Parting company

Many divisions occurred and new denominations were formed because of serious doctrinal disputes among people of good faith. The two sides could not come to agreement regarding some doctrinal matter and there was no mutually respected authority to settle their differences. There were no apostles to answer their questions or tell them which way was right. There was no church council to issue a formal creed and set the matter straight. So, the disagreeing parties simply parted company and began to worship separately.

This is not dissimilar to the problem Moses faced with the Israelites during their wilderness wanderings back in the Old Testament. Moses found that he had to spend most of his waking hours dealing with a steady stream of disputes among the people. The task was wearing him out. Eventually, based on the advice of his father in law, Jethro, Moses appointed others to make the smaller judgments and thereafter he handled only the harder cases.

For nearly 500 years, Protestant churches have been without a respected authority to settle their disputes and the end result has been division after division. In the day in which we live, when Christians disagree with one another, they part ways. They do not forbear. They do not say, "I disagree with you but I love you and need you and will not let this matter separate us." No, they just say "goodbye" and walk away as if their division is of no consequence.

But not all divisions were about doctrine; some were simply about "who's going to be in charge," or about the form of church government the church would have. As we mentioned earlier, church government is a subject discussed little in the New Testament. None of the apostles laid out an elaborate system or discussed any kind of ecclesiastical hierarchy. They simply appointed elders in every city and those elders governed the local church. The system that the apostles designed worked for the early church, but in more modern times we have been unwilling to accept such simplicity. We structure and organize and then we fight about it all.

Who's in charge, and who "calls the shots" usually involves the control of the money and budgets. Where humans are involved, things like money and budgets can lead to heated disputes and heated disputes can lead to division. The "who's in charge" debate often carries over to the question of who owns or controls the church's property, especially the real estate. Whether at the beginning, as the cause, or at the end when the separation occurs, church splits eventually come down to, "what happens to the property and money?"

Just to cite one example of a split over this issue, one large Pentecostal denomination suffered a major division over the question of whether the denomination or each local church should own the church's property and building.[38] The denomination insisted that it owned the real estate, so several churches broke off and launched a separate organization, largely because they believed the local church should own its own property. (We will discuss the church's ongoing real estate wars in the chapter on church property.)

Martin Luther may have broken the power of the Roman Catholic Church, but all too often, Rome's power was replaced by the power of some distant denominational headquarters. As denominational powers began to dictate doctrine and policies, some within the movement inevitably would reject the denomination's edicts, just as Luther had done with the Roman Church, and in no time at all, a new revolt was launched and a new denomination birthed. This cycle was repeated over and over.

Efforts to force doctrinal uniformity

At first, even within the Protestant Reformation, efforts were made to force uniformity of doctrine. So-called heretics were executed for their "errant" beliefs. Both Luther and Calvin employed violent means to stop what they considered the spread of false doctrine. The thugs of the Spanish Inquisition, who tortured and killed those out of favor with the Catholic Church, were not the only ones who executed errant souls; early Protestants did so as well. Church history is replete with godly men and women going to a cruel death at the hand of other "believers" over some doctrine he or she would not recant.

Many of those same doctrines were embraced decades or centuries later by the very churches which had earlier executed the pioneers who had first preached them. Eventually, executing "heretics" was replaced by merely excommunicating them or kicking them out of the movement. Those exiled often went somewhere else and started a new church of their own and preached the very thing for which they had been rejected.

It is interesting to note that very early on it was recognized (with very little effect) that church divisions were not scriptural. Leaders of a movement would state publicly that they absolutely did not plan on starting a new denomination, but simply wanted to preserve the truth or *emphasis* around which their movement had begun. The word "emphasis" should not be passed over too quickly. Sometimes, churches or groups would agree regarding a particular doctrine or practice, but not agree regarding the degree or extent to which it would be practiced in their services. Disagreement regarding the degree of emphasis often resulted in a new division. Some Methodists, for example, wanted to focus more on helping the poor than on evangelizing or preaching the gospel, so they split. Some Pentecostals wanted the operation of the gifts of the Spirit to be the focus of their meetings, while others were willing to allow the gifts to operate, but more in the background, so they parted ways. Some large denominations exist today as monuments merely to an emphasis around which its adherents gathered decades or centuries ago, even though doctrinally they are in agreement with the group from which they split.

Denominational names

Over time, almost all Bible-believing Protestant denominations have come to embrace the same essential doctrines, meaning that today they are not really all that different from one another in their basic beliefs. Nonetheless, they remain divided over fringe or secondary issues that most agree are not essential to salvation. Although at one time, the names of their organizations were reflective of major differences among them, that is less true today. In fact, the names of many denominations do not reflect who they are today. Baptists are not just about water baptism. Pentecostals are not just about spiritual gifts. Lutherans are not just about Luther.

And yet, the fact that denominations hang on to their different sounding names says something about them; it says something about the Christian church in general. Our names make it clear that we are not ashamed of our divisions and do not care what the Bible says about sectarianism.

Paul rebuked the Corinthians for saying, "I am of Paul; I am of Apollos; or I am of Cephas." After reading this passage, why would any of us say we are of Luther, of Calvin, or of Wesley? In fact, Luther passionately pleaded with his followers not to name the church after him, but they did it anyway. *(See last part of chapter 22.)*

But it's not just men we name our churches after. Baptist churches name themselves after the ordinance of water baptism, which is but a single truth within the larger body of Baptist doctrine. What does it say when we call ourselves Presbyterians or Congregationalists? How is a form of church government a basis for naming a church? Are Presbyterian and Congregationalist churches about Jesus Christ or church government?

The Seventh Day Adventists base their entire name on their belief in a New Testament Sabbath day. Why? Adventists would agree that they are about much more than the doctrine their name emphasizes.

The Pentecostals base their name largely on an experience, speaking in tongues or the baptism of the Holy Spirit, which initially occurred on the Day of Pentecost. Pentecostals believe the same essential doctrines as Bible-believing Baptists, Lutherans, and Presbyterians, but they all call themselves by names that keep them separated.

The Methodists were given their name by their critics. They were initially viewed as the "holiness movement," but their methodical approach to the Christian life became their signature characteristic. The "Methodist" name stuck and the movement embraced it.

It may appear that I am making too much of the issue of names, but church names matter; they foster and reinforce divisions among believers. They draw attention to our differences. Even when we agree on all of the essential things, we use our names to emphasize minor differences and keep us apart.

Labeling a church by the name of any person other than the Lord Jesus Christ is wrong. Rallying around a particular doctrine or emphasis is equally wrong. Both are sinful acts of disobedience. When a church puts up a sign that identifies itself with a doctrine or person so as to make itself distinct from other genuinely Christian churches around it, it reinforces division. In so doing, it defies the New Testament command that we all be one. It says to our Lord and Savior, *We don't place much value on the prayer for unity that you offered just before you went to the cross.*

Diversity in taste and style

None of this means that local churches cannot or should not have different personalities and flavors. That would deny the uniqueness that is inherent in creation. God has made it clear by the things He has made that He loves variety. Variety in personality and style, however, is not the same as variety in doctrine. We are not to be diverse or creative in our doctrines. The opposite is true; we are commanded to say and believe the same things. We are not commanded to sing the same way or to wear the same clothes, but we must believe the same things.

Local churches should be free to reflect differences in taste and style. Even though we are required to say the same things, we are not required to say them with the same flair or lack thereof.

The tendency toward personality cults

Another major reason for division is human idolatry. There is a very strong propensity in the human species to exalt strong or charismatic personalities, sometimes to a cult status, and then identify with them on a personal level, as if our perceived association with them somehow makes us more significant. We feel more important when our hometown team wins the state championship, the World Series, or the Super Bowl. Maybe we didn't go to any games or have anything to do with the team's victories, but when the mercenaries who play for our team beat the mercenaries who play for the other team, we grasp at that victory, identify with it, and draw some personal significance from it due to some barely existent association.

Paul recognized this weakness and told the Corinthians:

[10] I appeal to you, brothers, by the name of our Lord Jesus Christ, that all of you agree, and that there be no divisions among you, but that you be united in the same mind and the same judgment. [11] For it has been reported to me by Chloe's people that there is quarreling among you, my brothers. [12] What I mean is that each one of you says, "I follow Paul," or "I follow Apollos," or "I follow Cephas," or "I follow Christ." [13] Is Christ divided? **Was Paul crucified for you? Or were you baptized in the name of Paul?** [14] I thank God that I baptized none of you except Crispus and Gaius, [15] so that no one may say that you were baptized in my name. (I Cor. 1:10-14)

As we have mentioned before, Paul intentionally did not baptize converts in Corinth, expressly so they wouldn't be bragging about the fact that Paul had baptized them. That's a pretty sobering thought when you consider how many public ministries today are named after the man who does the public speaking. The leader's name is up front and center, sometimes placed above or in larger letters than the name of Christ himself. Does the man of God do this because of his ego or does he do it because it is easier to build an organization around a flesh and blood, visible human than around the invisible Son of God?

This may have been the problem the Corinthian church was experiencing. Apollos was known as an eloquent orator. People loved to hear him speak. For this reason some claimed, "I am a follower of Apollos." Paul was known far and wide as the apostle to the Gentiles and a prolific writer of inspired letters. Thus some claimed, "I am a follower of the great apostle Paul." Cephas, or Peter, was known as one of the greatest of the apostles. He worked many miracles, so much so that even his shadow passing over people resulted in physical healings. He had walked very closely with the Lord and along with James and John, had been part of the Lord's inner circle of three. Thus some said, "I am a follower of Peter." Another says, "I can trump you all - for I am a follower of Christ."

In the final analysis, it makes no difference why the people gravitated to Paul, Apollos, or Peter. Whatever their reasons, they all stood rebuked for creating divisions. Paul spared none of them.

I have often wondered why Paul added those who said, "*I am of Christ,*" in with the others. They sound like the good guys, don't they? I am merely speculating here, but perhaps the ones who said, "I am of Christ," should rather have said, "We are all believers and share the same faith, so we are *all* of Christ." Saying, "*I am of Christ,*" implies that the others are not, or are somehow lesser Christians than the one who made this claim.

We might not admit this or even realize that we are doing it, but most of us probably do the same thing. Most of us secretly believe that our church has something the others don't and that our practices and beliefs make our church at least a little superior to all of the other churches. We think our pastor is the best preacher or our choir is the best. If we didn't think these things, we would probably attend somewhere else.

One says, "My family came from Scotland. We have been Presbyterian for many generations. In fact, I might even be related to John Knox."

"Well, we are Lutherans. Our ancestors hailed from Germany. Old German Lutheran stock, we are...and proud of it."

"I'm Pentecostal. There are a lot of lesser Christians out there, but we are the ones with the spiritual gifts. Others profess a form of godliness, but deny the power thereof. Not us. We are *full gospel*."

Another says, "I don't believe in denominations. I go to an independent church. Our pastor is a great speaker and we only follow the Holy Spirit at our church. No headquarters tells us what to do."

"I'm Methodist. We practice what we preach. The rest of you spiritual nuts talk about how much you love Jesus, but we are the ones feeding the poor while you spend your time at Bible studies and prayer meetings."

On and on it goes. "We're the best and you're not." Maybe we don't come right out and say it, but we think it. After all, why go to a church if you don't think it's the best one around, right?

This has been the history of the Christian church. Fighting is what we do. We fight for the right. We fight for the truth. Why spend time fighting the devil when there are plenty of Baptists, Pentecostals, Calvinists, and Arminians to battle?

Yes, there are many reasons why Bible-believing churches have divided and split, but they all are an outgrowth of our carnality - in all the meanings of that word. Before we move on, let's take a look at a hypothetical move of God and its evolution from a movement into a full-fledged denomination. Observing this development in a short span might give us an insight into how a denomination came to be, even when no one had any intention of forming one.

How denominations come into existence

In the beginning, there is a genuine move of the Spirit and hearts are stirred. Believers begin to repent of sins they have ignored for a long time. There is a renewed vision for reaching the lost and the Gospel is preached with a new passion and boldness. The conviction of the Holy Spirit falls upon the hearers and many lost souls come to the Lord for salvation.

During this time there is a vibrant church life and the focus is on Jesus Christ and doing His will. People with gifts exercise their callings and there is a time of blessing and growth. Revival is in the air. Everyone can feel it. It is a great time to serve the Lord.

Other Christians come and join in what God is doing and they too are blessed. Others, however, do not comprehend what the movement is all about, and begin to attack it. This makes the group draw closer together and feel separate from other Christians. Those who do not understand what God is doing, are looked down upon as rejecting the move of the Holy Spirit.

The group grows increasingly separated from other Christians and eventually feels it does not really need them. Members of the group feel complete in themselves. Not being joined to other members of the body of Christ, the life of the group weakens. After a while, the revival fires grow dim. There is still life, but it is not as fervent.

After a period of time, there is a perceived need to formalize what God has done in order to preserve it from those who would dilute it or pervert it. Doctrinal statements are created to set forth what it is the group believes and stands for. This also helps protect against the extremes and distortions that some are prone to. The leaders of the group decide that it is important to know who is with them and who has the right to represent them and associate with them.

An organizational structure is created to preserve the movement, lest it die, but the leaders of the group make it clear that they are not going to start a new denomination. Structure, by its very nature, requires organization and a recognized hierarchy with the authority to enforce whatever orthodoxy the group has adopted. In order to ensure that outsiders do not come in and split churches and steal their property, the group retains ownership of the buildings and property of all of the local churches that identify with the group, as well as the right to ordain ministers who can preach or teach in those churches.

With the increased structure, the move of the Holy Spirit diminishes even more and increased dryness is experienced. This is troubling, but it is mostly the old timers who miss the golden days of revival. New people are put into place and vested with organizational authority by virtue of the office they hold, rather than the gifts they possess. This doesn't really bother those who were not around back in the days when the Spirit was really moving. The new people have no recollection of what it was once like, back when every service was a life-changing experience.

The new structure takes on a life of its own apart from the move of God and eventually the structure can exist without Him, provided that the money continues to flow into the organization's coffers. The group's doctrines become statements of what members of the group share in common more than expressions of what they are experiencing together in the move of the Spirit. Over time, allegiances inure more to the organization than the cause of Christ. That is not viewed as a bad thing, because members have the sense that, "We have really built something here, something we can pass on to future generations."

The group starts schools to teach future ministers the group's doctrines. These trainees come from all of the local churches who are part of the group's network and fellowship. Mission boards are set up and all of the churches contribute so missionaries can be sent out across the nation and throughout the world. In order to ensure that those working full-time in the ministry are not left desolate in their old age, a shared pension plan is created for all of the group's full-time ministries. More structure is needed to maintain the mission outreach and the pension plan and to oversee the schools that are training the new ministers.

Without realizing it, those leading the organization become more committed to expanding the reach and influence of the group than spreading the Gospel of the Kingdom. The new priority is to have as many churches affiliated with the group as is possible. The efforts of other Bible-believing churches are ignored. New churches are launched in towns that already have plenty of other Christian churches, but not one representing the group.

The empty shell, where God once moved, continues on in perpetuity. The Holy Spirit begins to move elsewhere, where people are hungry and hearts are open. The group, of course, formally condemns the new move of God because it is happening outside of its sphere of influence. "After all, if this new thing really was of God, it would be happening here - for our group is the place where God has moved before."

No one ever planned on starting a new denomination. It just happened. Everyone had the best of intentions and the purest of motivations, but somehow a denomination was formed, and another group of Christians was walled off from all the others.

Justifiable divisions

In recent years, some of the older, mainline denominations have suffered a major loss of local congregations due to their liberal theology. We will talk about this more in the chapter titled "Churches that are not really churches." But since we are speaking here of how denominations form, let's take just a quick look at why some new denominations are forming as a way for conservative congregations to escape denominations which have embraced liberal theology, and in addition to rejecting the inspiration of the Scriptures and the deity of Christ, have also begun ordaining gays and lesbians to the ministry.

Rather than trying to reform giant but wayward mainline denominations, the Bible-believing congregations are abandoning them, adopting the motto, "It's easier to create babies than to raise the dead." In other words, it's easier to start over than try to reform a dead denomination that has abandoned the faith.

Over the past decade, the "gay clergy" issue has led to the formation of a number of new denominations. One new group, the Anglican Church in North America (approximately 700 congregations) was formed in 2008 to escape the Episcopal Church (7,000 congregations), when the larger denomination consecrated an openly gay bishop. On another front, the North American Lutheran Church (300 congregations) was organized as a new denomination in 2010 after the Evangelical Lutheran Church in America (10,500 congregations) voted to allow partnered gays and lesbians to serve as members of the clergy.

The larger Presbyterian and Methodist denominations also have been losing congregations due to the same issue, though in most of these cases, the gay clergy issue was merely the straw that finally broke the camel's back. The departures really represent an overall rejection of the larger denominations' liberal theology, which usually includes rejecting the deity of Christ, the miracles of the Bible, the resurrection of Jesus from the dead, and the inerrancy of Scriptures.

I would argue that it would be better, rather than starting a new denomination, if the departing churches simply became autonomous local churches. Nonetheless, the kind of division these splits represent is justifiable when the alternative is being joined with churches that have abandoned the faith.

As we shall discuss in detail later on, breaking away from a wayward denomination is not always an easy thing, no matter how justifiable. Denominations sometimes react to defections in harsh ways. The Episcopal Church, for example, has been suing to seize the buildings of its departing congregations. The litigation has been expensive and nasty and the larger denomination has been winning most of the cases, leaving the departing congregations with no place to worship. Even when the split appears justified, there can be a heavy cost to undertaking it. (*We will discuss these ongoing real estate wars in greater detail in the chapter titled "What about all of those buildings?"*)

The Fractured Church – chapter 11

When disputes never divided

A lthough disputes and divisions have ruled the day for the past 500 years of church history and have given birth to thousands of new denominations, there was a time when major disagreements never led to divisions.

There was a time when church divisions were carefully avoided and serious disputes, which today would rip churches apart, did not result in church splits or the formation of new denominations. We should be able to glean from that time useful clues to help us find the way back to such a place. The Book of Acts tells us of such a time.

It is logical to assume that when the Christian church was in its infancy it was the most vulnerable to division. In reality, we find the opposite was true. There were serious disputes when the church was young, but no division resulted. Why was that?

People were no less human then, and where there are humans there will be sin. Where there is sin, there will be disagreements, and where there are disagreements, there will be excuses for division. The early church proved all these things to be true and yet was not divided. Let us see if we can discern why.

The early church's first crisis

The first recorded strife in the early church, the first opportunity for division, was in regard to the way food was being distributed to the needy believers in Jerusalem.[39] This was a time of great poverty in and around the city. In the Book of Acts, we are told that the Greek speaking Jewish converts (the Hellenists) were complaining to the apostles that their widows were being neglected by the ones passing out the food, which was a daily task.

Keep in mind that the players in this dispute were all believers and were all Jews. At that time, Jews were the only ones to whom the gospel had been preached. Even though both sides were believers and Jews, they apparently could not ignore their language differences. The Greek speaking Jewish widows were being neglected because they spoke Greek, which in the minds of some, made them less Jewish than others.

This was a unique time. Believers who had the ability were voluntarily selling their land and other worldly goods, and bringing the proceeds to the church to help provide for the poor. In this dispute, emotions were particularly high, because basic human needs were at stake. Poor widow ladies were going hungry because they were being treated unfairly. This was not a doctrinal or theological quarrel, but it pitted believer against believer and had the potential to tear the church apart.

This dispute could easily have resulted in the first church split. The two sides could have turned away from each other and divided the early church into two separate groups based on language, but this didn't happen. No division or split occurred. The dispute was brought to the apostles, who acted quickly to resolve the dilemma and end the tension.

Please don't pass by that last sentence too quickly. It is important. The apostles ended the dispute quickly and easily, because they had the authority to do so. The matter was laid before them with the expectation that they would provide a solution, and they did. The apostles didn't really resolve the dispute; they simply told the people how to do it. All the people wanted was for someone with authority to tell them what to do to end the tension and the injustice.

The problem should not have existed in the first place. The Hellenist widows should never have been neglected based on their language or ethnicity. The responsibility for distributing the food was apparently not in the right hands. The apostles ended the dispute by instructing the people to choose out from among themselves seven men who were of "good reputation and full of the Holy Spirit" to oversee the business of distributing the food. These deacons, as they were called, were the first official positions within the early church - other than the apostles themselves.

It is interesting to note that the apostles required that deacons, men whose sole task at the time was to handle daily food distribution, be honorable men, who were "full of the Holy Spirit." Even food distribution was considered a spiritual undertaking in the early church and required a good heart and good character.

It is also interesting to note that the first dispute in the early church was a fight based on language, the same basis for the divisions intentionally created by the Lord himself at the Tower of Babel. Language is a natural basis for division, a perfect excuse for separating from others, which is what the Lord obviously intended for the world. However, when a language based dispute threatened to divide the body of Christ, the division was immediately quashed. That which divides the world was not allowed to divide the church.

The Jew versus Gentile controversy

This was not the only challenge the early church faced.

As the gospel spread beyond Jerusalem, a new basis for division arose. This time, rather than language, the issue was race. For at least 1,500 years, Jews had kept themselves separate from Gentiles (non-Jews). Gentiles were like dogs to them. In fact, a Jew could not go into the house of a Gentile or sit down and eat a meal with a Gentile without being ceremonially defiled. This was the Old Testament way, the only way Jews knew.

Jesus, however, did not always follow such rules. The Gospels detail several stories of Jesus performing miracles for non-Jews. More than once, He marveled at the great faith some Gentiles displayed. In one case, Jesus made it clear to a certain Phoenician woman, who came to Him seeking healing for her daughter, that she was considered by the Jews to be but a "dog" and thus not entitled to the "children's" bread.[40]

The woman may have been a Gentile, but according to Jesus she had "great faith," and thus He gave her the miracle she desired.

The notion that the Hebrew God might love the Gentiles had not yet occurred to the early church, which was comprised solely of Jews. They had not yet considered the possibility that there might be a larger plan, i.e. that the Gospel of salvation would extend far beyond their own ranks and indeed go out to all the nations of the earth. Early church converts had accepted the Gospel message as it related to a Jewish messiah, but to them the Gentiles were still dogs and of no consequence.

It is likely that even the apostles had not yet grasped the idea of salvation being offered to the Gentiles. The thousands who had come into the church thus far were all Jews or Jewish proselytes. They had been saved, baptized in water and baptized in the Holy Spirit. There is no indication that they had any intention of sharing this good news with the Gentile dogs, even though the commission Jesus had given them included instructions to make disciples of all nations.

As we learn from the story of Peter and Cornelius in Acts 10, it took divine intervention for just one apostle to begin to accept the possibility that the God of Israel might also love Gentiles and want to offer the plan of salvation to them, as He had to the Jews. Peter received a marvelous vision from heaven and heard the voice of God speak to him, telling him that he was not to call unclean what God called clean. It took a vision from heaven for Peter to overcome his innate abhorrence of the Gentiles, and go and preach the Gospel to the household of Cornelius.

While Peter was still preaching, the Holy Spirit fell upon Cornelius's household and for the first time in history a bunch of Gentiles began to speak in tongues and prophesy. What happened that day was a truly historical event. The Holy Spirit was poured out on the Gentiles, as He had been on the Jews.

When the apostles and the other brethren back at Jerusalem heard the news that the Word of God had been preached to uncircumcised Gentiles, there was contention. This was contrary to their basic understanding of God. Some believers even rebuked Peter for going into a Gentile household and eating with them.

Of course, none of the objectors had been present when Peter received his heavenly vision. From their perspective, it was just plain wrong for Peter to go to a house full of Gentiles and preach the gospel to them; it violated everything they knew about Jew/Gentile relations.

Peter's actions could have resulted in a split in the early church. There could have been a faction that chose to "maintain the purity" of the Christian church and another faction that embraced the radical notion that Gentiles could be Christians. A division easily could have occurred, but none did.

The question is: Why not? Many churches have split permanently over far less controversial matters than this one. The answer is gleaned from the text. When Peter returned to Jerusalem and shared with the leaders there that the Holy Spirit had fallen on the entire household of Cornelius, and that these Gentiles had experienced the baptism of the Holy Spirit just as the 120 Jewish disciples had on the Day of Pentecost, the apostles made a decision.

The other eleven apostles listened to Peter's story and then simply accepted the new reality that he described. It was that simple. The acceptance of the twelve apostles put to rest what could have been a major dispute.

The scriptures sum up this historic event with one simple statement: The leaders at Jerusalem became silent and glorified God that He had "granted repentance to life to the Gentiles."[41] That was it. The matter was settled. Gentiles could be saved just like Jews could.

The world had just changed and all it took for this new move of the Holy Spirit to be accepted was for the apostles to give it their okay.

Simply put, the apostles had the authority to prevent the Gentile issue from boiling over and resulting in a major rift in the early church. All they had to do was hear the matter and make a decision and the issue was put to rest. As they had done in the dispute over the distribution of food to the Hellenist widows, the apostles settled the matter because they had the authority to do so.

The contention over Gentiles keeping the law

The issue of Gentiles coming into the church was a complex one, and was not entirely resolved by accepting the fact that Gentiles could be saved. It was one thing to allow Gentiles into the church, but it was quite another to allow them to come in without keeping the Jewish law, as Jewish believers thought they were required to do.

Before long, some Jewish believers were demanding that Gentile converts be circumcised, keep the Sabbath, obey the Jewish food laws, and participate in Jewish feasts, such as the Passover. Keep in mind that the New Testament had not yet been written. There was no "chapter and verse" that spoke to the issue. Today, we can refer to the books of Galatians and Colossians to answer these questions, but early church believers could not.

Questions regarding the Law were legitimate ones and had this new dispute been left unresolved, the early church easily could have split into two factions, with one side demanding that Gentile converts keep the Jewish law, and the other side saying the opposite.

In fact, it's entirely possible that more than two factions could have developed over this issue. Some could have claimed that Gentile converts must only keep some parts of the law, but not others. Maybe they should be required to keep the Sabbath, but not the food laws. Maybe they should be required to keep Passover, because their salvation was by means of the blood of the Lamb, but perhaps not be circumcised because in the opinion of some, Gentile believers weren't really Jews or heirs of the Abrahamic covenant. Many divisions could have resulted from this dispute, because there was no obvious answer to the question before them, except to say that in the Old Testament, a non-Jew wanting to join the Hebrew faith had to keep all aspects of the Jewish law.

Yet, given all that, and given how volatile this situation was, no splits resulted from it. There is no record of a new church or denomination forming. Why? Because the early church held a council to address the matter and successfully put it to rest.

In Acts 15, it is recorded that the apostles and elders held a conference in Jerusalem to decide this very contentious question. The issue was a hot potato. Tensions were high. The Scriptures tell us that Paul and Barnabas "had no small dissension and dispute" with those Jewish believers who had demanded that the Gentile believers come under the law. (The Jewish believers raising this ruckus were from the sect of Pharisees. After Pentecost, many Jewish priests and Pharisees had become believers in Christ, though some remained very legalistic.)

At any rate, we can safely infer from the text that there was a very heated debate over this issue. People were hardly of one accord. There were very strongly held differences of opinion. Doctrinally and emotionally, a perfect storm was brewing. (I emphasize this point, because I want you to see that today a heated dispute such as this one would almost certainly result in many church splits.)

The council at Jerusalem was a major event. Everyone in all of the churches recognized that the question at hand had to be addressed, and that whatever answer was arrived at would have far reaching consequences. It was a complicated issue and the apostles and elders at Jerusalem would have to settle the matter lest the church be divided by it. So, before it went any further, they ended it.

The apostles and elders heard the matter and made a decision. They issued an official decree, which was distributed to the Gentile churches. The decision was not represented to the churches as merely the decree of the elders and apostles at Jerusalem. The letter they sent out declared that "it seemed good *to the Holy Spirit and to us*" that you will be doing well if you do these four things: abstain from things offered to idols, from blood, from things strangled, and from immorality.

There were four things; that's all. No mention of circumcision, the Sabbath, animal sacrifices, Passover, or those elaborate Jewish food laws. While there is much debate as to why only these four were deemed "necessary things," the relevant point for the purpose of our study is this: This dispute, which easily could have resulted in major splits and divisions within the early church, was resolved because there was a body of men of sufficient spiritual authority to resolve the conflict and settle the matter.

The Jerusalem council spoke and the question was answered, and what's more, it was answered with the seal of the Holy Spirit's approval.

What lesson can we learn from the early church?

Is there a clear pattern we can draw from these three examples from the Book of Acts? Are there lessons we can glean from seeing how the early church settled disputes? I think the answer to both questions is, "yes," but it is not entirely clear how what we just saw might transfer over to the church today. We need to step back and look at the principle and not the specifics.

The principle seems to be that divisions are allowed to continue today because there is no recognized authority to demand that they cease. There is no authority to resolve disputes as they arise, or to answer the difficult questions, so we part company. We go our separate ways like sheep lacking a shepherd.

Sure, there are denominational authorities who offer answers, but their authority is not recognized outside the group for which they speak. Their answers only settle disputes within their particular segment of the body of Christ. This is not all that helpful and in fact in a very real sense, may serve to perpetuate the divisions among the denominations. Answers which are embraced within one denomination or group become that group's settled orthodoxy. However, when those answers are not commonly shared by other groups, the divisions between the groups become fixed and more permanent because they now are *officially* at odds.

Go back to our Acts 15 story again. Let's postulate for a moment that the Pharisees who caused the dispute decided to meet together and settle this dispute themselves. Does it not stand to reason that they would have reached, perhaps unanimously, a conclusion that was the exact opposite of the one the apostles and elders at Jerusalem had reached?

The Pharisees who stirred up the dispute were obviously teachers. Pharisees were known for their "head knowledge" of the Scriptures. They were trained debaters, so obviously, they could have settled the question themselves. They didn't because they lacked one key element, the spiritual authority to do so. They knew they could not enforce their opinions, because they had no real authority, at least no authority that was recognized outside the confines of their own group.

The same could be said of denominations. Denominations create their own authority. Denominations can "pull the papers" or withdraw the ordinations of pastors or ministers who stray from the doctrinal positions adopted by their organization. This kind of authority does little to further church unity in the broader sense of the term. All a denomination can do, after all is said and done, is maintain a consistency *within its own little division* of the body of Christ. However, if that division is in fact a prohibited one, then its authority cannot be real. (We deal with this matter in greater depth in the chapter on denominational doctrines.)

The body of Christ does not need hundreds of separate councils and boards making contradictory decisions regarding weighty matters. Decisions that maintain uniformity only within a denomination's own ranks do nothing to further the cause of church unity. As we noted earlier, they have the opposite effect.

Could we hold church councils today?

But think about this: What if there was today, as there was in the early church, a recognized council of apostles and elders (or if you hang up on the term "apostle," just a council of elders or highly respected men of God) with the authority, or at least the respect, to settle doctrinal disputes by reason of their obvious callings and gifting. Most if not all of the disputes that divide the church today, could be settled.

It seems safe to say that the lack of such authority is precisely why churches are so divided today and why they have been blown about by every wind of doctrine for the past five centuries. As we discussed earlier, Moses installed 70 elders in ancient Israel to settle disputes and the twelve apostles and elders at Jerusalem met in council to settle matters that threatened to divide the church. Why would we suppose that the church today should not have a council to resolve our differences?

Imagine for a moment a recognized body of godly leaders with the wisdom and spiritual anointing to answer authoritatively such questions as whether women should be allowed to preach; whether gays should be ordained; whether the gifts of the Spirit, such as speaking in tongues, prophesying and working miracles, are still in operation in the church today; and matters such as the true meaning and significance of communion and water baptism.

In an atmosphere where genuine believers are earnestly seeking real and lasting unity with other believers, many of the walls that separate us could be demolished and the shame our divisions bring to the name of Christ could be put behind us. At least, as a starting place, the walls that separate Protestant churches from one another could be broken down.

The greater the participation in such a council, the more unity there would be after its decisions, and the reasons for them, were announced. Serious steps toward restored unity could be taken – at least incrementally.

I do not pretend to have an entire roadmap in mind here, but there could be, for example, a requirement that decisions flowing from such councils be unanimous or perhaps be passed by an overwhelming majority. The goal would be to walk out of a council at its conclusion with a statement that those participating could say, in good faith, was "of the Holy Spirit," as the apostles did in Acts 15. In other words, a council that could say at its conclusion, "We believe with one accord that we found the mind of God regarding the matter." And let that be the end of it.

While such a council was in session, which could be for several months, millions of Christians around the world could be praying for wisdom and guidance. As the apostle James wrote, **"If any man lacks wisdom, let him ask of God, who gives to all liberally and without reproach…"**[42] If we believe God gives wisdom to individuals, could we not believe that He would give wisdom to a council of godly church leaders who were making decisions which would affect the entire body of Christ?

Early church councils took on tough issues

As we saw in the chapter on church history, for hundreds of years the early church settled their differences by utilizing councils. They did so even after the twelve apostles had passed on. Should we be afraid to trust a church council to address our issues, considering the early church trusted councils to address issues such as:

Who was Jesus Christ? Of what nature was He? Was Jesus God or was He a man? Was Jesus half man and half God? Was He part of both? Was He a hybrid mixture of the two and thus some new kind of being such as had never existed before? Did Jesus have a real human body or did He merely appear to? If He is the Son of God, was there a time when He was born, and if so, when? Did He remain God when He took on human form and became a man? Did Jesus cease being human when He ascended back to heaven?

These were weighty theological questions and yet all of them were decided by church councils 1,500 to 1,700 years ago, and the vast majority of Christians on this planet today accept, at least substantially, the conclusions those councils reached.

The stakes were high, and the councils had to get these things right. Believers could not be left on their own to come up with their own answers, lest there be hundreds of different views regarding the nature of Christ, and thus mass confusion within the church. So, the councils met and reached conclusions that ended the vast majority of the disputes.

Overcoming your doubt about church councils

I am certain that many will be skeptical of the notion of modern day church councils. Let's see if we can overcome that skepticism. Imagine creating a council with representatives from across Christendom, but throw in these two caveats: One, the decision at the end must be unanimous; and two, you or your church gets to place on that council the person of your choice, the one man (or woman) whom you respect and trust the most. Think about that. No decision could be reached unless your delegate, a person you know would not compromise the truth, signed off on it. Do these two caveats not make the entire concept more palatable, or at least conceivable? Whether complete unanimity should be a requirement for councils is not for me to say; it certainly wasn't in some of the early church councils. Such a policy might be necessary today, at least at first, due to the deep suspicions many of us hold for one another.

If, in our hearts, we are not willing to take serious steps to work out our differences and reach a decision that settles a matter that is of some contention and is causing division, then it is possible that we do not place a high enough value on unity and do not grasp the seriousness of our disunity.

In the interest of disclosure, there is some ongoing debate regarding the political influences that came to bear against some of the early church councils, as Roman emperors sought to force unity within the Christian church as a way to hold together the far-flung, seriously struggling Roman Empire. This appears to be a historical fact. However, such pressure has not been shown to have caused those serving on the councils to adopt some false doctrine, so as to please the emperor, at least not in the earlier, "pre Dark Ages" councils. Likely, an emperor's ultimate goal was more to maintain church unity than to dictate a specific doctrinal position.

It is this author's opinion that during this foundational period, God, in His sovereignty, ensured that the basic truths regarding the nature of Christ and the Godhead were preserved by church councils and the correct New Testament books were canonized. Otherwise, there would have been nothing left to restore at the end of the Dark Ages.

Here is what we should be able to take from this period: If hundreds of years after the twelve apostles died, but before the Catholic Church went far astray, the early church could convene councils to establish such essential doctrines as the nature of Christ, the Trinity and the Eternal Godhead, and decide matters as substantive as which of the many gospels and epistles circulating amongst the churches would be canonized into the New Testament, it seems that we ought to be able to settle together most of the things that divide us; that is, if we have the collective heart and will to do so.

Early church councils were comprised of highly respected teachers and scholars who met together to discuss doctrines and to exegete Scripture. Sometimes, they convened for years, but they stayed at it until they came to an answer. The creeds these councils formulated a millennium-and-a-half ago, comprise, still today, the basic doctrines of the church regarding the nature of Christ and the eternal Godhead.

It was easier for the early church to form councils

Perhaps this suggestion makes sense to you. If so, you should recognize the challenges such an undertaking would face. During the third through the sixth centuries of church history, when church councils were convened, the church was not as divided as it is today. A few prominent city churches could choose the scholars who would sort out these weighty matters and the smaller churches would accept those choices. The leading churches were respected enough that afterward they could confirm the conclusions of the council and proclaim to the entire Christian world what was right and wrong doctrine regarding the matters at hand.

Let us not pretend that as great as the rewards might be, there is not some risk in convening church councils in modern times. Sure, the early church councils got it right, or at least substantially right. Centuries later, however, the church that appointed those councils had become so corrupt that it could not be trusted to get even the basics right. We are dealing with humans and humans do make mistakes. But let us not leave God out of the equation. It is, after all, His church and He has a vested interest in guiding those who seek His will with pure hearts. Thus we should not discount His sovereign intervention in the affairs of men when it suits His purposes.

Let me illustrate why I say this. There is some continuing dispute regarding the books that were canonized into the New Testament 1,600 years ago. Some believe that three or four of the 27 books should not have been included or that a handful of other books should have been. I find it interesting, however, that those who canonized the Bible, so many centuries ago, came up with 39 Old Testament books and 27 New Testament books for a total of 66 books. You might assume that the number itself is meaningless, and perhaps you are right. I am of another opinion. So, for those who are open to considering Old Testament typology, I offer you the following indication that the canon is correct:

<u>Canonization and the golden lampstand</u>

In the Old Testament, the only light in the Holy Place of the Tabernacle was the golden lampstand or candlestick, which God told Moses to have constructed according to the pattern shown to him on the mountain. Now according to the New Testament, the Word of God is the light of the world[43], so we shall assume that the specific directions God gave Moses for making the golden lampstand are important and symbolic of the Word of God or the Scriptures. Keep in mind also that, according to the Psalmist, the Word of God is a lamp unto our feet and a light unto our path. If the golden lampstand in the Holy Place of the Tabernacle was a symbol of the Word of God, its design should reflect that.

According to the instruction Moses received from the Lord, the entire lampstand was to be made from one piece of pure gold. Gold in the tabernacle symbolized deity, and it is God who is the divine author of the Scriptures, not the 40 or so men who wrote the various books[44], as they were moved on by the Holy Spirit. Now, God told Moses to make the candlestick with a specific pattern, placing a golden seed at the base with a golden bud on top of the seed and then a golden flower on top of the bud, a clear indication of a progressive unfolding or progressive revelation, which is the precise way God says His doctrines come, i.e. line upon line, precept upon precept, here a little there a little[45]. These seeds, buds, and flowers were to be stacked on top of one another so that a total of twelve seeds, buds, and flowers would comprise the center stem of the lampstand. Protruding from the sides of the stem, the artisan was to construct three arms protruding from each side for a total of six arms. Each arm was to have the same pattern of seeds, buds, and flowers, except instead of twelve pieces, as with the stem, there were to be nine on each of the six arms[46].

If you add the twelve seeds, buds and flowers that comprise the stem to the 54 seeds, buds, and flowers that comprise the six arms of the lampstand, you get a total of sixty-six seeds, buds, and flowers, the precise number of books canonized into the Old and New Testaments combined. In other words, according to the Old Testament type, those who canonized the Bible 1,900 years after the golden lampstand was constructed, got it right when they settled on sixty-six books.

Finally, the lamps on the six arms of the golden lampstand and the one lamp on the center stem made a total of seven lamps; in Scripture seven is the number of completion and perfection. It stands to reason that God would not let Christianity follow a Bible that was made up of books that didn't belong there and were not really the Word of God, so He intervened in the affairs of men and made sure they got it right.

I offer this illustration only to suggest, for those who can receive it, that God can and does work through fallible men. He leads them to right answers when they are inclined to hear Him. And, as King Nebuchadnezzar discovered in Daniel's prophecy, God, at least on some occasions, intervenes to bring His will to pass, even when people are not inclined to listen.[47]

Moving cautiously towards consensus

It is reasonable to fear the creation of some kind of ecclesiastical super structure, or "world council of churches," which might compromise essential doctrines for the sake of ecumenicalism. That would be a step backward. That's not what I am suggesting. I am merely saying that church councils have been held before and with success, even when none of the original twelve apostles were around to oversee things.

Keep in mind that the Acts 15 council at Jerusalem worked because there were respected, gifted leaders conducting and overseeing the affair, and because the Holy Spirit was present. Is it not reasonable to conclude that the Holy Spirit was also present and overseeing matters when the New Testament was canonized in the fourth century, and also when the Athanasian Creed was formulated by means of a church council in the fifth century, establishing the doctrine of the Trinity and the Eternal Godhead.

Are we capable of choosing godly men (and women) to undertake such a task today? Keep in mind that the early apostles empowered the believers in Jerusalem to select godly, Spirit-filled men to end the first dispute in the early church. The believers chose the first deacons. The apostles trusted them to do that.

Of course, if councils were held today, great wisdom would have to be exercised in choosing those who would comprise it. Rather than picking proud men, those prone to argue their own positions to prove they are right, pick humble men who want only to find the mind of God. A council should be comprised of the kind of believers Paul spoke of in Ephesians 4. Believers who:

> *"...walk in a manner worthy of the calling to which you have been called, ² with all humility and gentleness, with patience, bearing with one another in love, ³ eager to maintain the unity of the Spirit in the bond of peace."*

Obviously, what we are considering is but a suggestion, but we can see from Scripture and from history that it is not altogether without precedent. Alternatively, we could do nothing. We could continue to behave as if every man or woman with a Bible, and every denomination, has every right to come up with their own set of doctrines without regard to what other Christians believe, and without regard to centuries of time tested orthodoxy. We could continue to ignore the New Testament admonition against devising "private interpretations" of Scripture and continue to see the body of Christ divided into countless denominations and independent churches tossed to and fro by every wind of doctrine. That appears to be our future, unless we take definite, albeit measured steps to change the way we handle our differences.

Perhaps we do not realize how precarious our present condition is. Some of us are vulnerable to religious fads and doctrinal trends that could throw us completely off track. All it might take is the right personality and the right piece of literature to throw thousands of churches into a tailspin. Recently, one prominent author proposed that God is so loving that no one will go to hell, because God's love will prevail in the end. Many believed his message. What defense does the body of Christ have when such doctrines start blowing about? Certainly, we cannot speak to such a matter with one voice, because we are not one.

Is this man right, or is his teaching rank heresy? If he is found to be teaching heresy, he would still be free to say what he wishes, but if the Christian church could "with one voice" answer him, one way or the other, many would receive valuable understanding and perhaps be kept from serious error.

It is time to recognize that if we continue on the path we are currently on, there will be no end to our divisions. Our disagreements will continue to divide us, plague us, and hinder our mission. If Christians are ever truly going to speak the same thing and be of the same mind and judgment, as we have been instructed, this will come about because we have found a way to resolve our differences.

There is a way to do this and it is quite possible that the apostles and the early church have already shown us that way.

The Fractured Church – chapter 12

Obstacles to church unity

ভৈ৺৶

I
f genuine church unity was an easy thing to achieve, would we not have achieved it already? Obviously, this is not an easy thing. There are serious obstacles standing in the way. There are challenges to overcome, or in Old Testament terminology, there are giants to overcome. It will take faith and courage to possess this New Testament "promised land" called unity, a place where the Lord says He will "command a blessing."

It is without controversy that in the world of spiritual things, the greatest battles are won and lost in our hearts and minds. That's where our misguided attitudes are firmly entrenched, where we have been taken captive and bound in chains of discouragement and deception. If we are going to come to a place of unity with believers who are not part of our current circle, there are several wrong attitudes or perspectives which must be overcome. In our hearts and minds, that is where the most powerful giants lurk.

Is it wrong to seek unity?

The first giant we face is the widespread belief that we should *not* seek unity; that it would be wrong to do so. This belief is more widespread than you might think. The fact that many believers have this attitude is compelling evidence that they do not see division and sectarianism as the grievous sins they are.

To be fair, blindness regarding church division is almost understandable. The contemporary church is like a baby that was born blind and does not know that it cannot see. Division and disunity are to us like water is to a fish. It's the world we live in. It's the world we grew up in. We do not see the disunity that is all about us, because we have nothing with which to compare it. It's just the way things are and the way they have always been, or so we think. Hopefully, this study has been dispelling at least some of the blindness which has surrounded this issue.

Is church unity possible before we get to heaven?

Another giant or obstacle we face is the fact that many church leaders believe that genuine unity among believers will not be achieved until we get to heaven. This view is widespread and may be the result of a flawed or incomplete doctrine regarding the end times.

This perspective is a serious challenge and the entire next chapter has been dedicated to answering it. The next chapter discusses "God's Big Picture" and outlines more fully the obstacle that an incomplete view of the end times poses. That chapter will be challenging to many readers, especially those who are constantly watching Jerusalem and the Middle East for signs of the end. They will find in the next chapter a new list of "signs of the end" to add to their list. So please, when you get there, try to have an open mind. Allow the Bible to trump your pet doctrine, if you find that the two are in conflict.

Should we forget about unity and just keep our eyes on the Lord?

Another obstacle is the fact that many believe it is wrong to seek unity, because "we should simply keep our eyes on the Lord." Although this sounds like a lofty mindset, when closely examined it is a difficult position to defend. In promulgating this view, one debater quoted the esteemed A.W. Tozer, as follows:

"Has it ever occurred to you that one hundred pianos all tuned to the same fork are automatically tuned to each other? They are of one accord by being tuned, not to each other, but to another standard to which each one must individually bow. So one hundred worshippers meeting together, each one looking away to Christ, are in heart nearer to each other than they could possibly be were they to become unity conscious and turn their eyes away from God to strive for closer fellowship. Social religion is perfected when private religion is purified. The body becomes stronger as its members become healthier. The whole church of God gains when the members that compose it begin to seek a better and a higher life."[48]

I do not wish to pick a fight with Brother Tozer for he is certainly right in what he says. Of course, we should all keep our eyes on the Lord. If we did everything else right, but skipped this one thing, we would be lost and floundering. To that end, seeking unity solely for unity's sake would be ill advised and perhaps even downright dangerous.

Having said that, let us examine this perspective a little more closely, as it directly relates to the premise of our study. Many of us have been in settings where Christians from different traditions were worshipping together and sensed a wonderful spirit of unity - simply because everyone was in tune *for that moment* with the same Lord. However, when the moment or the meeting was over, we went back to our own churches with all of our same disagreements and separate doctrines, and we kept our separate denominational names and labels. In short, everything was pretty much like it was before. The unity "of the moment" did not last.

The unity did not last, because this kind of unity is by its nature temporary and fleeting. It's special while we are in it, and indeed the Holy Spirit can move in our hearts and change our lives in such an atmosphere. In another sense, however, it is as if we merely declared "a temporary truce." Our differences were there with us, but we set them aside for the moment while we focused our hearts and minds elsewhere.

This kind of unity can only be maintained by temporarily agreeing to ignore the things that divide us. This kind of unity is earnest money. It's a down payment on the real thing; a taste of what is to come. What is to come will not be temporary and it will not be just in heaven. It will be in the here and now and by the grace of God, it will be lasting.

We should recognize that keeping our eyes on the Lord, as Brother Tozer advised, should not exclude striving for and believing for a lasting and genuine unity, a unity that doesn't just put our divisions on the back burner for the moment, but ends the root cause of them.

Keeping our eyes on the Lord must include striving for unity

Keeping our eyes on the Lord should not preclude conscious efforts at unity. Allow me to illustrate this point. We would never say, "Let's ignore the poor and needy and just keep our eyes on the Lord." That would be an act of disobedience. James tells us that faith without works is dead. He also tells us that pure religion, undefiled before God, includes caring for the orphans and widows in their affliction. So we keep our eyes on the Lord and care for the poor at the same time.

We would never say, "Let's not worry about preaching the gospel to the lost. Let's just keep our eyes on the Lord." This would be akin to saying, "I love the Lord so much and I desire Him so much that I don't need to do the things He tells me to do. He has told us to spread the good news, but I am just going to keep my eyes on Him instead."

So, what should we do about the poor and the lost? We should keep our eyes on the Lord while providing for the poor and reaching the lost with the Gospel. Keeping our eyes on the Lord should never prevent us from doing His will; it should only purify our motivations in what we do.

Understanding this principle, why would one then say, "Let's not worry about all of the divisions that exist among us. Let's ignore our disunity and just keep our eyes on the Lord?" Did Jesus not say, "If you love me, keep my commandments?" Keeping His commandments includes caring for the needy, sharing the gospel, and giving of our finances to the work of the Lord. Keeping His commandments also includes loving one another, forgiving those who sin against us, and *not allowing any divisions among us.*

Not allowing divisions is a command of the Lord. Apparently it is an important one, because the Lord told us that if there is a brother against whom we have grievances, we are to leave our gift at the altar and go reconcile with our brother, and then come and offer our gift. If this is true of Christian believers, should it not be true of the organizations Christians form? Should denominational entities allow their grievances with other denominations to remain unresolved and yet presume that the Lord accepts their service?

The New Testament is absolutely packed full of admonitions and pronouncements against divisions, strife, and disunity. We are strictly commanded not to allow divisions among us. How then can we *keep our eyes on Jesus* and ignore the fact that we are at odds with most of our brothers and sisters in Christ and acting before the world like we don't at all like one another?

To say as some have, "Let's not worry about unity. Let's just keep our eyes on the Lord," is to ignore the log that is in our collective eye, a log which the world sees more clearly than we do.

The misguided attitudes we discuss here are serious obstacles to unity. We cannot begin to make real progress until we first see how far short we have fallen. There can be no repentance and turning away from division until we begin to see division for what it is... until we see our divisions as God sees them. Until we see how debilitating this disease is, until we come to loathe it as the Lord must, we will not turn from it; we will not repent of it. Instead, we will live with our disunity and perhaps even embrace it.

Are we already in unity, because we are all Christians?

Another obstacle to unity is, in a sense, a more technical one. Some mistakenly believe that we are already in perfect unity because we all serve the same Lord Jesus Christ. That is enough, they say, for that makes us one. For those with this perspective, visible unity is not necessary. The obvious response to this position is: Why would there be a single verse in the Bible admonishing Christians to be *one* or in unity, if oneness was automatically accomplished simply by virtue of our having become Christians?

It is a strange thing, but in regard to some matters, the world sees the church more clearly than we see ourselves. The world sees us as hopelessly divided, mired in petty disagreements, and self-centered. It is also safe to say that the world does not think of Christians as people who have great love one another. How could it? When unbelievers see the lengths to which Christians go to avoid one another and avoid worshipping together, they are not likely to think, "My, how they love one another."

No, the world dismisses us, ridicules us, and ignores us. The world rejects our message because our actions contradict everything we say. We say one thing, but our separate buildings, our separate names, and our constant bickering over doctrine; say the opposite.

For many years, I played on one of the better softball teams in Oregon. We won several city championships in Portland and routinely went to regional and sometimes national tournaments. We started out in the city's church league, but eventually left the church league and joined a commercial league, where we played a lot of business and tavern teams. Why did we stop playing against other churches and move to the tavern league? Because of the bickering and fighting.

Never in my life have I seen such poor sportsmanship as when Christians played sports against each other. It was embarrassing. When we played non-church teams, we were on our best behavior. We had to show the other team that Christians are different. We had to show that we were good sports. But when we played other church teams, it was the opposite; it was Katie bar the door. We fought and argued like only brothers can. God have mercy on the poor umpires who drew our games. They often saw the worst side of "Christianity."

If we would have said to guys on the tavern teams the things we said to one another in the church league, we would have had fists in our faces. Perhaps we knew that. All I can say for certain is that we were, all too often, an embarrassment to the name of Christ.

The point is, it's okay if the world hates us because they hate the truth and despise the light. It is not okay that they hate us because we deserve it. It is one thing for the world to reject our message, it is quite another for us to make sure they can't hear that message because we are drowning it out with a contrary one.

Focusing on pet issues is an obstacle to unity

Another obstacle standing in the way of church unity is our tendency to focus on pet issues. We act as if minor issues are more critical than they really are. When we "major on minors," we tend to emphasize the issues about which we disagree. When we focus on nonessential minor issues and ignore the major, essential truths that unite us, we are picking fights with one another. We are inviting controversy, building walls, and reinforcing our divisions.

We do this in many different ways. The only issues some believers want to talk about are election, predestination and the sovereignty of God. They live to preach against free will and they find no shortage of believers on the other side, who are ready and willing to do battle "in defense of God's character." Both sides stress the extreme views of their opponents, when in fact, if semantics were laid aside they would find that they are probably not all that far apart. But what fun is there in that? It is more stimulating to argue and fight with our spiritual siblings while the world watches and shakes its head.

There are many such issues. Some love to criticize claims of divine healing and the miraculous, as if their criticisms could not possibly be wrong. They claim unequivocally that God has not done anything miraculous in modern times, even though to know this with any degree of certainty, it would be necessary to have investigated every claim of healing everywhere in the world and proven them false, which is of course an impossibility. There is not a single verse in the Bible that says in any clear way that miracles would cease after the original apostles died or after the New Testament was written. Those who hold this view infer it from verses that could mean something else entirely. On the other hand, those who believe in the miraculous often criticize those who don't and claim they are spiritually dead or don't have the Holy Spirit in their churches. They say, "Those other churches have a form of godliness, but deny the power thereof." Neither attitude is helpful, respectful, or loving.

The same applies to the debate over speaking in tongues and the operation of the gifts of the Spirit in modern times. The two sides of this debate spend a lot of pulpit and air time denigrating the other side. One side says tongues are not for today and the other says you can't be baptized in the Holy Spirit without speaking in tongues. Both sides use the Bible to prove their point and neither side persuades the other. I have observed this debate for forty plus years now, and in my opinion, the wall between those who believe in tongues and the operation of the gifts in the modern church, and those who reject such things, is as high as the wall between the Jews and the Gentiles, which threatened to divide the early church. If God can demolish that wall, as Paul describes in Ephesians 2, then He can break down the wall between modern day Bible-believing Christians over the matter of spiritual gifts.

I am reminded of two things Jesus said about the Holy Spirit. Jesus said that when He comes, He (the Holy Spirit) will testify of Me and glorify Me. Some churches have forgotten that. When the Holy Spirit moves, it is not to put the focus upon the Holy Spirit or the things He does. When churches magnify what is going on in their midst and make spiritual manifestations the focus, they are straying from the Spirit's purpose. The Holy Spirit points people to Christ, not to Himself. When churches forget that principle, they invite criticism that is to some degree earned.

Ultimately, both sides of the spiritual gifts debate cannot be correct, so resolving the matter is important. But what good does it do to find answers if we do it separately? History has shown us that when we find our answers separately, we reach different conclusions; meaning *we* have found no answer at all.

Talking without arguing

If we desire unity with other genuine believers, we must learn to talk to one another without fighting. That seems rather obvious, but we do not act as though it is. This problem lies at the heart of so much of our division. Sometimes, people who profess to love the Lord get pretty far out there in the things they choose as "their cause." Sometimes they focus on an issue that has never even crossed the minds of most believers and they make defending that issue their reason for getting up in the morning. It is as if they just want to argue with someone. When I was a kid, we unlovingly called such Christians the *"fighting fundies."*

I will use what I believe to be an extreme example to illustrate the way an obscure issue can be used to create unwarranted division. Recently, I engaged in a series of lengthy email exchanges with a group that publishes a newsletter proclaiming the King James Version to be the only "inspired" translation of the Bible. One of the leaders of the group, a man who said he has been a Baptist preacher for more than forty years, said that he doubts the salvation of anyone who heard the gospel from any Bible translation other than the King James Version. You can imagine my amazement.

Now, I love the KJV. Overall, it is my favorite translation, though I often use other translations as study guides, and generally prefer to quote publicly from the New King James Version. In all fairness to the KJV, it would be impossible to measure the positive influence it has had on the English speaking world over the past four to five centuries.

However, the problems inherent in claiming that the KJV is the only inspired version are too numerous to name here. For starters, the King James Version was not completed until the 1,500s and thus was not available to the early church. Yet somehow, first, second, and third century Christians were able to save countless souls without a KJV Bible in hand. The apostle Peter led 3,000 souls to the Lord on the Day of Pentecost and all he could quote was the Old Testament, so he preached from what he had and thousands were added to the church.

And then there is the fact that most of the world doesn't speak the English language, let alone King James English. Souls are being saved in such places as Uganda, Brazil, China and India through the use of interpreters and preachers using Bibles translated into languages that do not sound at all like King James language.

Sure, some translations of the Bible are better than others and some are actually harmful or of questionable intent, but the church ought to decide such matters together. No single group has the right to tell the entire church what translation of the Bible they must use.

We could take a few pages and rattle off a list of other issues Christians use to pick fights with one another, but I trust that you get the point. Someone standing afar off and watching us might get the impression that it is not really the issues which are dividing us, but rather our attitudes toward those issues and our hearts toward one another. Too often we do not approach controversial matters with an attitude of love for the brothers who hold opposing views. We do not discuss controversial issues with the appropriate dose of humility. Instead, we play to win. We do not play for the Lord to win or for truth to win; we play for us to win. We play like the church teams played back when I was a young athlete. I say to our shame that, back then, we sometimes acted like jerks, as my wife would plainly put it. We treated our brothers in the Lord in ways we would never treat the guys down at the local tavern. Many of us do the same thing with doctrine.

This brings us to an important point: There can be no unity without true lowliness of heart and gentleness of spirit. Most of us are quite aware that we have not always entered theological or doctrinal discussions with the humility such discussions require. Plain and simple, we have gone to war with one another over matters of the faith and should not have been surprised by the results of all our bloodletting.

Are church divisions merely signs of diversity?

Another obstacle to unity is the belief that our divisions are really a form of diversity and as such, are a good thing. While it is true that God loves diversity in its place, what we see in our denominational splits is not diversity. There may be beauty in a diversity of dress and style of music, but these things should not be compared to divisions based on doctrinal differences.

It stands to reason that not every church will worship exactly the same way or sing the same songs or follow the same liturgy. Some churches might have no liturgy at all and be perfectly biblical. Diversity in style should not lead us to conclude that Christians everywhere should not believe the same things. The opposite is true. We worship the same God. We share the same Scriptures. These are the things which connect us to one another, and for that connection to exist, the essence of our faith must be the same. We must believe the same things.

You will find in the Bible references to the doctrine of Christ, the doctrine of the apostles, and the doctrines of demons. You will not find anywhere in the Bible a statement that gives Christians the right to believe whatever they want or the right to create their own doctrines.

When I teach Basic Doctrine (Systematic Christian Theology), I tell each new class on the first day, "This is a '*Basic* Doctrine' class; it is not a '*Creative* Doctrine' class." The students always laugh and I laugh with them, but in reality doctrine is not a laughing matter. None of us is free to make up our own. Doctrine is not an art form. It is not subjective. Creativity is not a plus when it comes to the truths of the faith.

In the next chapter, we will deal with eschatology, the biggest obstacle we face in our quest for genuine church unity. Before we go there, I want to pass on a story a friend shared with me.

Singing "Hallelujah" breaks down entrenched barriers

This story was relayed to me by an older minister, a man of worldwide renown. A group he was working with (not a denomination), had gathered several pastors together from various European countries to pray for revival across their continent.

When the ministers came together for the first time, many would hardly speak to one another. There were many offenses separating them, often regarding matters which had been buried for several decades. There were even issues of contention between brethren who had no previous connection. Some issues were, in fact, nationalistic and related to things one brother's country had done to the other brother's country, going back as far as World War II. Some European countries had lost millions of lives to the war and suffered untold billions of dollars in damages. The war had ended decades earlier, but the bitterness and hostilities had not.

Another barrier separating those in attendance was language. Several of the ministers spoke different languages and thus could not understand one another. The divisions in the room were palpable, and before long it was apparent that the meeting was going nowhere. Nothing any of the leaders said could break through the tension.

Finally, one of the organizers asked a music leader go to the piano and lead the pastors in a worship song. That in itself was no easy task due to the language barriers. The worship leader settled on the song, "Hallelujah," a song which is comprised solely of one word, a word that is universally known and is the same in every language.

The group sang that one word over and over. Eventually, hands began to be raised, (which was okay in their circles). Gradually, voices were raised in volume. In time, tears began to flow as the presence of the Holy Spirit filled the room. The men gradually became lost in their worship of the One who alone is worthy of all praise and adoration.

Before long, the men began to recognize that they all loved the same Lord, and with that, the barriers began to melt away. Eventually, the men were hugging one another, asking for forgiveness, and offering to pray for one another and for revival in their various countries, using interpreters where needed.

This simple story illustrates the potential that exists where the Spirit of the Lord is. Where the Spirit of the Lord is, there is liberty. Where the Spirit of the Lord is, there is freedom from division and strife. In fact, division and strife are imposters and intruders when the brethren are dwelling together in unity. This is the kind of unity Brother Tozer spoke of. It is not the full unity we will eventually enjoy, but it is powerful and can change hearts, break down walls, and open doors. It is a starting place.

Perhaps you are struggling with believing that genuine church unity can be achieved here on earth because it seems so impossible. If so, remember this: It is only impossible if we attempt it on our own. Ultimately, it is Jesus who will build His church. It must be this way, for "Except the Lord build the house, they labor in vain that build it." God will use us and work through us, but ultimately only He can bring all of the living stones together and build from us a spiritual house, a temple for the Lord.

We will direct our attention now toward our biggest challenge, misguided or incomplete eschatology. For many of us, it is our view of the end times that leads us to believe that the church is ready, right now, for the "rapture," or the return of the Lord. But what if it isn't? What if where we are today does not fit with God's ultimate intention for the body of Christ? What if we are not yet ready for His return? What if Christ will not return for a divided church? Let's explore that possibility next.

God's "big picture"
Will Christ return for
a divided church?

Flawed "end times" doctrine can hinder church unity

In the interest of full disclosure, I will begin this chapter by telling you that I am a long time student of eschatology and am familiar with all of the major views of the end times. Yet, for all my study, I have not yet embraced wholly any of the views I have studied. I see strengths and potential flaws or weaknesses in all of them. I am not claiming to be "above the fray." I do have my leanings, but not decidedly so. There are two things, however, which I have concluded about the end of days: First, the Lord will return, just as He promised, and second, the church is not yet ready for His return. No matter how it all unfolds, whether by secret rapture or by a visible coming that every eye beholds, or both, there are some things that must happen first, and they have nothing to do with the Middle East or Jerusalem.

For many readers, this will be the most controversial chapter in the study. What I say here will likely challenge the fundamental way many Christians view the world and current events. You might even be tempted to stop reading and toss this book aside, but I hope you will hear me out.

The premise of this chapter is: Eschatology matters because our view of the end times can be a major hindrance to church unity. A flawed eschatology can make one of the most important themes in the New Testament all but irrelevant.

If we accept the notion that Jesus Christ could return to rapture the church at any moment, a view that is widely preached and commonly held in evangelical circles, then we must believe that the church today is ready for the return of the Lord. What we see is what He gets. To believe this is to embrace the view that a church, which is broken into thousands of denominations, a church that is at war with itself over a vast array of doctrines and practices, a church that is telling the world by its actions that Christians dislike one another so much that they won't even worship in the same building, is a church somehow "good enough" for the Lord. We are saying in essence that the Holy Spirit, try as He might, could not fulfill the prayer of Jesus when He asked that those who believe on Him would all be one, even as He and the Father are one.

Far too many believers look around them at the status quo of the church, see our fractured and somewhat anemic condition, and shrug it off as if where we are today is "good enough for God." In their view, all we have to do now is share the Gospel with as many as we can and hold on until we are raptured out of here. There are solid reasons why you should doubt this scenario. That's what this chapter is about.

This is going to offend some, but it's entirely possible that books like "The Late Great Planet Earth" and the "Left Behind" series left some believers with an incomplete view of the end times. Those books made popular the view that there is soon going to be a secret rapture of the church followed by a tribulation, during which 144,000 Jewish evangelists will preach the gospel to those left behind after the rapture. Underlying that view is the assumption that the church is already what she is supposed to be and is ready for the end.

It is not necessary to prove or disprove the pre-tribulation rapture theory here, but readers would be wise to take note of the fact that there are many qualified scholars, who have an altogether different view of the way things will end. Their books are not as famous, but they are every bit as interesting and scholarly. Many Christians would be shocked to discover how scholarly and persuasive some of those books are. Some of them argue persuasively from Scripture that there will be no rapture, just a second coming at the end of the tribulation. Some argue that the tribulation Jesus described in Matthew 24 occurred in 70 A.D., when Jerusalem was destroyed by the Roman army and a million-and-a-half Jews died during the three-and-a-half year siege; thus there is no tribulation to come. I dismissed that view out of hand – until I read some of their books.

In my opinion, there are so many different views of eschatology, with learned scholars supporting each of them, that an open-minded student of the Word of God might conclude that end time doctrine is simply not as settled as many Christians have been led to believe. The Lord might return soon, or he might return centuries from now. Seriously. In the end notes at the back of this book, you will find references to authors and books you might want to read, if your view of the end times is too narrow and limiting.[49]

For our purposes here, it is not necessary to sort out how things will unfold in the last days. It *is* necessary, however, to examine the belief that the Lord might return imminently or *any day now*. Some readers have assumed that this is a settled issue and that Christians were always supposed to believe that the Lord could come at any moment; that the Lord intended this mindset to keep believers in a constant state of preparedness or watchfulness. I am asking you to lay that assumption aside for the moment, so you can consider it with an open mind. Keep in mind that many authors and learned scholars have attempted to prove that we are living in the last of the last days or *the final generation*, but have been embarrassed when their predictions failed to come to pass. This includes some of the more popular authors who have sold millions of books.

It isn't just the odd radio preacher here and there who has predicted the end and been wrong. Some of the stars of eschatology have fallen from the sky and crashed and burned trying to predict the timing of the end. Speaking to this phenomenon, Kenneth Gentry, Jr. wrote in, "He Shall Have Dominion," (a defense of post millennialism):

"Furthermore, why has not dispensationalism and premillennialism been wholly discredited by its constant cry of "the end is at hand"? (Tim) LaHaye wrote with no hesitation: *"The fact that we are the generation that will be on the earth when our Lord comes certainly should not depress us.... [I]f you are a Christian, after reading this book you ought to know the end is near!"*

We see the clearest examples of date setting in Hal Lindsey's *The 1980s: Countdown to Armageddon* (rapture expected before 1990), Edgar C. Whisenant's **88 Reasons Why the Rapture Is in 1988** (rapture expected in 1988) and *The Final Shout: Rapture Report 1989* (rapture expected in 1989), and Richard Ruhling, M. D., *Sword Over America* (rapture expected in early 1990s), and Grant R. Jeffrey, *Armageddon: Appointment with Destiny* (rapture expected in A.D. 2000)."

I am not saying that we are not living in the last days or that this might not be the last generation. I don't know one way or the other. But many who believe these things are not aware of how many generations throughout history have known for sure that they were living in the last days. In *"Last Days Madness,"* author Gary DeMar recounts the history of this belief and shows how pervasive it has been throughout history. For example, those living in Europe when the black plague was wiping out nearly half of the population were certain they were living in the end times, though obviously they were not. DeMar offers several historical examples, which serve as a worthwhile reminder that we ought not be too quick to assume that we can discern God's timetable by reading the newspaper or watching the nightly news.

The early church was not taught the imminent return of Christ

It seems clear that at the time the apostle Paul was writing much of the New Testament, he did not believe in an imminent return, because he spoke and wrote of future things that had to happen *before the return if the Lord;* thus those reading Paul's writings had no reason to expect the Lord to come back "any day now."

When early church Christians read Paul's statements regarding future events, they would have been watching for those things to happen not for the Lord to come and "snatch them away" at any moment. This is an important point to consider. Before we get caught up in what those things were, keep in mind that in a sense it doesn't matter what they were. If something had to happen first, anything at all, before the Lord would return, then early church believers could not have been expecting the Lord to come right away. There was going to be some delay.

The following two passages make that point a little clearer. First, here are Paul's words to the elders of the church at Ephesus, which he delivered to them in person, rather than by letter:

> [28] *Therefore take heed to yourselves and to all the flock, among which the Holy Spirit has made you overseers, to shepherd the church of God which He purchased with His own blood.* [29] *For I know this, that **after my departure savage wolves will come in among you,** not sparing the flock.* [30] *Also from among yourselves men will rise up, speaking perverse things, to draw away the disciples after themselves. (NKJV Acts 20)*

Paul is speaking somewhat prophetically and describing things that would happen after he was gone. Presumably, he meant after his death, but, at any rate, he told the Ephesians of things that would happen later. If you were a Christian in Ephesus and heard Paul's words, would you not assume that the Lord could not come today or tomorrow, because the apostle Paul, speaking by the Holy Spirit, had just told you of future events that would need time to come to pass?

Of course, if by saying, "after my departure," Paul meant his literal death, then the early church knew that the Lord would not return right away, because Paul wasn't dead yet. Also, savage wolves had not yet come and attacked the flock and Paul had said that was going to happen. This may seem a simple matter, but it shows, as does the next passage, that Paul was not telling the Ephesians to expect the return of the Lord momentarily.

Here's what Paul said by way of a letter to the church at Thessalonica:

*"Now, brethren, concerning the coming of our Lord Jesus Christ and our gathering together to Him, we ask you, ² not to be soon shaken in mind or troubled, either by spirit or by word or by letter, as if from us, as though the day of Christ had come. ³ Let no one deceive you by any means; **for that Day will not come unless the falling away comes first, and the man of sin is revealed**, the son of perdition, ⁴ who opposes and exalts himself above all that is called God or that is worshiped, so that he sits as God in the temple of God, showing himself that he is God."* (II Thessalonians 2 NKJV)

In short, Paul told the Thessalonians that there had to be a falling away before the Lord returns, and also the "man of sin" had to be revealed. Consider what this meant to Christians living then. If Paul himself had to die and there had to be a falling away before the end would come, and if wolves had to attack the flock and the "man of sin" had to be revealed before the end came, then early church Christians would not have been expecting the Lord to return any time soon. There are several other examples which could be offered, but it seems clear that after hearing Paul's words, neither the Ephesians nor the Thessalonians would have been expecting the Lord to return for His church imminently. (I realize that some popular schools of eschatology attempt to separate the "rapture" from the second coming to make room for a perpetual sense of imminence, but their arguments are hardly conclusive.)

Many Biblical scholars believe that the falling away of which Paul spoke was the Dark Ages, a one thousand year period during which even the most basic and essential parts of the gospel would be lost, a time during which the authority of the scriptures would be replaced by the edicts of men and people would be required to pay money for forgiveness of sin. If the "falling away" meant something other than the Dark Ages, and there are, as you might expect, several other interpretations, the falling away was nonetheless a future event and thus precluded the imminent return of Christ.

The things we have been considering are, in a sense, old news, things that happened hundreds or even thousands of years ago. Let's direct our discussion more towards our time period. Some believers' view of the end times leads them to believe that the world we live in must get worse and worse until the end. In fact, the worse things get in the world, the happier they are, because it means the end is near. This is the view most premillennialist and dispensationalists hold. But there are others who believe the opposite; that the gospel is going to prevail and the church will eventually disciple all the nations and bring about a lengthy period of peace and hope. This is what post millennialists believe. Still others believe that the world will get worse and worse but the church will get better and better as the wheat and the tares mature side by side in the same field. Rather than seeing the church decline in the last days, they quote Proverbs 4:18.

> "But the path of the just *is* like the shining sun,
> That shines ever brighter unto the perfect day."

Let's consider the possibility that it makes no difference which way you lean in that debate. It seems clear from Scripture that even if the world is going to get darker and darker in the coming days, the church of Jesus Christ is no less obligated to be of one mind and judgment and void of all divisions. In fact, Paul delivered his message of unity to believers who were suffering terrible, life-threatening persecution at the hand of Rome. Whether the church is in hard times or good, tribulation or peace, we are commanded by the Word of God to all be of the same mind and judgment and to say the same thing. This must be our constant testimony: In whatever state we find ourselves, we will maintain unity with one another so that the world will know who Jesus really is.

Sure, it is enticing to believe that Jesus might come and take the church out of the world any minute now, but to believe that, we must ignore several powerful passages of Scripture that suggest otherwise, as we shall see next.

Signs of the end times which many have ignored

When I suggest that, still today, there are things which must happen before the return of the Lord, I am *not* speaking of earthquakes, wars and rumors of war, or Jerusalem being surrounding by armies. I am speaking of issues that relate directly to the church and the topic of this study. Having laid that foundation, it is time now to enter the very heart of our study.

Paul told the church at Ephesus that the work of perfecting the church would not be completed *until the body of Christ had reached the level of maturity of a perfect man, to the stature of the fullness of Christ.* This passage is, I believe, the key to understanding God's big picture and what He plans for the final wrap up of the age, whenever that is. If Paul was right and God's ultimate plan is to bring the church to a level of maturity or perfection to which it has not yet arrived, then we should not be looking for the end to come. Right? If God's plan is to accomplish in us something that has not yet been accomplished, we should not be looking for an early or premature escape, but rather focusing on becoming what our Lord desires us collectively to become.

The apostle Paul tells us in Ephesians 4 that when Jesus ascended back to Heaven, He gave certain ministry gifts to the church for the express purpose of bringing the church to a full measure of maturity, as we discussed earlier in Chapter 2. The gifts Jesus gave to the church were not silver or gold or fancy buildings. They were ministries; four or five of them. (Some prefer to combine the last two.) Jesus gave the church apostles, prophets, evangelists, pastors and teachers. He gave us these gifts because the church was immature and easily blown about by winds of doctrine and He wanted it to grow up to be a mature man, rising to the same level as Himself.

Now, I realize that many modern day teachers have said that ministries like apostles and prophets do not exist today, but their position is hardly provable. There is no passage of Scripture that says that any of the five ministry gifts which Jesus gave the church would disappear before the church had reached the level of maturity that Paul described in Ephesians 4. If the early church needed all five gifts, there is no reason to believe they are not needed today.

According to the Ephesians 4 text, which we will examine in a moment, these ministry gifts were given for a duration of time and for a specific purpose. They were given *until* the body of Christ becomes, *"a perfect man, unto the measure of the stature of the fullness of Christ..."* Think about those words for a moment. They are *impossible* sounding words: the *stature of the fullness of Christ*. How could there be a higher level of maturity or perfection than the stature of the fullness of Christ? Stop for a minute and look around you at the church and think about what you see. In your assessment, have we arrived at the place the apostle Paul described or are we collectively still very much children, tossed to and fro and blown about by every wind of doctrine?

Many scholars pride themselves on what they call their literal approach to the Bible, but skip right past the standard of maturity Christ set for His church in this passage. Taken literally, this passage means that collectively we, as a body, will be matured to the stature of Christ himself. It makes perfect sense that it would be so, given the fact that we are, after all, His body. Even if we are nowhere near that level of maturity, how can we deny that this is exactly what Paul was describing? Paul is describing something, which to the best of our knowledge, has never happened, not even in the early church.

Now keep in mind, you cannot go off into some corner with an "elite" bunch of super-Christians or "manifested sons of God," and accomplish this level of perfection. What Paul described was the entire body of Christ coming to this level of maturity, not just you, your friends, or even your church.

Completion of the New Testament did not bring perfection

I must take a brief diversion here and address a common error that is in broad circulation today. Note that Paul does not say, *"Once the New Testament is completed, you will all be perfect and be just like Jesus."* Of course, that would have been an easier way, but that is not what the passage says. Paul makes it clear that it would be the ministry gifts that Jesus gave to the church, i.e. apostles, prophets, evangelists, pastors and teachers, which eventually would bring the body of Christ to full maturity, not the completion of the New Testament.

The teaching that the completion of the New Testament somehow managed to make us all perfect and no longer in need of these four or five ministries is highly debatable and does not appear to align well with what Paul said in Ephesians 4. I do not say this to lessen the importance of the Scriptures. God forbid. But, the church had the Scriptures all through the Dark Ages, and it simply ignored them.

Think of the Bible as the sharpest sword in the world. Indeed, Hebrews 4 says that the Word of God is "sharper than any double-edged sword." If, however, that sword lies on a shelf or hangs unused on a hook, it is of no effect. In the hands of men and women who know how to wield it, that sword can accomplish great things, but it is only powerful when it is used, and used rightly. The Scriptures are indeed "*profitable for doctrine, for reproof, for correction, and for instruction in righteousness, that the man of God may be complete, thoroughly equipped for every good work.*[50] But the Scriptures are the tool which the apostles, prophets, evangelists, pastors and teachers utilize to do their jobs. The mere completion of the New Testament did not make the church perfect or mature, at least it hasn't yet. That notion defies both logic and the clear words of Ephesians 4.

Here's the question that must be answered: If the dispensationalist view is wrong and all five ministries are necessary for the work to be completed, does it not follow that the lack of any of them weakens the church and forestalls its eventual maturity?

Apostle Paul shows us God's end game

Now, let's read Ephesians 4:7-16 and see exactly what the Holy Spirit said. (You may wish to read this passage in several translations.) As you read through these verses, look for the big picture, the one that transcends the first century and the Church at Ephesus. Look for what God is saying about His long term purpose and His "end game" for the body of Christ.

Ephesians 4: [7]But grace was given to each one of us according to the measure of Christ's gift. [8]Therefore it says,
"When he ascended on high he led a host of captives, and he gave gifts to men." [9](In saying, "He ascended," what does it mean but that he had also descended into the lower regions, the earth? [10]He who descended is the one who also ascended far above all the heavens, that he might fill all things.) [11]And he gave the apostles, the prophets, the evangelists, the shepherds and teachers, [12] to equip the saints for the work of ministry, for building up the body of Christ, [13]until we all attain to the unity of the faith and of the knowledge of the Son of God, to mature manhood, to the measure of the stature of the fullness of Christ, [14]so that we may no longer be children, tossed to and fro by the waves and carried about by every wind of doctrine, by human cunning, by craftiness in deceitful schemes. [15]Rather, speaking the truth in love, we are to grow up in every way into him who is the head, into Christ, [16] from whom the whole body, joined and held together by every joint with which it is equipped, when each part is working properly, makes the body grow so that it builds itself up in love.

There it is: God's end game. This is where He wants to go. Given that reality, external things such as wars in the Middle East, rapture doctrines, theories about the tribulation and a millennial reign, might not be the most important things for us to focus on. These things are exciting to discuss and ponder, but if you are looking for God's big picture and how things will wrap up in the end, you might want to ponder this passage for a while. Read it over and over and meditate on it. What Paul told us is that God wants the body of Christ, the church, to be brought to the stature of his Son! Unless God has abandoned this plan and admitted defeat (Lord, please forgive me for speaking thusly), there is something still to come that has nothing to do with what goes on in the world around us.

Ephesians 4 paraphrased

You have read the passage in Ephesians for yourself; now let us see if we can summarize what Paul said in this passage in simpler words. I will paraphrase the passage and let you judge whether I am adding or taking anything from what Paul said.

The Apostle tells us that when the Lord Jesus ascended back to the Father, He gave each believer grace sufficient for the gifts that He gave us. Some of us He gave the grace to be an apostle, some a prophet, some an evangelist, and to some of us He gave the grace to be pastors (or shepherds) and teachers. The purpose of these ministries was to prepare believers to carry out the work of the ministry and build up the body of Christ. This process was to continue (a) until all of us come to the unity of the faith, (b) until we all truly know the Son of God, (c) until all of us together reach mature manhood, which is measured by the stature of the fullness of Christ. We will be at that place when we are no longer children who are tossed to and fro by every wind of doctrine that comes along. When every part of the body of Christ is joined together, all speaking the truth in love and all properly functioning; the head of the body, which is Jesus Christ, will make sure the body grows and builds itself up in love. This is how the body will grow to maturity.

Notice the role which love plays in this plan. Love is the life-blood of the body of Christ. His love flows down from the head and through the body, builds it up, and makes it strong and mature. Of course, for that process to work, the ministry gifts must be functioning and the body parts must all be connected, both to one another and to the Head, which is Christ.

There is still work to do

Granted, one can approach Ephesians 4 predisposed to make it say something else, but taking this passage at face value, it's obvious that there is serious work left to be done before we arrive together at the level of maturity that the Lord intends. Whether you believe in a rapture before the tribulation, in the middle of the tribulation, or at the end, or if you are a Post Millennialist and don't believe in a future, worldwide tribulation at all, at least consider the possibility that there is a maturity which must come to fruition in the church before the purposes of God have been accomplished and the end can come.

If this is true, some of us should start a new list of "end time events." Following are some additional things that must happen before the Lord returns for us. First, Paul has to die and wolves have to come and attack the church, both from the outside and the inside. Okay, we can probably check those two off. Second, there has to be a great falling away. We can probably check that one off, too. A thousand years of gross spiritual darkness probably qualifies as a falling away.

You may have been watching the Middle East and events such as Israel becoming a nation again in 1948, and if so, you can make that number three on your list, if you are so inclined. You can add wars and rumors of wars and earthquakes and all that, though there is more scholarly debate about the historic meaning of Matthew 24 than you may realize.

Next, considering what we just read in Ephesians 4, we might want to add to our list: The ministry gifts that Christ gave the church must bring the body of Christ to *the stature of the fullness of Christ before the end will come.* Until this has been accomplished and we are no longer tossed about by every wind of doctrine like children, there will still be work to do. Consider this passage from Acts 3, which says that Jesus is not coming back, but is being retained in heaven, until everything God wants to restore is restored:

[19] Repent therefore and be converted, that your sins may be blotted out, so that times of refreshing may come from the presence of the Lord, [20] and that He may send Jesus Christ, who was preached to you before, [21] whom heaven must receive until the times of *restoration of all things*, which God has spoken by the mouth of all His holy prophets since the world began.

The meaning of this passage has been oft debated, but it clearly informs us that Jesus is not coming back until everything that *all* of the prophets spoke of has been restored. What is actually meant by the phrase "restoration of all things" is unclear, but it is a rather sweeping statement and at a minimum suggests that we should be looking more for a fulfillment of everything the prophets foretold than for a soon return.

Finally, we will add one more item to our list. If we believe that the prayer of Jesus in John 17 will be fully answered and His followers will be one, as He and the Father are one, and as a result of this oneness the world will know that Jesus really was sent by the Father, then we should not expect the end to come before that happens.

It is likely that what Jesus prayed for in John 17 and what Paul described in Ephesians 4 are really one and the same thing. The fulfillment of one is the fulfillment of the other.

Chapter summary

When I first contemplated this book and the idea of laying out for my fellow believers a vision for true church unity, I immediately saw something powerful blocking the path. That "something" was and is the incomplete eschatology which so many believers hold. This problem is pervasive in the church today. It is an "escapism" mentality. People just want out of here. They want it all to be over. They see the world getting worse and rather than combating the darkness with an eye to victory or seeking to overcome it, they assume that the darkness will overcome the light. One renowned radio preacher has said that when Jesus asked the question, "When the Son of Man returns, will He find faith on the earth,"[51] He was asking a rhetorical question with the answer being an implied, "No." This is not true. The way the question was stated in the original language, the answer was not an implied *Yes,* and not an implied *No.* It was a wide-open question with an undetermined answer.

There is often a different way of looking at passages than that which first occurs to us. For example, in the parable of the wheat and the tares, an enemy sowed tares in the man's wheat field and his servants wanted to know whether they should remove them. The master said, "No," lest they damage the wheat while trying to remove the tares. Now, compare your view of the world around you to that parable. Do you optimistically consider the world a wheat field with some tares in it, as the parable states, or do you pessimistically consider the field a "tare field" with some wheat in it?

I don't know whether the world is going to get continually worse, or if instead there is going to be a large scale revival that turns everything around. But know this: The early church was hiding in catacombs and Christians were being tossed to the lions, if discovered. Those brave souls had no reason to be optimistic about their lot in this world. Yet they kept the faith without wavering and eventually, the seemingly all powerful empire that was persecuting them was overcome by the simple truth they preached. In other words, it is not given to us to know how our generation will respond to the message; nonetheless, it remains our responsibility to demonstrate to it *by our oneness* that Jesus Christ really was sent by the Father and *by our love for one another* that we indeed are His disciples.

There is no telling how the world will respond to that reality when they truly see it demonstrated, because it has never fully been done before. I am persuaded that it will be. This is why I say that some of the most popular views of the end times, beliefs that are widely promulgated by published authors and radio and television preachers, stand as a roadblock to church unity. For them to say, as so many do, that Jesus can come back today, is to say that the church is as ready as she needs to be. If this is so, we can ignore the prayer of the Lord Jesus in John 17, and we can forget the level of church maturity Paul described in Ephesians 4, for we have robbed those words of their plain meaning. What they describe seems too powerful and too lofty to be possible, so we have dismissed them or interpreted away their meaning.

Ponder this thought for a moment. What if Jesus Christ is not going to return for a bunch of bickering believers who don't love each other, won't worship under the same roof, and don't agree on what they believe? What if the Holy Spirit is not willing to wait 2,000 years for something beautiful and perfect to be completed, and then just give up in the end and proclaim, "Oh well, I couldn't do it. I guess what we see will have to be good enough?"

Frankly, I don't see that happening. What we see in the fractured church today cannot be the crowning achievement of the indwelling Spirit of Christ. This can't be as good as it gets. I believe it is time we stopped ignoring our divisions and started obeying the Word of God. When we begin to do that, the Holy Spirit is going to move upon us. He will move powerfully. When believers across the globe begin to catch the vision, when we begin to repent in mass of our grievous divisions, then the Holy Spirit will move in our midst in ways we have not imagined, and barriers that have stood for centuries will fall. The dissension will begin to melt away and the unity of the faith will be restored.

For that to happen, we must begin to see division as we see adultery, homosexuality, idolatry, lying, and stealing. We must not ignore that which the Scripture strictly forbids. We may be accustomed to our divisions. They may seem normal to us. But they are nonetheless a grievous sin.

Jesus is going to come for a glorious church without spot or wrinkle or any such thing. Her beauty, the level of her perfection, her holiness, her unity, her strength and power, and her maturity are all spoken of in Scripture. Some of those things will be completed in their fullest and ultimate sense only at His coming, but much of what our Lord intends for us is meant to be accomplished in the here and now by His Spirit and by the anointed ministries He has given us.

Toward the end of this study we will discuss the two possibilities by which unity will come, by revival or by persecution. In the meanwhile, let us pray, "*Lord, help us to see this truth and believe it according to your Word. Amen.*"

Denominations and the nature of God

"Hear, O Israel, the Lord thy God is one."[52] This 3,500 year old declaration has long been the rallying cry of Judaism, the religion from which Christianity sprang. Like the ancient Israelites, Christians have only one God, not three and not a hundred. The God we serve, the God of the Bible, is a God of perfect unity. The Father, Son, and Holy Spirit co-exist as one God who is manifest in three Persons. As we discussed earlier, those three Persons are distinguishable, but forever inseparable from one another.

The Father, Son, and Holy Spirit never disagree. They cannot. It would be inconsistent with their nature for them to do so. They are all of one mind and one purpose in all things, so much so that there is only one God and one cannot say, as a matter of orthodox Christian doctrine, that there are three.

It is part of the nature of our triune God that He hates discord. There is no discord in His heaven. There are no warring factions or competing elements. Lucifer, the angel who tried to introduce such things, was forever banished. Because division is contrary to the nature of God, to the extent to which we, as a church, are divided, we are not like Him and misrepresent His nature to the world.

It is clear from Scripture that we are divided from one another because we are carnal and immature, but the God we are to emulate is not carnal or immature. To the extent we remain carnal, to that extent we misrepresent God before the world.

We are easily blown about by winds of doctrine. Our God cannot be blown about or changed by anything, for He is immutable. We compete with one another and work against each other. Our God never works against Himself. It is not in His nature to do so.

Here's the point of all that: Denominations are a sign of our carnality because denominations are by definition divisions; as such they represent to the world an image of God that is not real. God is not divided, thus a divided church portrays a distorted image of God. As bold as it may seem to say so, denominations ought not to exist, because by their very existence they contradict the nature of the one true God.

There are of course those who do not agree with this assessment. The challenge to ending denominationalism will come primarily from those conducting denominational affairs. Those running them and expanding their influence have rationalized certain defenses to justify their existence. Let's look at one statement made in defense of a denomination. In 1950, J. Roswell Flowers, a former General Secretary of the "Assemblies of God," said of denominations:

> *"Sectarianism is a heart matter. If, because of denominational association, we despise our brother because he is a member of another denomination, we are sectarian in spirit. Being associated in a fellowship with those of like minds is not necessarily sectarianism...It is possible to belong to a denominational body for the purpose of accomplishing the will of God for the evangelization of the world in the most effective manner without at the same time having a sectarian spirit,"*[53]

That sounds like a pretty good rationalization. In fact, it is almost persuasive. But in reality, we see in this statement our problem in a nutshell. According to Secretary Flowers, denominations are not necessarily "sectarian in spirit," but are merely people "...associated in a fellowship **with those of like minds**..."

It is admirable that Secretary Flowers wanted to avoid the sectarian spirit. But did he succeed? Is his defense not the very problem we are seeking to end? Let me explain. Secretary Flowers spoke of a *fellowship of like minds*. Well, what mind is that? Is it the mind of Christ? Is it the Pentecostal mind? Is it just the Assemblies of God mind? You see, we have broken up into clubs *comprised of those who think like we do*, those who are *of like mind with us*, and in so doing we have ignored all of the other believers; Christians who don't think like we do, and yet serve the same Christ. If believers are to be of the same mind, how can we break up into clubs of different minds?

Is unity within a denomination unity at all?

Is it really okay to break up into sects or denominations, as long as those who belong to each particular club are of the same mind with the other members of the club? Is such a club, group, or organization the body of Christ? You've heard the saying, "I really gave him a piece of my mind." Maybe that's what denominations represent, a piece of the church's mind. Not the whole thing; just a piece.

We gather in denominations with people of like minds and as a result do not have the mind of Christ, just a piece of it. It is of course the nature of men to gather with those of like minds. That is the natural thing for mere men do. But we are not called to be mere men. We are not called to gather only with those of like minds; we are called to gather with all who call upon the name of Christ, and we are to become of one mind and judgment with them. That will not happen while we are gathered in our echo chambers and fellowshipping and worshipping only with those who agree with us on every point. This is precisely the mindset denominations embody, which makes them a fatally flawed institution.

Is there some other justification for our denominations? Secretary Flowers defends denominations as existing for the purpose of evangelizing the world "in the most effective manner." We have dealt with that defense elsewhere, so let it be sufficient to say here that for all the evangelizing denominations have accomplished, their very existence has prevented the world from knowing that Jesus was sent by the Father for they have demonstrated to the world that His followers are not one.

I will say it plainly: It is time for the denominational age to come to an end. Denominations might not diminish or fade away willingly or quickly, but they must pass from the scene. All of those things which hinder the purposes of God must be discarded. Denominations must decrease so that the body of Christ may increase. It is time for the church of Jesus Christ to come together and walk in a more perfect way.

Finally, denominations are by their very nature wasteful and God is not wasteful. For example, a denomination considers a city or town that does not have a church affiliated with its brand of Christianity to be a wide-open mission field, no matter how many Bible-believing churches are already thriving and growing in that community. Denominations train ministers to go into cities and towns with dozens or even hundreds of existing churches and start one that is affiliated with them. This requires not only the expense of training the ones sent, but also requires the cost of buildings and furnishings. This is a waste of resources which could be expended in places where the Gospel has not yet reached.

Furthermore, starting unneeded churches in cities full of churches discounts the work of God's servants who are already ministering there. It says that their efforts are worth less than ours because they are not affiliated with the *our* denomination, by which we really mean the *right* denomination.

While it is the basic premise of this book that denominations should not exist at all and that they are by their very existence undermining the fulfillment of the Great Commission, it is important to note that throughout Scripture and throughout church history, God has used flawed vessels to accomplish His purposes. Times of ignorance God has sometimes winked at, as Paul told Athenians, but the time comes when He calls on men everywhere to repent.

We should not pretend that denominations have not done good things or that at times they have not been used of God. Most have, and that is the subject of our next chapter.

Were denominations stepping stones?

God uses flawed vessels

Thousands of years of human history stand as proof that some-times the Lord uses a particular office or structure for a period of time, and notwithstanding its imperfections it accomplishes good things while the hand of God is upon it.

In the Old Testament, for example, the Aaronic priesthood was used by God under the old tabernacle and temple worship system. That priesthood, with its incense, animal sacrifices, and ceremonial washings, served the purposes of God for a millennium and a half. It was, however, a system designed to be temporary.[54] This truth is made abundantly clear in the New Testament, where we are told that the Law was added to the Abrahamic Covenant as a temporary stepping stone, a schoolmaster or tutor to bring the people to Christ.

When Jesus died on the cross, the Aaronic priesthood and animal sacrifices became obsolete. That entire system, which at one time had been ordered by God, became defunct. When its time of useful-ness had past, the veil in the temple was torn by the Lord, from top to bottom, and a new way to approach God was made available.

Sure, even after the veil in the temple was rent, it was possible for a Levitical priest to continue to perform the same duties he had performed the day before. Those very same actions, however, were no longer blessed by God. What God had accepted before, He no longer accepted. What was okay one day became a sacrilege the next. To offer the blood of a sheep or goat after God had offered his own Son was an affront to God.

In like manner, denominations, which may have served a useful purpose for a season, must decrease so that the body of Christ may increase. The imperfect must give way to that which is better. In the coming days, denominational boards must begin to adopt the attitude of John the Baptist and recognize that their time in the sun is coming to an end. John recognized that he had to decrease for the sake of the One "whose shoe latchet he was not worthy to unlatch;" and so must every division in the body of Christ. Denominations must not do this begrudgingly, as if they were losing their little kingdoms, but happily, recognizing that they are gaining a better one.

As we begin to repent of our divisions, the Lord will begin to bring His body together and unite His people. Denominational boards may play a pivotal role in that outcome, if they are willing. One way or another, all barriers preventing the unity of the body of Christ will crumble. As God broke down the wall of separation between the Jew and the Gentile (Ephesians 2) and made them all one man in Christ, so must the denominational walls come down, so that the church of Jesus Christ may be one.

Divisiveness within the church, a thing which God *may* have ignored for a season, will be seen for what it is. The sin of division will come under the spotlight of God.

Over the past 500 years, God has worked through denominations and countless independent churches to spread the gospel, establish missions around the globe, and establish training centers for evangelists, pastors, and missionaries. Denominations have built hospitals, clinics, and retirement homes for the elderly. They've opened and staffed shelters for the homeless. Obviously, these are good things.

If, in fact, denominations were merely organizational structures for efficiently providing these kinds of services and ministries, they might somehow be justifiable. Unfortunately, this is not the case. Denominations are not primarily service providers. They are more akin to little kingdoms existing as "self-sufficient subsets" of the larger Kingdom of God.

Denominations may have had their time and purpose

Earlier on, we said that many of the major denominations exist as monuments or memorials to past moves of God. As such, they may have been used by the Lord, before they became denominations, to progressively restore important truths that had been lost during the Dark Ages.

It is also likely that the existence of denominations has allowed and facilitated more open discussion and exploration of doctrinal issues than could have occurred under the rigid structure of the Roman Catholic Church, which, at times, met any effort to restore biblical truths with an iron fist - or a sword.

It is also true that the abundance of Christian literature available today, speaking to a vast array of faith and doctrinal issues, exists as a testimony to the progress the church, including denominations, has made in expanding our understanding of matters of doctrine that might not have been explored otherwise. Absent the existence of Bible colleges and seminaries, which in many cases were established and funded by denominations, it is unlikely that all of this abundance of worthwhile literature would be with us. Of course, there are two sides to this coin, but we must acknowledge that good things have been done.

Having accomplished some measure of good cannot justify staying past one's allotted time. No one would deny the role of John the Baptist in preparing the way for the One who would follow, but John knew when his time was up and he willingly decreased. Perhaps this is why Jesus said there was no greater prophet than John.

Denominations and the Period of the Judges

The church's denominational era may have served as a permissible transitional period in the same manner as the Old Testament period of the judges served as an interim transition leading up to the establishment of the united kingdom of Israel under David. As was true with the period of the judges, which was morally and spiritually quite spotty, the church's denominational phase has not been a perfect time.

Like the judges, denominations have only been able to win partial victories for a limited few. They have not been able to bring victory to the entire body of Christ. The judges, acting on their own, could not drive all of Israel's enemies out of the land and bring about a time of lasting peace and prosperity for all of Israel. The united kingdom under David and Solomon, which followed the period of the judges, could and did accomplish that.

Denominations working separately have brought a measure of success here and there, but they cannot take the church to where it must go. A divided church simply cannot get there. It is important that we not pass over that last sentence too quickly. A divided church cannot get to where the Lord would take us for it is a place of oneness, a place of unity.

There is a time and a season to every purpose under heaven; a time to scatter stones and a time to gather stones together. Even if there was a time for the stones of the church of God to be scattered into thousands of denominations and countless independent local churches, there must also be a time for those stones to be gathered together. As the Lord assembles the living stones of His church in the days ahead, His ultimate intention for the body of Christ will be fulfilled as all the parts are fitted and joined together.

Have denominations outlived their usefulness?

It is not our purpose to decry the faults of denominationalism so much as to move past such institutions. If denominations have been a permissible stepping stone to what lies ahead, still we must recognize that at such time as they have outlasted their usefulness, they become a hindrance. Notwithstanding any good they might have done over the centuries, we must also recognize the following about denominations:

(1) Jesus prayed for his followers to be one as He and the Father are one. Denominations do not further this purpose; they reinforce divisions, and in so doing they prevent the world from knowing that Jesus was sent to earth by the Father in heaven.

(2) Denominational divisions proclaim to the world that Christians do not love one another. The world is to know that we are His disciples because of our love for one another; denominational divisions say the opposite.

(3) The existence of so many church buildings with different names tells the world that not only do Christians not love one another; they do not agree with one another. In fact, they disagree so passionately that they will not even worship God under the same roof.

(4) Denominations are unmistakable signs of the church's carnality and its humanness. According to the apostle Paul, we are not to behave as "mere men," but denominations prove that we have not yet risen above our carnality.

(5) Finally, denominationalism robs the church of the power that is inherent in real unity. As we learned from the Tower of Babel story, unified, there is nothing the body of Christ cannot accomplish. The gates of hell cannot prevail against a unified church.

For all of these reasons, denominations must cease to be.

Will denominations willingly diminish?

The coming days will be a test for many within the denominational structures. Their deepest loyalties will be tested. The Gospels tell us that there were many Jews, especially those of the priest class, who rejected the message of Jesus the Messiah. They saw His miracles. They heard His teachings. They tried to prove Him wrong, but they couldn't. They had to bring forth false witnesses in order to convict Him. Even when they learned that He had risen from the dead, the priest class tried to conceal the truth, paying the guards to lie about what had really happened.

Why did they do this? Because Jesus was a threat to the established order, to their way of life, to their power and influence. They were professional clergy, if you will, and they refused to open their hearts to any truth that diminished their power and influence.

It is hard to predict the extent to which self-serving human nature will delay the end of denominationalism. It is possible that men and women who have served the Lord for many years will choose to cling to some dead body because they have grown to love their denomination more than their Lord or have learned to depend on it to supply their earthly needs. I pray that it shall not be so. Consider the wisdom of A.W. Tozer:

"Millions call themselves by His name, it is true, and pay some token homage to Him, but a simple test will show how little He is really honored among them. Let the average man be put to the proof on the question of who or what is ABOVE, and his true position will be exposed. Let him be forced into making a choice between God and money, between God and men, between God and personal ambition, God and self, God and human love, and God will take second place every time. Those other things will be exalted above. However the man may protest, the proof is in the choice he makes day after day throughout his life."[55]

These are hard words, but they are true. The proof of our love for God is not in our words, but in the choices we make day by day, especially those that cost us something.

The Book of Acts tells us that many of the Jewish priests eventually became believers. That should be music to our ears as we contemplate the end of the denominational era. It suggests that many who have walked in the denominational way while it was perhaps okay to do so, in the days that lie ahead shall put the will of God above their own personal interests. With careers, status, and security at risk, this will be a challenge for many and it may take time for some to do the right thing, but let us pray that they do. When the cloud of His presence moves, believers must not stay where they are. It may have been okay to live there yesterday, but none of us should be found there tomorrow.

What about all those buildings?

M any Christians do not realize the prominent role real estate plays in any serious discussion of church unity. We usually think of church unity in a spiritual sense; so it is easy to forget the tangible elements of the discussion. There is much more to the issue of church property than meets the eye and few are aware of the battles that have been and will be waged over church-owned land and buildings.

Denominations and independent churches own real property valued at hundreds of billions of dollars. There are advantages and disadvantages to this reality. It is nice to have a place to worship, but often, very expensive buildings are half-full on Sunday morning and then sit empty and unused the rest of the week. Some church facilities are so underutilized that it is a disgrace that so much of God's money is tied up in them.

The church's ongoing real estate wars

There are several ways in which church owned property poses a real challenge to church unity. Here's one that many do not realize: Congregations often believe they own property that they do not. Many congregations, who thought they owned their buildings because they bought and paid for them or are obligated to pay the mortgage, are surprised to discover that their buildings are actually owned by their denomination.

The story I am going to share with you has happened many times over. You can decide for yourself the right and wrong of it.

After much prayer and deliberation, a certain congregation decided that being part of a denomination was wrong, at least for them. They decided that the right thing to do was to end their affiliation with their denomination and become an autonomous local church. They had come to believe that this was the biblical pattern and that they had a responsibility to follow it.

The church sent a formal letter to their denomination's headquarters announcing its decision. The reply they received was essentially: *You are free to leave us if you believe you must, but we are keeping the land and buildings.*

The church was shocked. It promptly informed headquarters that the church's property had been wholly financed with money donated by members of the local church and that no denominational funds had been used. They reminded the denomination that from a legal perspective, the mortgage and the deed to the property were in the local church's name, not the denomination's name.

To make a long story short, the matter went to court and the court ruled in the denomination's favor, saying that the money used to pay for the building had been raised "under the banner" of the denomination's name and thus it didn't matter that it had been raised locally. If the congregation wanted to terminate its affiliation with the denomination, it would be required to surrender all of its real estate.

In this case, the congregation decided that becoming independent and autonomous was the principled thing to do, even if it meant they had to start over. The church had an "ace in the hole," or at least it thought so. The church had been planning on expanding its facilities for some time and had accrued several hundred thousand dollars in a separate fund, which it assumed it could now use to purchase a new building. Alas, this was not to be. The denomination not only seized the church's existing land and building; it also seized its building fund, employing the same legal grounds; i.e. that this money also had been raised under the denomination's name.

In any serious discussion of church unity, the ramifications of cases like this and the fairly consistent court rulings in favor of denominations, must be considered. Churches wishing to join with other churches in a spirit of unity might not be able to do so without being at risk of their denomination seizing their buildings. Denominations do not always employ the strong arm tactics we saw in the story above, but cases like this are not at all uncommon. In fact, the building issue is spilling over into struggles over certain doctrinal issues.

There is an ongoing battle within the older, mainline denominations over the subject of ordaining homosexuals and lesbians to the ministry. More conservative congregations are attempting to withdraw from denominations which have adopted the more liberal position. The mainline denominations in turn are suing the departing congregations and seizing their buildings. Such actions make it abundantly clear that church real estate can and will be used as leverage in doctrinal disputes.

A church planter who tried to do the right thing

There was an evangelist in the United Kingdom who held revivals from town to town. His efforts to win souls for the Kingdom of God were very successful and he became quite famous in the British Isles.

When it came time for a local crusade to close down and for the evangelist to move on to the next city, rather than leave the new converts to fend for themselves, his organization would establish a local church to shepherd the new flock. The evangelist's crusades were so successful that within a few years more than a hundred new churches had been established.

One day, the evangelist went to his board of directors and informed them that he believed they were violating a scriptural principle by owning the real estate of all of those local churches. He informed the board that it should turn the land and buildings over to each local church so that they could truly be autonomous and self-governing, according to the pattern he saw in the New Testament.

The board refused. They insisted that they would continue to own and control all of the real estate and would not entrust such wealth to local congregations or their local boards of elders.

The evangelist stood by his guns. He told the board that he felt so strongly about this principle that he would resign if the board was not willing to take this important step. The board refused to let go of even one building. True to his word, the evangelist resigned from the very organization he had built. He continued to evangelize and start new churches wherever he went, but this time he ensured from the beginning that the buildings were owned by the local churches, not some organizational headquarters in another city.

This battle goes on quietly all over the globe. Churches attempt to do what they believe the Lord is directing them to do, but find that their denomination is standing in their way. Many a denomination has seized the buildings of a defecting local church, even though the denomination often has had no congregation to place in the empty building. They seize the buildings because they can.

You've heard of the golden rule: He who has the gold makes the rules. In some cases, that is what denominations are doing. They use a church's land and buildings as leverage to force the congregation to continue its identification with the denomination. If the congregation follows what it believes is the leading of the Lord, the denomination steps in, takes its case before the secular courts and collects a windfall, essentially reaping what it did not sow. Apparently, some denominations believe they have to treat a congregation graciously only if the congregation is willing to remain connected to their brand of Christianity.

Things might be viewed differently if the denomination had paid for the real estate, wholly or in part; then it might have a case that it was owed back what it had invested. But to seize a local congregation's property simply because the secular courts allow it, seems scripturally wrong on several fronts.

The struggle over church-owned property will become an increasingly volatile issue as we move forward. Readers should keep in mind that denominations vary on this issue. Not all denominations demand control or ownership of a local church's real estate. However, where people are involved, matters such as position, money, power, and control can become quite heated. I know of one large group of Pentecostal churches that broke away from a major denomination primarily over this issue. The departing group refused to be part of a denomination that insisted on owning and controlling the real estate of all of its local churches.

Given all this, it is probably safe to say that those who control the land and buildings control the church. Unfortunately, many churches are not aware of who that really is.

Should churches own so much real estate?

It is difficult to speak broadly about the practicality of church-owned real estate. As we saw earlier, churches did not own buildings at all until sometime around 250 A.D. Given so many varied circumstances, it is not easy to pass judgment on this issue today. Some churches have large buildings and use them all week long. Others have beautiful, expensive buildings and except for maybe a small office, use them for an hour or two a week. Granted there is every appearance that God, at times, has blessed churches with facilities that seem vital to their ministries. And yet, it seems equally true that billions of dollars of God's money have been wasted on expensive buildings that are grossly underutilized.

We do well to remember that God does not dwell in temples made with human hands; He dwells in the hearts of humble men and women. It should go without saying that God is more interested in our hearts than some fancy structure we are willing to build for Him. Buildings at times can be a blessing, but there is an undisputable fact of human nature that we must recognize: Building buildings for God is almost a reflex for religious people. You might want to read that last sentence again. We like to show our devotion by building God a house, whether He wants one or not. It is, after all, easier to build God a house than to give Him our hearts.

Do you recall the story of Jesus on the Mount of Transfiguration? The three disciples who were there with Him experienced a sight no human had ever seen. They saw the Lord Jesus speaking in person with Moses and Elijah, two of the greatest men of the Old

Testament. Jesus, Moses, and Elijah were all bright and shiny. What an amazing sight it must have been.

How did the disciples respond to this marvelous experience? Peter's first words were, "Let's build three tabernacles here on this place." God must have rolled His eyes. The building reflex was on full display. Jesus is standing there talking with Moses and Elijah and the first thing the disciples think of is building a building. Apparently, God was not all that interested in Peter's building project, because His voice was heard from heaven telling the disciples that what they were to do was listen to the words of his Son.

Do buildings reveal our true priorities?

Forgive me for repeating here something I have said several times already, but all of those church buildings with their different brand names are a bigger problem for us than we realize. They really do declare to the world, day after day, that Christians are too divided to worship together. They stand as a constant testimony to the world of our disunity and lack of love for one another. But, that's not all they say.

Having so many buildings also says to the world: Churches have too much money. It says we have money to fritter away on beautiful buildings with nice rugs and stain glass windows, while people around us are going hungry and homeless. Expensive buildings that are used for only a few hours a week say something about our priorities.

A modest building designed for frequent use is one thing, but a crystal cathedral? Why? If our vision is to reach the lost, feed the hungry, or teach new converts the basics of the faith, how does spending money on an obscenely expensive or ornate cathedral assist in our mission? I suspect that God is not impressed with such behavior, at least not favorably.

In his book, "*Radical, taking back your faith from the American Dream*," author David Platt describes a Christian news publication he received in the mail. There were two headlines. On the left, the headline read, "First Baptist Church Celebrates new $23 Million Building." A lengthy article described the exquisite marble, intricate design, and the beautiful stained glass of the new building. On the right, was another headline, which read, "Baptist Relief Helps Sudanese Refugees." That article described 350,000 starving refugees, who might not live to the end of the year. Further down, the story told readers that the Baptists had raised $5,000 to send to the starving refugees.

David Platt's response was,

"Five thousand dollars. That is not enough to get a plane into Sudan, much less one drop of water to those who need it. Twenty-three million dollars for an elaborate sanctuary and five thousand dollars for hundreds of thousands of starving men, women, and children, most of whom are dying apart from faith in Christ. Where have we gone wrong?"[56]

In conclusion, church buildings must be a component of any meaningful discussion of church unity. The real estate holdings of some of the larger denominations are enormous and the holdings of the Catholic Church are almost unfathomable. In the days ahead, there will be struggles over who owns all this property and what should be done with buildings that are not needed. It stands to reason that as churches come together in Christian unity, there may not be a need for quite so many buildings. If more believers are worshipping together, facilities which are not needed or are under-utilized today could be converted to homeless shelters or day care centers, or they could be sold and the money used to finance missions or to minister to the poor.

Would your church be open to doing that? Would your denomination allow you to do that? As things stand today, we might not like the answer to either question.

Visible unity and disunity

Must church unity be visible to be meaningful? Can't we all just be "one in spirit" and forget about the technical stuff? That is the fallback position of those who do not want to face the reality of church division or take meaningful steps to remedy it. This opinion is widespread enough to justify a considered response.

Let's approach this subject by examining (once more) the opening words of Paul's first letter to the Corinthians. Notice the two "groups" Paul describes:

> [2]To the church of God that is in Corinth, to those sanctified in Christ Jesus, **called to be saints together with all those who in every place call upon the name of our Lord Jesus Christ**, both their Lord and ours: [3] Grace to you and peace from God our Father and the Lord Jesus Christ.

Paul's greeting to the Corinthians speaks of the church in two regards. First, he addresses the local church in Corinth, the body of believers in and around that city. Then he makes it clear that the Corinthian believers are simultaneously "saints together" with "all those who in every place" call upon the name of the Lord Jesus. Do you see the two groups? Paul speaks of both the local church and the universal church. One is visible; the other exists, but is not visible as a specific entity, except to the Lord, of course.

When Paul writes admonitions to believers, he writes to the visible, local church. In a very real sense, this approach is an acknowledgement that we cannot fix or change the universal church, except by addressing the local churches of which it is comprised.

True unity must be visible to the world

In another letter, Paul told the church at Ephesus that they were to *endeavor* to keep the "unity of the Spirit in the bond of peace." It stands to reason that the Ephesians would only have to *endeavor* or *work* at maintaining unity, if it was possible for them to lose it, and if unity was not something all Christians automatically enjoy because they have called upon the name of the Lord. Right? Why would the Ephesians be told to *endeavor* to keep or maintain unity, if they automatically experienced and enjoyed the kind of unity Paul was describing simply by virtue of being Christians?

Obviously, the kind of unity Paul describes is a real world experience, one at which believers could fail.

That being the case, here is the question we must address: Does our mutual calling *to be saints together with believers everywhere* make us one in the sense that Jesus prayed for *oneness* in John 17? Does the fact that we are all Christians, redeemed by the same Savior, make us visibly one with one another or does God want us to exhibit something more tangible?

Renowned Christian philosopher Francis Schaeffer answered this question as follows:

"We make a mockery of what Jesus is saying unless we understand that He is talking about something visible."[57]

Visible unity. Is this not the only sensible way of understanding the prayer of Jesus? How will our *oneness* make the world know that Jesus was sent by God the Father, if it is not visible to them?

Francis Schaeffer went on to say:

"In theological terms there are, to be sure, a visible church and an invisible church. The invisible Church is the real Church -- in

a way, the only church that has a right to be spelled with a capital. Because it is made up of all those who have thrown themselves upon Christ as Savior, it is most important. It is Christ's Church. As soon as I become a Christian, as soon as I throw myself upon Christ, I become a member of this Church, and there is a mystical unity binding me to all other members. True. But this is not what Jesus is talking about in John 13 and John 17, for we cannot break up this unity no matter what we do. Thus, to relate Christ's words to the mystical unity of the invisible Church is to reduce Christ's words to a meaningless phrase."[58]

In other words, Jesus was not praying for a mystical unity. He had something both real and observable in mind, something the world could not easily ignore.

Christians are proclaiming two contradictory messages

Evangelical Christians acknowledge that the primary responsibility of the church is to preach the gospel and thereby see men and women converted to Christ and then discipled. That's the Great Commission. Not all churches do this, but churches which have discounted their charge to preach the gospel eventually have withered away and died or they have devolved into mere social clubs, purveying a social gospel that only feeds men's temporal bodies, but neglects the salvation of their eternal souls.

If you have stuck with me this far, you should have concluded by now that preaching the gospel and evangelizing the world involves more than just telling people who Jesus Christ is. The Christian church must also *show* them who He is. The world must see our love for one another and they must see our unity and be thoroughly impressed with what they see. According to Jesus, that's how they will know that our words are true.

The world will not know that our message is true simply because many people are responding to it. Numbers do not prove veracity. They never have. Cults are often very successful at bringing large numbers of people under their spell, swelling their ranks with tens of thousands of new converts every year. Hitler persuaded millions to follow him, even though there was only death and destruction at the end of the road he traveled.

Jesus proved unequivocally that numbers can be meaningless. He exited this earth after three and half years of ministry and left behind only 120 committed disciples. As David Platt says in *"Radical, Taking Back Your Faith From the American Dream,"* Jesus would be labeled a failure by today's mega church standards. One hundred and twenty souls in three and half years would be deemed downright unimpressive.

In one place, Jesus said that the road to destruction is a broad road and many travel on it, but the way that leads to life is narrow and few find it. While numbers matter on the one hand, on the other they are irrelevant. Not once did Jesus say, "The world will know you are my disciples and that the Father sent me, because your churches will be really, really huge." No, He said the world will know that the Father sent Him and that we are His disciples *when they see our love for one another and our unity.*

To today's skeptical world, words are cheap. People can say and prove anything, especially on the internet. So, how are we to persuade the world that our message is true? How are we to show them that we really have the goods? Jesus answered that question two thousand years ago. All the world has to do is observe how we behave towards one another.

Unfortunately, the world has done exactly that and as a result has largely dismissed us. It is entirely possible that the church's lack of unity is the primary reason the world has passed us by and is now calling our time the "post Christian" era. I do not believe we live in a post Christian world, but in a world that has been shaped by a terribly but temporarily divided Christian church.

Our failure to *love one another* and *be joined to one another* in a spirit of unity has been visible to the world for hundreds of years now. We must show them the opposite. Our love and our unity must be visible; they must be on full display. When they are, the world will see and know that Jesus Christ is the Lord. I do not know what they will do with that knowledge, but they will know.

The Fractured Church – chapter 18

Denominational doctrines - by what authority?

D enominations keep Christians separated into different camps. It is their nature to do so. Denominations encourage fellowship primarily among their own kind, with those who are of a like mind. Here's just one example of how that plays out. Denominational youth leaders routinely arrange trips for their youth groups. They travel long distances to fellowship with other youth groups within their denomination, even though there are other Christian youth groups, often just blocks away, with whom they have established no connection whatsoever. They do this because of doctrinal conformity.

Agreement regarding doctrine forms the primary basis for denominational fellowship. Fellowship is not based on shared faith in Christ, but agreement on denominational doctrines, otherwise we would all fellowship with the churches closest to us. Denominations utilize doctrine to draw lines; we should say *official* lines, which ensure that their members will remain separated from "inferior or flawed" Christians from other denominations. They may not do this consciously, but they do it.

I'm asking you to stop for a minute and consider a question that you may not have pondered before. Where does a denomination obtain the right to establish its own doctrines and create its own articles of faith? By what authority do they do this?

Unless a denomination believes that its members are the only Christians in the world, it has absolutely no right to establish doctrines of any kind. A denomination cannot speak for the entire body of Christ, because it does not represent the entire body of Christ. A denomination can't even speak for its own little division of the body of Christ, because divisions within the body of Christ are expressly prohibited by Scripture. If divisions are prohibited, how then can a division speak authoritatively about anything?

The Bible speaks of two sources of sound doctrine, Christ's doctrines and the apostles' doctrines. (The Bible also states that there are doctrines of devils.) Nowhere does the Bible speak of "doctrines of denominations" or give any group or organization the authority to establish its own unique set of beliefs.

If denominational doctrines are not the doctrine of Christ and not the doctrine of the apostles, then whose doctrines are they and where did those establishing them obtain the authority to do so? Did they vote themselves the authority? That would be the height of presumption. Are they claiming that God gave them the authority to establish doctrines for their group, even though their doctrines are different from the doctrines of other believers? That is not believable. It is unlikely that the Holy Spirit would lead one group to establish beliefs that are different from those of another Christian group.

Even if the Holy Spirit was present in a denomination's board meetings and kept the group from going too far astray when it drafted its articles of faith, it does not automatically follow that He wanted the group to establish a set of denominational doctrines in the first place.

Denominations have no authority to establish doctrine

Once we recognize that all believers are members of the body of Christ at large, it makes denominational doctrines entirely irrational. How can a man or woman believe one thing as a member of the worldwide body of Christ, but something different as a member of a particular denominational body? It is not possible to do so. Christians are supposed to be of the same mind and of the same judgment and to speak the same things. They are to embrace the same body of truths. Those truths are not a matter of opinion or personal preference, because no scripture is of private interpretation. No individual and no committee is free to make these things up. We can only agree on them together.

As Paul told the Ephesians, there is one body, one Spirit, one hope, one Lord, one faith, one baptism, and one God and Father of all, Who is above all, and through all, and in you all. Can we truly say that we share "one faith" with other believers, if we believe different things?[59]

All arbitrarily established doctrines lead to division. Wait, that's not strong enough. Denominational doctrinal statements do not merely lead to divisions; they cause divisions. They cause divisions and then they make those divisions "official" and cement them into place. They make members of a denomination *officially* at odds with the members of other denominations. To that end, any doctrinal statement that is unique to a certain group, usurps an authority that only the church as a whole should possess.

Doctrine is too important for us to play so loosely with it. God has so ordered things that what we believe determines our eternal destiny. Because doctrine is so vitally important, it is a usurpation of authority for any subset of the church to establish its own. There is one Christian orthodoxy and no other orthodoxy. We must begin to acknowledge that. There cannot be a Baptist orthodoxy, a Presbyterian orthodoxy, a Pentecostal orthodoxy, and a Methodist or Lutheran orthodoxy. There can only be one. For that reason, a denominational orthodoxy is no orthodoxy at all.

We are not so free to disagree, as we suppose

This brings us to one of the most important things I am going to say in this book. This may sound simple, but what I am going to say next runs contrary to our entire system of theology.

Pentecostal Christians are not free to believe different things than Baptist Christians or Methodist Christians or Presbyterian Christians. Members of the Churches of Christ are not free to believe different doctrines than Episcopalians, Adventists, Lutherans or Reformed Christians. We must all believe the same thing. We must all speak the same thing. The Bible is clear about that. There are not many faiths or many versions of the truth; there is but one. If we believe there can legitimately be different beliefs within the one body of Christ, we deceive ourselves.

This concept may seem foreign to our thinking, but it must be so. The Bible says unequivocally that we are all to be of one accord and that we are all to be of the same mind and judgment. The fact that we are not, but rather have adopted thousands of different doctrinal statements, only demonstrates how far we have strayed from the biblical pattern and thus, the Word of God.

We have been told that it is okay to disagree with fellow believers regarding nonessentials, but there is obviously some danger in this philosophy. You may be familiar with this 1,600 year old quote:

"In Essentials, unity. In non-essentials, liberty. In all things, love" Augustine (354-430 AD)

The question I put before you is this: If there is such a thing, what makes a doctrine non-essential? Who determines that? We know that *all* Scripture is given by inspiration of God and is profitable for doctrine, reproof, for correction and for instruction in righteousness, that the man of God might be perfect..."[60] If we are going to have liberty in our opinions regarding matters that are non-essential, then we must determine what those non-essential things are. Of course, in so doing we arbitrarily relegate some truths to a lesser status. If this must be done, and to some extent it appears that it must, it must be done by the Christian church and not by each of us individually or by some denominational body with artificial authority. Disagreement regarding "what is essential and what is not" can result in division as quickly as disagreement regarding the details of an essential doctrine, such as belief in the bodily resurrection of Christ.

To remedy this, the Christian church at a minimum must come together and determine what real orthodoxy is and decide which doctrines are essential and which are non-essential and end all divisions based on non-essential doctrines. This would be an historic undertaking, but it must be done. I am not calling for a new Inquisition or for burning heretics at the stake, but Christians must begin to speak as one and in order to do so we must decide together which things are "most surely believed among us," to borrow a phrase from the Gospel of Luke. After that determination has been made, Christians must refuse to divide over any matter which the church decides cannot be resolved with certainty.

In the next chapter, we will discuss a difficult issue. We will talk about churches that are not really churches, at least in the Christian sense of the word. We will talk about a line that must be drawn so that people will know that there are those who call themselves Christians, but are not. We must not seek to be one with those who are not part of the body of Christ for we are not to be unequally yoked with unbelievers, for what fellowship does light have with darkness?

How do we make this determination? Who will decide where the line should be drawn and who is on the other side of it? Two things are certain. First, such a decision will have meaning only if we make it together. Second, in this time of diversity training, multi-culturalism, and political correctness, we will be hated for calling darkness "darkness." However, the fact that we will at times be despised for speaking the truth must not cause us to shrink from doing so.

Churches that aren't really churches

For there to be genuine Christian unity, there must first be division. This may seem counterintuitive, but it is so. The same Jesus who preached love and unity also said that He came not to bring peace, but a sword.[61] The sword was not to divide one believer from another, but to separate those who love the truth from those who hate it, even if that division is between father and son, mother and daughter.

It follows then that not all attempts at unity are good or advisable. Some efforts at ecumenicalism are not only a waste of time and resources, but also violate the very principle of Christian unity. Consider the words of one of the greatest Christian thinkers of the last century:

"...exactly the same thing is true in the Protestant ecumenical movement. There is an attempt to bring people together organizationally on the basis of Jesus' statement, but there is no real unity, because two completely different religions -- biblical Christianity and a "Christianity" which is no Christianity whatsoever -- are involved. It is perfectly possible to have organizational unity, to spend a whole lifetime of energy on it, and yet to come nowhere near the realm that Jesus is talking about in John 17."[62] (Francis Schaeffer)

True unity is not organizational unity. True unity is a oneness that is based on a shared faith in Christ and surrender to his Lordship. Sadly, there is a so-called Christianity in the world today, which, as Francis Schaeffer said above, is no Christianity at all.

I am not attempting here to divide the wheat from the tares, which is something Jesus said the angels will do at the end of the age. I am not suggesting that we should presume to judge whether a person who professes the Christ of the Bible is really a Christian. That is for God to decide; He alone knows the hearts of men. I am speaking of dividing truth from falsehood, as it relates to essential doctrines.

Unity that should not and, in fact, cannot be

This is a difficult thing to say, but how can we have a meaningful discussion of church unity without recognizing that there are churches which are Christian in name only, churches with whom genuine believers should not be joined? As light cannot be joined with darkness, so it is with churches. Some should not, and in truth, cannot mix.

A church is free to call itself anything it wishes, at least in the western part of the world. (This is not so true in countries where national Orthodox Churches rule as the only official church.) In the west, a church may place any sign it wants out front, but writing something on a sign does not make it so. Just as the apostle Paul found that *they were not all Israel who said they were of Israel*, so it is true that not everyone who claims the name of Christ is indeed His.

The Bible speaks of ravenous wolves coming into the church, dressed like sheep.[63] Jesus and the apostles warned believers of such men. Paul further warned the church that Satan's ministers come as ministers of righteousness and Satan himself comes as an angel of light.[64] In other words, people are not always who they say they are.

It may be politically incorrect to deny that a church is Christian when it says it is, but the body of Christ cannot bow to political correctness, especially when the church claiming to be Christian does not believe in Christ. Jesus stated unambiguously, in one of the

230

most sobering verses in the Bible, that in the final judgment He will announce that He never knew *many* of those who claimed loudly that they were working for Him.

We must recognize that there is a doctrinal line over which one cannot cross and still be a Christian. It is possible to draw that line. It is a tragedy that some churches and denominations have strayed so far from the truth that true, Bible-believing churches must identify them as outside the body of Christ, but there is no other choice. In one place, the apostle Paul said that he *feared* that churches would "put up with" false teachers.

Consider II Corinthians 11:3-4.

> *³ **But I fear**, lest somehow, as the serpent deceived Eve by his craftiness, so your minds may be corrupted from the simplicity that is in Christ. ⁴ For if he who comes preaches another Jesus whom we have not preached, or if you receive a different spirit which you have not received, or a different gospel which you have not accepted—**you may well put up with it!***

There are churches and denominations that preach an entirely different Jesus than the one the apostles preached. We must not put up with their doing so or allow them to go unchallenged. As we shall discuss momentarily, the Jesus they preach is not found in the Bible; they made him up. They fashioned him to be what they wanted him to be, because they had rejected who He really is. To those who have devised a different Jesus, we must not fail to speak the truth in love. We must speak against their doctrine; we must speak plainly and boldly; but we must do it together.

It is important, however, not to use too wide a brush when doing so. Just because a denomination has left the faith does not mean that all of its member churches have. Sometimes a majority of the congregations comprising an organization (or their delegates) vote to adopt a non-Christian doctrine or policy, though some number of other congregations within the same denomination vigorously opposes that position. Some congregations within a denomination stand for the truth, but are simply on the losing side of a denominational vote.

Mainline churches are at war over the basics

There are several high stakes doctrinal and policy battles being waged right now within some Lutheran, Presbyterian, Episcopalian and Methodist denominations headquartered in the United States. The more conservative congregations, primarily from southern states and African countries, are fighting to make their denominations truly Christian. The more conservative congregations are losing many of these battles, but in the case of the United Methodists, the theologically conservative congregations have sufficient numbers to prevent the denomination as a whole from formally adopting several theologically liberal policies, including ordaining gay and lesbian ministers. For this reason, we must be careful not to assume that an entire system of churches has departed from the faith, even though a majority of those comprising it has.

To further illustrate this important point, note the difference between the Presbyterian Church (USA) and the Presbyterian Church in America. Both are Presbyterian denominations, but the Presbyterian Church (USA) is theologically liberal. It is the larger of the two and has more than 10,000 congregations. The Presbyterian Church in America, on the other hand, is much smaller, being comprised of around 1,500 congregations. It is clearly the more theologically conservative denomination.

What is true of Presbyterians is true of many mainline denominations, which should suggest to us that brand names alone may not tell the whole story. There are committed Christians languishing within spiritually shipwrecked denominations and even under non-Christian pastors. In some cases, these "stranded" Christians are not merely languishing; some are fighting the good fight in difficult places and speaking out for the Christ of the Bible where they can. It is a strange thing to be in a position where one has to pray that his or her pastor will someday become a Christian, but I have personally prayed with believers for that very thing.

Political correctness and the fear of man

In our day of diversity training and multiculturalism, passing judgment upon another person's beliefs is viewed as bigotry and intolerance. We are told that we must accept everyone's opinion as equally valid and that there are "many paths to God." This may be the politically correct thing to profess, but it is a lie.

Claiming that Jesus Christ is the only way for a man or woman to come to God may make the unbelieving world see red, but what choice do we have? For us, that is not a debatable matter. Jesus said He was the only way to the Father.[65] Do we believe Him or not? The Gospel of John says unequivocally that we either believe in Jesus Christ or we remain under the wrath of God.[66] The apostle Peter said the name of Jesus is the only name under heaven whereby a man must be saved.[67]

We cannot run from such clear statements or dilute them. All we can do is proclaim them. A church can only become so "seeker friendly" before there is nothing of value remaining for the seeker to find.

How anemic the Christian church would be if it could not define what someone must believe to be a Christian, or if it were to meekly allow the true Gospel to be replaced by a watered down counterfeit? It is not the church's role in the world to ignore the darkness, but to stand against it and dispel it.

The lines between doctrinal right and wrong are not really as blurred as some might think. Churches that deny the inspiration of the Scriptures, the virgin birth, the deity of Christ, and His bodily resurrection are not Christian and preach another Jesus than the one found in the Bible. Their Christ did no miracles. He didn't claim to be the only begotten Son of God or the only way to the Father. He didn't rise from the dead.

Churches which preach this Jesus may claim the name "Christian," and no one can prevent them from doing so, but they only get away with their deception because the real church is so fractured that it lacks the authority to declare, with one voice, the difference between the truth and a lie, between the broad path of destruction and the narrow one that leads to eternal life.

Churches that deny the essentials of the faith are so well hidden amongst the real ones as to be camouflaged. People who attend these churches often do not know that their own minister, pastor, or priest does not believe in the deity of Christ or his literal, bodily resurrection from the dead. There are many atheists pastoring so-called Christian churches today, though not all of them have announced their disbelief from the pulpit.

Churches which have rejected the Christ of the Bible and yet call themselves members of the "faith community" are disingenuous. It is difficult to understand why they insist on being called people of faith. They are more skeptics than believers. They are known more for what they don't believe than what they do. Rejection of the truth usually begins with rejecting the authority of the Scriptures. When a church or denomination rejects the infallibility of the Scriptures, it arrogantly places itself in the position of judging the Word of God rather than the Word of God judging it. There is no easy way to reach such a church with the truth, because it does not accept the basis by which the truth was delivered. Unbelief is the one thing that closes all doors and makes it impossible for a person, or a group of persons, to come to God.[68]

Where should the line be drawn?

The question we must now ask is: Whether we are speaking of an individual or a church, where should the line between Christian and non-Christian be drawn? Several Bible-believing Christian leaders have suggested that unity begin with something as simple as the Apostles' Creed, which dates back to the middle of the third century, even before the New Testament was canonized. The Apostles' Creed declares the basics of the Gospel. It is more than 1,700 years old and is not overly complicated. In fact, it is so simple and basic that it should be a red flashing light if a group claims to be Christian but has a serious problem with the Apostles' Creed.

There are several variations of the Creed, but they are all similar. The following is a good version with one notable change from the original. This version uses the term "holy Christian church" instead of "holy catholic church." Even though *catholic* was used in the small "c" sense of the word, many Protestants object to the use of the word in any form. (The word "catholic" simply meant "universal" and originally did not refer to the Roman Catholic Church.) Here is the Apostles' Creed:

I believe in God, the Father Almighty,
Maker of heaven and earth.
And in Jesus Christ, his only Son, our Lord,
who was conceived by the Holy Spirit,
and born of the virgin Mary,
suffered under Pontius Pilate,
was crucified, died and was buried.
He descended into hell.
On the third day He rose again from the dead.
He ascended into heaven
and sits at the right hand of God the Father Almighty.
From thence He will come to judge the living and the dead.
I believe in the Holy Spirit,
the holy Christian church,
the communion of saints,
the forgiveness of sins,
the resurrection of the body,
and the life everlasting. Amen

No one knows the origin of the Apostle's Creed, but it is one of the oldest statements of the Christian faith known to man. Granted, there are important doctrines not covered in this statement, but it seems to set forth the essentials around which unity could be built.

Most Bible-believing Christians embrace every part of this creed without reservation - with one possible exception. There is a good faith objection made by several respected theologians to the statement, "He descended into hell." Even though the belief that Jesus descended into hell after his death on the cross has been around for a long time, there is scant biblical evidence for it and even some of the early church fathers, Augustine to name one, struggled with that doctrine. There are a handful of verses of Scripture which have been interpreted to convey this thought, but they are hardly clear and can reasonably be interpreted otherwise. Personally, I believe that Jesus did descend into hell during the three days His body lay in the tomb, but there is no proof text that ends all debate and thus there is room for honest discussion.

With that one possible exception, the Apostles' Creed may be sufficient to form the basis for Christian unity, although, as with any statement, there are some technical concerns that the language of the creed might not be sufficient to address. Some churches, for example, accept the words and phrases that comprise the Apostles' Creed, but mean other things by them. Some theologically liberal churches, for example, teach that Jesus Christ was the son of God, but only in the same sense that Buddha, Confucius, and Mohammed were "sons of God," making theirs a substantially different Jesus than the One the Creed describes. The same goes for the Mormon Church and the Jehovah's Witnesses and their heretical interpretation of these same words, which we shall discuss momentarily.

What happens when the Scriptures don't matter

I recall a conference I attended at a theologically liberal United Methodist Church in Portland, Oregon several years ago. As memory serves, the subject of the conference was something like, "How should the church respond to the cult explosion that is overtaking our youth?" The group was especially concerned with New Age and eastern cults, such as the Hari Krishnas and the Rajneeshees.

The Rajneesh cult was of particular interest to churches in the Pacific Northwest, because oddly enough that group had headquartered itself in the rough and tumble ranching country of Central Oregon. Its adherents were predominantly well-educated professionals, who had given up their wealth and positions to move to a 64,000 acre ranch in Oregon's high desert to meditate and "seek enlightenment" with an eccentric Indian guru.

Hundreds of ministers from many of the older, mainstream denominations attended the conference. There were Lutheran pastors of different persuasions, and ministers from various Episcopalian, Methodist, and Presbyterian churches. The United Church of Christ was also well represented, as were many others. A professor

236

from the Harvard School of Divinity, one Harvey Cox, was the keynote speaker.

The conference on cults was a two or three day affair. Panel discussions were conducted. Many speeches were given. Expert testimony was received from professional psychologists and sociologists. An expert specializing in in eastern cults made a presentation. It was all quite informative.

It did not take long, however, to ascertain that many, if not most, of the ministers attending the conference had personally rejected the infallibility of Scripture and represented theologically liberal, mainline denominations. They wore expensive suits and looked altogether learned and distinguished, but there was something seriously missing.

I attended the conference with a Bible-believing Baptist brother, who had been invited to the conference and for some reason was inclined to drag me along. We both listened intently to everything that was said.

I must tell you, I have been to countless Christian meetings and conferences spanning several decades and have rubbed shoulders with many thousands of people I didn't know. Generally, I have known that I was among brethren, people who knew the Lord and loved Him. Knowing that the brother or sister standing next to you loves the same God and shares the same faith in his Son as you, creates a powerful kinship, even when you have never met before. At this conference on cults, however, I did not sense that shared faith. In fact, I felt entirely out of sync with everything that was said and even with the way things were said.

I recollect that there were 300 to 500 ministers at that conference. They discussed the topic of cults forward and backward. They heard from the experts and then they answered the question they came there to answer.

What do you think this theologically liberal "faith community" decided they should do in response to the cult explosion that was overtaking their youth and drawing some astray? To what conclusion did all of the panel discussions and expert testimony lead? It all led them to this: *We should not do anything. Who are we, after all, to say that the young people joining these cults will not find their way to God on the path they have chosen, just as we have found our way on the path we have chosen?*

When you stop and think about it, what else could a group like this have concluded? Once you have decided that the Scriptures are not the infallible Word of God and the final authority for determining how we should live and what we should believe, one man's opinion really is as good as the next man's. Once you reject the deity of Christ and His resurrection from the dead, which is the very heart of the gospel, you have nothing left but human opinions, which are of course "all of equal value."

They were the blind leading the blind. They were like men trying to build a house without a level or a square or a plum line. There was simply no place to start. There can be no such thing as a cult if there is no absolute truth. It would have been an act of unmitigated, narrow minded arrogance for this group to have concluded that their view was correct and the views of the gurus and eastern mystics were wrong. To be consistent with their own philosophy, they, above all things, had to be tolerant of other opinions.

Mormons and Jehovah's Witnesses

So we come back to the point where we started: There is a doctrinal line that cannot be crossed without putting one's self or one's church outside the body of Christ. Accepting a statement such as the Apostles' Creed might be sufficient, in most cases, to make a delineation, but the Creed in and of itself might not be enough. For example, Mormons might embrace each of the statements set forth in the Apostles' Creed and yet mean something entirely different when they say those same words. Recently, one of the most well known preachers in the United States said on a CNN news show that he believed that a prominent political figure is a Christian, even though he is a Mormon. Was he right? He justified his assessment because the man said that Jesus Christ is his Savior and that Jesus rose from the dead. The question is, can a church use the same words as are contained in the Apostles' Creed and mean something entirely different by them?

We will come back to the Mormon Church in a moment. The problem with Mormon or Latter Day Saints' doctrines regarding Christ is in some ways more subtle than some of the other non-Christian "churches," such as the Jehovah's Witnesses. It's an easier call with the Jehovah's Witnesses. If Christians cannot be joined in unity with churches which reject the deity of Christ, then there can be no unity with the Jehovah Witnesses, plain and simple. Jehovah's Witnesses teach that Jesus is not divine, but rather a created being, a sort of super angel. This is not a Christian doctrine and yet it is this group's primary focus; it is what they are about.

Jehovah's Witnesses have gone so far as to change the wording of their *New World Translation* of the Bible to obscure clear statements about the deity of Jesus Christ. For example, where the Gospel of John says, "In the beginning was the Word and the Word was with God and the Word was God," the Jehovah's Witnesses have changed the text to read, "In the beginning was the word and the word was with God and the word was *a god.*"

I know several decent people who are Jehovah's Witnesses, but it is unlikely that they are Christians. Some of their *Watchtower*[69] publications say some good things, but when you dig deeper and find what Jehovah's Witnesses really believe regarding essential Christian doctrines, theirs is clearly a different gospel, and thus, there can be no Christian unity with this group.

Now, back to the Mormons. No church is more difficult to write about than the Mormon Church. The false doctrines they espouse are too numerous to name. Mormon television commercials often say things so close to the truth that they appear to be entirely Christian. It is only when converts are taught what the Church of Jesus Christ of Latter Day Saints truly means by the things it says that it becomes clear that the gospel the Mormons teach is not biblical Christianity. In fact, it's not even close.

Because Mormons use so many of the same words and terminology that Bible-believing Christians use, some have suggested that there may be Mormons who have heard those words and believe the true Gospel because they have not yet been introduced to real Mormon doctrine. If it is possible to be a Mormon and be a Christian, it is probably not possible to be a *good* Mormon and be a Christian. Mormons share one belief with theologically liberal churches; both believe that the Bible is not the inspired Word of God. Both believe that the Bible is so flawed and so full of errors that it is not reliable scripture. Both replace the words of the Bible with their own opinions.

The apostle Paul warned the Christian church not to accept any gospel other than the one he preached, *even if an angel from heaven delivered it*. The Mormons have ignored Paul's warning. The angel Maroni, whether real or fabricated, allegedly brought the Mormon gospel to Joseph Smith. The message Maroni presented to Smith was, however, radically different from the one found in the pages of the New Testament. If an angel, claiming he was sent by God, appears to you and tells you that Jesus and Satan were brothers up in Heaven, you ought to walk away. You ought to *run* away. The founders of Mormonism didn't. Consider the following statement by Brigham Young:

"Who will redeem the earth, who will go forth and make the sacrifice for the earth and all things it contains?" The Eldest Son said: "Here am I"; and then he added, "Send me." But the second one, which was "Lucifer, Son of the Morning," said, "Lord, here am I, send me, I will redeem every son and daughter of Adam and Eve that lives on the earth, or that ever goes on the earth."[70]

And there is this Mormon statement describing a council that they allege was held in heaven before Jesus was born in Bethlehem:

"The story of Lucifer is the most terrible example of such apostasy. Lucifer, son of the morning, through diligent search for truth and the use of it, had become one of the foremost in the assembly of those invited to undertake the experiences of earth. But, in that Great Council, his personal ambition and love of power overcame him. He pitted his own plan and will against the purposes of God. He strove to gain the birthright of his Elder Brother, Jesus the Christ."[71]

Then there is the problem with Jesus being, to Mormons, a created being, which is similar to what the Jehovah Witnesses believe about Jesus. Of course, if Jesus was created, He had a beginning and could not be the Eternal Son of God. Consider the following statement from mormonchurch.com/587.

"God created both Satan and Jesus, and in that respect, they are brothers. But in that respect, every person who ever lived is a brother or sister to every other person, because we are all children of God."

So, you see, it is possible to use the same words as Christians use, and mean something entirely different by them. Christians believe, as John chapter one states regarding Jesus, "All things were made through Him, and without Him nothing was made that was made." Jesus was not created, as Mormonism teaches; rather He is the one who created all things. The Mormon Jesus is a different Jesus. The real Jesus is *the only begotten Son*, not the devil's older brother.

Eight heresies in one paragraph

The following excerpt from the "Journals of Discourse," which is a series of volumes considered to be scripture by the Mormon Church, should make it clear that the doctrines of the Mormon Church are far outside the teachings of the Word of God.

"Now hear it, O inhabitants of the earth, Jew and Gentile, Saint and sinner! When our father Adam came into the garden of Eden, he came into it with a celestial body, and brought Eve, one of his wives, with him. He helped to make and organize the world. He is Michael, the Archangel, the Ancient of Days! About whom holy men have written and spoken—He is our Father and our God, and the only God with whom we have to do. Every man upon the earth, professing Christians and non-professing, must hear it, and will know it sooner or later." (Published in "The Latter Day Saints' Millennial Star in 1853)

There are at least eight false doctrines in that one paragraph. This one brief statement contradicts the biblical teachings regarding God, creation, Adam, Eve, and Michael the archangel. When Adam is your god and the only god with whom you have to do; when Adam is also the archangel Michael and the "Ancient of Days," a biblical name for God; and when Jesus and Satan are brothers, your religion is simply not Christian. It is something else entirely. Mormonism may have some of the trappings of Christianity and use some of the same words, but its doctrines cannot be deemed Christian. My heart grieves that so many well meaning people are caught up in this deception.

It would require a sovereign act of God to do it, but would it not be a truly historic event if the Lord were to break through to the leaders of the Mormon Church, persuade them of the error of their ways, and turn that church into a truly Christian body? I have prayed for this many times and encourage others to do so, as well. If the enemy can lead Christian churches, including entire denominations, away from the truth, could the Holy Spirit not tear the Mormon Church from his grasp? What a prize that would be!

It is not the purpose of this book to deal with all of the errors of the Mormon Church. Suffice it to say that opening arms of Christian fellowship to the Mormon Church is neither possible nor prudent given their present belief system. Love them? Definitely. Be joined with them? Definitely not.

There are many fine human beings in the Jehovah's Witnesses religion and the Mormon Church, and if individuals within those organizations choose to turn from the errors of those groups and fellowship with Christians and worship in a spirit of unity, that would be a welcome event. However, it should be stated unequivocally that one cannot believe what these organizations teach and accurately be called Christian.

Christians can work with Mormons and other non-Christian organizations in staffing and funding programs which provide for the poor and needy. We can work together in areas of legislation and public policy, places where our goals might at times overlap, but not in any forum in which there is a suggestion that our beliefs and spiritual values are the same as theirs. I say this as one who knows many

LDS people who are fine individuals, have great families, and are upstanding members of society, something I can also say of some Buddhists I know. I grieve for the spiritual darkness in which Mormons are enveloped, but it would do them no favor to pretend that their doctrines place them safely within the body of Christ.

I ask readers to join with me in praying regularly that the Lord will break through to them and save many. It is at least conceivable that this might be one of the fruits of genuine church unity. When those on the outside see the unprecedented thing the Holy Spirit is doing in the body of Christ, it is likely that many will be drawn to know the Lord, as only a Christian can.

In summary, church unity can only reach as far as the Gospel itself reaches. There can be no real Christian unity with churches that teach another gospel or that deny the most basic tenets of the Christian faith. Where that line is drawn is not for me to say, except to say this: True unity must be based on a commonly shared faith in the Jesus Christ of the Bible.

Before we move to the next chapter, it might be helpful to share with you the following "current events" update by columnist Mark Tooley, who describes in more detail the struggle going on within some of the older mainline denominations, struggles between those holding to biblical Christianity and those rejecting the essential truths of the Gospel. This column may serve as a warning to mainline Christians in Europe and the United States, but at the same time it also offers a ray of hope.

Culture War and the Global Church

By Mark Tooley

Liberal Protestant denominations are increasingly no match for their conservative brethren worldwide.

Global Christianity is thriving, with one out of every 3 people on earth professing Christian faith, according to a Pew study released last month. But Christianity is shifting south. Two percent of global Christians 100 years ago lived in sub-Saharan

Africa. Today, nearly a quarter do, equal to Europe's percentage, and soon surely to surpass it.

Insulated secular elites in the U.S. remain largely clueless about thriving religion even in America, much less globally. To the extent they notice domestic religion, it is often the echoing voices of liberal Protestant elites who preside over increasingly empty churches.

The Presbyterian Church (USA) and the Episcopal Church, both of which are now likely below 2 million members, will have their governing conventions this summer (2012). They will probably solidify their liberal trends, especially in deconstructing traditional marriage. United Methodism, unique among the major liberal Mainline denominations for having not compromised its sexual teaching, will convene its General Conference in late April in Tampa. Its U.S. membership of 7.6 million is shrinking, while its overseas membership of 4.5 million, mostly in Africa, is surging.

Meeting at the same convention center where Republicans will nominate their presidential candidate a few months later, the United Methodists perhaps will offer a little more excitement than the GOP. Church liberals, as they have for 40 years, hope they will finally overturn the denomination's prohibition against same-sex unions and clergy sexually active outside heterosexual marriage. But 30 percent of the nearly 1000 delegates this year will come from Africa, and another 10 percent from the Philippines, Europe, and elsewhere overseas. The overseas churches, especially Africa, are overwhelmingly conservative.

Liberals will need over 80 percent of U.S. delegates to win. But about 200 of the 600 U.S. delegates are believed to be evangelical, making the odds almost insurmountable. The U.S. church's only growing areas are in the relatively more conservative South, while the U.S. church as a whole loses 50,000 to 70,000 members annually. The liberal West Coast and Northeast regions that are most adamant about "full inclusion" are the fastest declining. This year, the whole West Coast and Rocky Mountain region will have only 32 delegates, or only about 3 percent of the total. The Democratic Republic of the Congo will by contrast send 136. African churches gained more than 1 million members since the last General Conference, while the U.S. church lost about 300,000.

At over 12 million members and fast approaching 13 million, the United Methodist Church is now possibly the ninth largest denomination in the world. And arguably it is the largest global Protestant church. Catholics number over 1 billion, the Russian Orthodox Church reputedly has 125 million,[72] the Ethiopian Church (Oriental Orthodox) has 48 million, the Church of England claims 25 million, Germany's Evangelical Church (Lutheran) reports 24 million, the Romanian Orthodox cites 23 million, the Church of Nigeria (Anglican) has 18 million, and the U.S. Southern Baptist Convention has over 16 million.

All of the larger Protestant churches are mostly national churches. In contrast to a typical Southern Baptist governing convention or a Church of England synod, United Methodism's uniquely international General Conference will sometimes appear schizoid. Nigerians will denounce homosexuality as an abomination, while U.S. transsexuals will insist on the holiness of cross dressing and sex change operations. At a pre-General Conference news briefing last week in Tampa, a liberal Minnesota bishop presided over a panel on "holy conferencing" about civil disagreement. But the panel ended with an angry lesbian activist complaining she had been denied ordination 3 times and insisting the time for dialogue was over. The time for justice is now!

The Minnesota bishop, along with the briefing program, described the chief political issues before United Methodism as anti-Israel divestment, liberalized immigration, environmentalism, and opposing the Afghanistan War, including nuclear disarmament. The General Conference will focus especially on "repentance and healing" over mistreatment of American indigenous people. One church official described how Tampa was a "deportation center" for Cherokees and other tribes during the early 19th century's "Trail of Tears." He also bemoaned how an ancient Indian mound once blocks away from the convention center had been destroyed a century ago to extend Tampa's Jackson Street, named for the president who deported eastern tribes westward.

Meanwhile, an anti-Israel caucus invited participants at the United Methodist briefing in Tampa to attend a session on divestment proposals targeting companies that profit from Israel's "occupation," such as Motorola, Caterpillar and Hewlett Packard. A divestment spokeswoman faulted "campaign donations" and "arms sales" for bolstering pro-Israel policies in the U.S. The briefing was poorly attended, but the anti-Israel divestment proposal, aimed at the church's huge pensions fund, comes from the denomination's official lobby office. United Methodism already has officially denounced the "occupation," the spokeswoman pointed out, and its bishops have opposed U.S. arms sales to Israel.

Focusing on the historic crimes of America and Western Civilization, both real and perceived, is a favorite theme for politically correct U.S. church bureaucrats. But these mostly leftist themes will not resonate with most international delegates. For Nigerians and other Africans, discussing the threat of radical Islam would be more relevant to their own current situation. For U.S. church liberals, any conversation potentially negative about aspects of even political Islam would be anathema.

When African churches soon become a majority within the once all U.S. denomination, overshadowing U.S. liberals, the chronic debate about sex will finally recede. So too will the preoccupation with U.S. political themes. The increasingly global United Methodist Church will then confront new controversies. But at least it will then reflect the concerns of millions of Christians around the world, rather than the obsessions of a cloistered, elite few in the U.S.

(This column is reprinted with the permission of The American Spectator, where it first appeared in its online edition of January 31, 2012, at Spectator. org)

Lines are being drawn, even on a global scale, whether we like it or not. While it is both sad and frightening to see so many mainline congregations in the United States and Europe depart from the faith, it is at the same time heartening to see these "churches" challenged by those within their own organizations, churches which are not afraid to speak against the darkness.

A necessary tension between two principles

There are two truths *in tension* when believers are attempting to come together and end their divisions. The apostle James said it this way: **Wisdom from above is first pure, then peaceable.**[73] In other words, in our quest for peace with one another, we must not sacrifice the purity of the truth. Compromise is not an option when it comes to the essential truths of the faith.

Earlier we mentioned that the Lord Jesus said that he did not come to bring peace, but a sword.[74] A sword? For what purpose? Is the sword to divide believers from other believers? No, Jesus never said that. The sword is to divide those who love the truth and believe the gospel from those who reject it. In that sense there are only two kinds of people in the world, those who believe the report of Jesus Christ and those who are still under the wrath of God. Consider John 3:35-36:

[35] The Father loves the Son, and has given all things into His hand. [36] He who believes in the Son has everlasting life; and he who does not believe the Son shall not see life, but the wrath of God abides on him."

That is strong language and draws a clear line. To accept these words at face value is to acknowledge that every human is in one group or the other. We either believe in the Son and have surrendered our lives to Him, or we do not believe and are lost and without hope. It is a shared faith in Jesus Christ that binds Christian believers and Christian churches to one another, but that same faith also sets us apart from the unbelieving world and all of those churches, so called, which have rejected Him.

Calls to unity

S ome churches have begun to recognize the importance of Christian unity and are making it a matter of genuine concern. Consider the following statement by the Reformed Christian Church, which is excerpted from page 193 of "*The Unauthorized Guide to Choosing a Church*" by Carmen Renee Berry. (A very worthwhile read by the way)

The Reformed Christian Church sees itself as: "*one small part of Christ's church on earth. It recognizes as fellow-Christians all people who accept the teachings of the Bible as they are summarized so beautifully in the Apostles' Creed. This includes believers from many denominations such as Roman Catholic, Orthodox, Lutheran, Baptist, Presbyterian, and Pentecostal. We may disagree with these believers on some practices or teachings. But we recognize them as brothers and sisters in Christ if they believe in God the Father, Son, and Holy Spirit, and if they confess that Jesus died for their sins, rose from the dead, and ascended into heaven.*

"*On the way to achieving unity, major differences in the perception of biblical truth must be overcome. God must be trusted to teach all of us as we engage in ecumenical dialogue and thereby to unite us through a more common understanding of* *his truth. <u>In the search for unity the biblical message must not be compromised, but the presumption of possessing the truth in all of its fullness must be guarded against.</u> Churches must seek to heal past wounds by overcoming differences with those who are closest to them. The Christian Reformed Church in North America gives high priority to relations with other Reformed churches and after that to churches of other traditions such as non-Reformed Protestant churches, the Roman Catholic Church and Orthodox churches."* (emphasis added)

Within this brief statement, several important truths are set forth quite eloquently. This statement recognizes that (a) the Reformed Church of America is but a part of the body of Christ, (b) that differences in perception of truth amongst believers exist, (c) that we must not compromise the biblical message in our search for unity, (d) that we all must guard against the presumption that we possess the truth in all its fullness, and (e) that unity will likely be achieved incrementally or step by step.

There is much wisdom in this statement. If we cannot at this time achieve or even dream of achieving real unity with the Catholic and Orthodox Churches, which doctrinally are the farthest from Protestant Christian churches, then let us believe for an end to division amongst Protestant churches. Perhaps the genuine believers from those other entities will individually be drawn to reach out and become connected to believers outside their churches, to join in genuine Christian fellowship with them, and work with them towards achieving unity within the entire body of Christ.

When our focus shifts from how right our own church is to how wonderful our Savior is, our differences begin to fade to insignificance. This must be the starting place for unity for this is the common heart that Christians from all nations and cultures share. When we come together with other genuine believers, regardless of our differing backgrounds, we find that we share certain things in common: We all believe that Jesus Christ is the incomparable Son of God, that He died for our sins and rose on the third day, and that without His death and resurrection we would all be lost in our sins.

This is the thing we all share in common. This is the heart that binds us all together. It is this shared love for the Lamb of God that makes Christian unity possible. In the Book of Revelation, John describes a scene in which many millions are saying with a loud voice,

Worthy is the Lamb who was slain
To receive power and riches and wisdom,
And strength and honor and glory and blessing!
Blessing and honor and glory and power
Be to Him who sits on the throne,
And to the Lamb, forever and ever![75]

In the final analysis, Christianity has always been about Him. It is not about us or our organizations or our structures or pet doctrines. The extent to which we recognize this reality is the extent that we will open our hearts to one another.

A nondenominational denomination

We spoke earlier of the regularity with which those leading a particular movement would organize their efforts so as to avoid starting a new denomination – and yet in spite of their noblest intentions they would become a denomination and eventually wall themselves off from other believers. Let's look at one of those for a moment. You might notice that the distinction between a denomination and a non-denomination can be, in the final analysis, a non-distinction.

There is a widespread movement commonly known as the Churches of Christ. (*Note: churches of Christ sometimes do not capitalize the word "church" in their name. I do so here to make it clear that I am speaking of a particular group. No offense or deception intended.*) Many within this movement forbid the use of musical instruments in church worship. The group is strongly anti-denomination and always has been. Consider these statements by one of its founders, Alexander Campbell:

- *"I have no idea of adding to the catalogue of new sects. I labor to see sectarianism abolished and all Christians of every name united upon the one foundation upon which the apostolic church was founded."*

- *"Dear sir, this plan of making our own nest, and fluttering over our own brood; of building our own tent, and of confining all goodness and grace to our noble selves and the "elect few" who are like us, is the quintessence of sublimated pharisaism. The old Pharisees were but babes in comparison to the modern: and the longer I live, and the more I reflect upon God and man--heaven and earth--the Bible and the world--the Redeemer and his church--the more I am assured that all sectarianism is the offspring of hell; and that all differences about words, and names, and opinions, hatched in Egypt, or Rome, or Edinburgh, are like the frolics of drunken men; and that where there is a new creature, or a society of them, with all their imperfections and frailties, and errors in sentiment, in views, and opinions, they ought to receive one another, and the strong to support the weak, and not to please themselves. To lock ourselves up in the bandbox of our own little circle; to associate with a few units, tens, or hundreds, as the pure church, as the elect, is real Protestant monkery, it is evangelical pharisaism."*

- *"I have tried the pharisaic plan, and the monastic. I was once so straight, that, like the Indian's tree, I leaned a little the other way. And however much I may be slandered now as seeking "popularity" or a popular course, I have to rejoice that to my own satisfaction, as well as to others, I proved that truth, and not popularity, was my object; for I was once so strict a Separatist that I would neither pray nor sing praises with any one who was not as perfect as I supposed myself. In this most unpopular course I persisted until I discovered the mistake, and saw that on the principle embraced in my conduct, there never could be a congregation or church upon the earth."*

It seems abundantly clear that Mr. Campbell recognized the folly of launching yet another denomination. He clearly sensed the evil of sectarianism and railed against it, even when it reared its ugly head in his own heart. I applaud his words. Nonetheless, after all Mr. Campbell's pronouncements against division and sectarianism, and after all of his efforts to prevent the Church of Christ from becoming just another denomination, even labeling their meeting places the *Church of Christ*, which seems in some ways a nearly perfect name for a Christian church, what is the end result? Is the Church of Christ a denomination? You be the judge.

There is in town after town across the United States a church calling itself the Church of Christ to the exclusion of other Christian churches within the same town. These churches distinguish themselves from other Christian churches by such doctrines as a prohibition against using musical instruments in worship services (at least some of them do) and an insistence that one is not saved, except in extreme circumstances, unless he is first baptized in water, a view shared with some other churches.

Though Churches of Christ are not denominational in the formal sense of the word, they *very much are* in so far as church unity is concerned.

It is not my intent to single out this one group in some pejorative way, but simply to illustrate a truth: A denomination is a division within the body of Christ, no matter how large or small the organization and no matter what it calls itself or how it is structured. If a doctrine or name separates one group of believers from other Christians in the same area, it is a prohibited division. In other words, a group, with a sincere heart, may call for unity and yet all the while undermine unity by its actions. Saying that you do not mean to divide believers does not mean that you are not dividing believers.

Some things really are too deep for us

Often the things which divide us are greater than our capacity to understand, but we don't realize it. They are deeper than our minds can grasp and yet we quarrel over them, not realizing that none of us truly understands them and in reality cannot. Consider the eloquent words of Charles Spurgeon, known by many as the "prince of preachers," as he ponders certain doctrines that are admittedly too deep for us. In this case, he speaks of predestination and election, which are the primary focus of Calvinism or covenant theology. (You may have to read this piece more than once, as did I, to grasp the beauty of it. It will be worth it to do so.)

"Hast thou entered into the springs of the sea?" - Job 38:16

Some things in nature must remain a mystery to the most intelligent and enterprising investigators. Human knowledge has bounds beyond which it cannot pass. Universal knowledge is for God alone. If this be so in the things which are seen and temporal, I may rest assured that it is even more so in matters spiritual and eternal. Why, then, have I been torturing my brain with speculations as to destiny and will, fixed fate, and human responsibility? These deep and dark truths I am no more able to comprehend than to find out the depth which coucheth beneath, from which old ocean draws her watery stores. Why am I so curious to know the reason of my Lord's providences, the motive of his actions, the design of his visitations? Shall I ever be able to clasp the sun in my fist, and hold the universe in my palm? yet these are as a drop of a bucket compared with the Lord my God. Let me not strive to understand the infinite, but spend my strength in love. What I cannot gain by intellect I can possess by affection, and let that suffice me. I cannot penetrate the heart of the sea, but I can enjoy the healthful breezes which sweep over its bosom, and I can sail over its blue waves with propitious winds. If I could enter the springs of the sea, the feat would serve no useful purpose either to myself or to others, it would not save the sinking bark, or give back the drowned mariner to his weeping wife and children; neither would my solving deep mysteries avail me a single whit, for the least love to God, and the simplest act of obedience to him, are better than the profoundest knowledge. My Lord, I leave the infinite to thee, and pray thee to put far from me such a love for the tree of knowledge as might keep me from the tree of life.

Would that I had read this piece and comprehended it when I was in Bible College - for there is profound wisdom in brother Spurgeon's words. It did not occur to me when I was young that there is wisdom in recognizing the honest limitations of one's ponderings, and at times more wisdom in this than in reaching some personal conclusion, which a large share of equally sincere believers will probably never embrace.

While there remains some benefit in contemplating the deeper truths of some of the weightier doctrines, it is utterly foolish to place technical points of theology, which are not essential to salvation, above the love of the brethren and the unity of the Spirit. If we love the tree of knowledge more than the tree of life we are "ever learning and never able to come to the knowledge of the truth."[76]

The Bible speaks of predestination and election, thus these matters are ripe for discussion. It might be prudent to recognize, however, that for many centuries, men of good faith and scholarly credentials have differed greatly in what these doctrines mean and how they come to bear on the fate of each individual human on this planet. Neither side suggests that any man, whether he has a free will or not, is saved by his own works of righteousness, but rather solely by the grace of God and the blood of Jesus Christ. Why then would we separate from one another over this doctrine or name our churches after it? Why insist that we are right and the other man, who believes equally in the efficacy of the blood of the Lamb, is a heretic? If there is going to be unity, there must be a recognition of our limitations, even amongst theologians.

Let's not define "denomination" too narrowly

The word *denomination* means different things to different people. In the Christian context, we tend to think of a denomination as an organization of churches with a central headquarters which owns the property of all the member churches, controls their doctrine and policies, and in some cases installs and removes local ministers as it sees fit.

However, for purposes of this study, it is not useful to define the term so narrowly. It seems more worthwhile to recognize that any church name, unique set of doctrines, or doctrinal emphasis, which has the effect of distinguishing one Christian church from other truly Christian churches in the same geographical area, in effect causes a division within the body of Christ.

If yours is a Baptist church or is called a Baptist church, whether Free Will, Southern, American, Conservative, or some other kind of Baptist, then you are setting your church apart from other Christian churches based on a name and an emphasis, (and perhaps the convention or conference with which you identify). In so doing, you are dividing the body of Christ.

This is true even though Baptist churches are strongly "anti-denominational" and believe in independent, autonomous local churches. Being nondenominational or anti-denominational is largely irrelevant for purposes of church unity. By calling yourself a Baptist, you are telling people in your area that you are not like other Christians; you're Baptists. You are saying that you are different from Presbyterians, Methodists, Lutherans, Pentecostals, and so on. By using a name to distinguish yourselves from other Christians you are dividing the body of Christ. Call yourself whatever you choose, govern yourself however you choose, but if you distinguish your church from other churches, you are a division.

A denomination of one

Even a truly independent church, which is entirely a "stand-alone" entity and does not even so much as fellowship with or share a specific doctrinal position with other churches, is for purposes of church unity, merely a denomination of one. The fact that a church does not receive marching orders from some earthly headquarters does not make it any less a division of the body of Christ.

The sin is division. Denominations are merely a more organized and conscious form of division.

Think of it this way. If all denominations disappeared tomorrow, but the local churches in a particular area continued to be separated from one another by names and doctrines that set them apart from other Christian churches, the body of Christ would still not be one. There would be neither a unity of the Spirit, nor a unity of the faith.

The world would continue to see the church as divided, which is hardly the result Jesus prayed for in John 17.

In summary, divisions are divisions, plain and simple, and unless those divisions are based upon one side's error in the area of an essential doctrine, the adherence to which would exclude it from the body of Christ, then the divisions are scripturally forbidden and grieve the heart of God.

As churches across the world begin to catch the vision for genuine church unity and give this topic the attention it deserves, let's make sure that our cries and our prayers are genuine. Let us be careful to recognize division in all its forms, including our own.

Doctrine versus Truth

Right doctrine is a beautiful thing, even if the term has been abused and denigrated by those who wrongly believe that doctrine is the cause of much of our division. Doctrine does not cause division. The word "doctrine" simply means teaching. The doctrines of Christ, for example, are simply the teachings of Christ. What kind of faith would Christians have, if we had no teachings?

The problem is not doctrine; it is our misunderstanding of what doctrine is and with our tendency to separate doctrine from its source, the Lord Jesus.

I have had the privilege of teaching several college-level *Systematic Christian Theology* courses. In the process, I have observed the regularity with which students make doctrine a set of facts about God and forget that the end purpose of right doctrine is to know God, not to learn facts about Him.

It is easy for theologians to forget that truth is not the perfectly formulated doctrinal statement. Truth is a person. Truth is the Lord Jesus Christ. He is the treasure chest from which all truth springs. As Paul told the Colossians, "In Him are hid all the treasures of wisdom and knowledge."[77] Jesus is truth personified. To know Him is to know the Truth. To not know Him is to not know the Truth.

A person can graduate from Bible College and seminary and be able to recite all of God's essential attributes and expound upon His divine nature, but none of that ensures that the person knows God.

In fact, memorizing information about God can actually be harmful, if it does not lead to knowing Him. As the proverb declares, "knowledge puffs up." Being proud or puffed up is obviously not the goal of truth. If our knowledge about God makes us proud of what we know or what we think we know, we have gained nothing.

As Paul told the Corinthians, *"…and though I have the gift of prophecy, and understand all mysteries and all knowledge… but have not love, it profits me nothing."*[78]

If the knowledge we gain serves to separate us from other believers for whom Christ died, if it causes us to quarrel with them rather than love them, then perhaps our knowledge is not truth. Even if our knowledge is factually correct, it may not be truth.

A Bible college professor told his class of young, wannabe theologians, "If you're right in your head, but you're not right in your heart, then you're wrong." It always takes both. Our heads and our hearts must come into alignment. A man with a sincere heart towards God, who neglects gaining a foundational understanding of doctrine, is highly vulnerable to deception and can be led far off track. A man who gains knowledge of foundational doctrines but does not come to know God in his heart, may have an empty religion and never know the God he has studied.

Right doctrine is drawn from the Word of God, from scriptures which can be read and seen, but ultimately we must find that Jesus Christ is the Word of God. Think about that fact for a moment in the context of the body of Christ. If our doctrine divides us from other believers who are part of that same body, then our doctrine has somehow been moved to a place above the purposes of God, a place too high. If doctrine stands in a place in our hearts above the purposes of God, then doctrine has become an idol to us.

Should right doctrine separate the church from false churches and cults? Yes, of course. Should right doctrine separate us from churches that have abandoned the faith and rejected the truth? Yes. But should our perception of right doctrine cause genuine believers to separate from one another to the extent that they can no longer worship and pray together? The answer is emphatically, "No!" *His truth will not tear apart His own body.*

For that reason, we cannot continue to allow disputes over non-essential issues to separate us. Disagreements over nonessential matters must be resolved or they must be tabled. This may be a difficult pill to swallow. It may require us to take a pet doctrine, about which we feel very strongly and for which we have fought valiantly, and label it "nonessential."

If the Spirit of Christ dwells in a person, then he or she is our brother or sister in the Lord. We are joint heirs together with them and are cleansed by the same blood. That being the case, we are forbidden to break fellowship with them. We may disagree from time to time, as even the apostles did, but we cannot break fellowship with them.

The believers who attend other churches are owed the same love and loyalty as the people who go to our own church, because they have embraced the same Truth as we have. Let's say that again, slowly. Believers who attend other churches are owed the same love and loyalty as the people who go to our own church.

This must be true. We are not and cannot be complete without them. We literally cannot function perfectly as members of the body of Christ without them. We cannot fully accomplish the will of God in our communities without them. This is a powerful truth. We literally fail in our outreach to our city to the extent to which we are not connected to all of the other believers in our city. When we fully grasp this reality and act on it, we will change the world.

Let's bring this closer to home. Those other folks may speak in tongues and you don't. They may believe in eternal security and you don't. They may sing old hymns, and you don't. They may wear casual clothes to church, and you don't. But none of these things matters in so far as Christian love and unity are concerned.

It's the connection that is missing

You don't have to be a Methodist or a Presbyterian to be saved. You have to believe that Jesus Christ is the Son of God, that His death atoned for your sin, and that He rose from the grave for your justification. If you and I have declared from a sincere heart that He is our Lord and Savior and have submitted our lives to His lordship, then we are part of the same body. We may not be connected, and because we are not connected we may not be functioning as a body, but we are part of the same body. It is the connection that is lacking. There can be no unity and no completion without connection. This may offend your spirit of rugged individualism. It may contradict your belief that you are a "rock" or an "island," and that all you need is Christ, just you and Jesus; nonetheless it is so.

The indispensible role of humility

Paul told the Ephesians how they should approach the unity of the faith. He told them that they were to endeavor to keep the unity of the Spirit in the bond of peace and that they were to do so **"with all lowliness and gentleness, with longsuffering bearing with one another."**[79] We have not always done this.

Imagine a serious doctrinal discussion between a Calvinist and an Arminian with both sides endeavoring to keep the unity of the faith in the bond of peace and doing so with all lowliness and gentleness towards one another, as Paul described. The goal of the discussion would not be to prove that you were right and the other side wrong. Pride would play no role. Lowliness and gentleness would rule. The doctrine under discussion would not be made to sound more important than it is. No one would pretend that there are no weaknesses in his arguments and no merit to the other person's. Both sides would try to understand the other's perspective. Both would acknowledge the validity of any point the other side made.

Even if neither side persuaded the other, both would embrace afterwards in a spirit of brotherly love and go away from the discussion with a better understanding than before. No division would result from the discussion. Unity would not be broken.

Now change the topic of the discussion from Calvinism to say speaking in tongues or the operation of the gifts of the Spirit in the modern day church. How about women preachers or infant baptism? How about apostolic succession or the meaning or frequency of communion? Do you see how Paul's admonition regarding lowliness and gentleness could be applied to all such debates? The approach Paul set forth works for all of them.

Now, however, exchange the nonessential doctrine for an essential one, such as whether Jesus bodily rose from the dead. The same process doesn't work, does it? Unless the forum is a mock debate, a discussion regarding an essential doctrine cannot be approached in the same manner, because the two sides are not on the same team. If one side rejects the resurrection or deity of Christ, essential truths clearly set forth in Scripture, then that side is not Christian. The discussion cannot start from the same place, because one side believes something that is spiritually fatal, something that makes it non-Christian. In this case, the doctrine that separates the two sides, in fact, should separate them. There are biblical grounds for separation, because one side's view puts it outside the body of Christ.

This chapter is not meant to be overly or unnecessarily mystical. It is meant to convey one cohesive principle: Our relationship with Christ is powerfully tied to our relationship with other believers and His truth will never separate us from one another.

The apostle John asked, **"If a man says, I love God, and hates his brother, he is a liar: for he that loves not his brother whom he has seen, how can he love God whom he has not seen?"**[80] John was saying something powerful, but it is not easily grasped. As a kid, my response to that passage was, "God, that's kind of a dumb question. It's easy to love you, 'cause you haven't done anything to tick me off and that guy, whom I can see, has."

Childhood memories aside, John was making a serious point. We can't love God and hate our brother. When we hate our brother for whom Christ died, we are not loving God. Let's apply John's words to the issue of church unity. Do you think the Lord would understand if we said, "I love you God, but I want nothing to do with those Baptists and Lutherans? I don't like the way they do things."

How much love is enough?

Two children were quarreling. Mom interrupted their tussle and told them to stop fighting. "You kids, stop fighting, right now. Brothers and sisters are not supposed to fight. You are supposed to love one another. The Bible says so. Susie, you love your brother Tommy, don't you?"

Without a moment's hesitation, Suzie looked up at her mother with an angelic face and replied, ever so innocently, "Yes, Mommy, I love Tommy. I love him just enough to get to heaven."

"Just enough to get to heaven". Hmmm, I wonder how much that might be. Are we trying to love Christians from those other denominations *just enough to get to heaven*, as if there is some bare minimum that will get us by? But, what if there is no such standard? What if Christ's standard is that we love them so much that the world will see that love and know immediately that we are His disciples, and in fact, be so impressed with our love and perfect oneness that they cannot help but know that Jesus really was sent by the Father?

If that is indeed the standard, then I am afraid we have fallen far short of it. I don't think the world looks at all of our divisions, all our different names and all those buildings where we worship separately - and concludes that we have great love for one another.

Truth is a Person and it is around that Person that we must unite. We must not rally around pet doctrines or talented, charismatic men or different forms of church government. We must unite around the Son of God. It is all about Him and nothing else. He alone is worthy for He alone shed His blood to redeem us out of every kindred, tribe, tongue, and nation in the earth. If we love the Truth, then we will love all those whom He loves.

Let us remember that lowliness is the key ingredient to the unity of the faith. It is lowliness or genuine humility that attracts God. It brings Him near. The Lord draws nigh to the humble as surely as He resists the proud. This is likely why Paul prefaces his admonition for us to "keep the unity of the faith in the bond of peace" with his exhortation towards lowliness. Lowliness is the nature of Christ. It is how He came. It is how He lived.

Some of the worst sermons ever preached

S ometimes, the worst sermons are preached from the pulpits of Bible-believing churches. Sometimes they are hand delivered in books or brochures, the kind we hand out to people who visit our churches and show an interest in learning more about us. Wherever and however they are delivered, these sermons are always bad.

The sermons I am speaking of are pleasing to our ears. We like to hear them. They make sense to us. They make us feel special, as if we are part of an inner circle, perhaps closer to God than other Christians.

The faithful love these sermons and nod their heads in approval, especially the "old timers." Sometimes, we formalize them and put them into a curriculum so we can teach them to all of our new members. We deliver them to our children so they can learn of their heritage, and it makes us proud when they do.

So, what are these sermons that are always bad, should never be preached, and yet we delight to hear them? They are sermons about our denomination, our conference, or our synod and why it is the right or best one. You might be surprised to know how often such sermons are preached or how frequently parts of them are inserted into other messages.

Sometimes they have titles like this: *Why I am a member of the Assemblies of God. Why I am a Missouri Synod Lutheran. Why I am a Southern Baptist or an American Baptist or a member of the Church of Christ, et cetera.* These are not sermons about why I am Christian, but why I am a certain brand or kind of Christian.

These sermons emphasize our differences and explain to the faithful what it is that sets our group apart from (by which we really mean *above*) other Christians. These are sermons that make us proud of our special division of Christianity. They teach us not to root for the body of Christ, but for the home team, our segment of the body of Christ.

A large percentage of the Christians outside our group probably would not agree with all that is said in these sermons, but why fret that? After all, we are only delivering them to the troops. They are our "rallying cry," not rallying us to celebrate the church of Jesus Christ, but to remain faithful to our brand name.

There is harm here. Damage is being done. Our hearts swell with pride because these sermons make us feel safe and comfortable with our current affiliation. They confirm the things we already know and make us more sure of them. But there is a secret that few of us will admit. We would not dare say some of these things in front of an audience of scholars from other denominations, because they might be able to respond to the contrary with just as much eloquence and persuasiveness. Maybe even more.

Sometimes in these messages, we speak derogatorily about churches where the music is, in our opinion, too loud or too lively, where they don't sing the old hymns, the ones Luther or Wesley wrote. These are the sermons where we criticize those other churches where they don't speak in tongues, like we do, or where they do, but in our opinion, shouldn't; where we boast of how orderly our services are and how wrong it is for preachers to walk around the front of the church when they preach and not stand staunchly behind the lectern like we do in *our* church.

These sermons are about the idiosyncrasies which make our group *uniquely us*; the things we believe and do that other churches do not see quite the same way.

Sermons that cause division

The problem with these sermons and the reason they are of the worst sort, is that they reinforce the divisions that exist among Bible-believing Christian churches. More than anything else, they are designed to keep our sheep in our fold lest they stray off and go to some *inferior* church. These sermons ensure that everyone knows that we are the right church and that they are lucky to have found us.

These sermons do not further the cause of unity; they engender strife. They arouse pride in our hearts, a kind of false pride that is based on nothing that is really all that important, or in some cases, not all that defensible.

Perhaps there is nothing wrong with differences of opinion over the meaning of a particular passage of Scripture or some fringe doctrine, but should we build churches around such things? Should we emphasize them and set our members apart from the members of other churches based on controversial or debatable issues? When we do this, we make our church about something other than the Gospel of Jesus Christ.

There is so much that all Christians have in common. Teachings which emphasize differences and prioritize issues that many equally astute scholars dispute, serve only to divide. Controversial subjects may tickle our ears and excite our audiences, but keep in mind that each time we indulge ourselves and our home team audience, we are laying another brick on the wall that separates them, and us, from the rest of the body of Christ. We are laying bricks and carefully mortaring them into place.

The messages I am speaking of prepare our people to go to war, not with the enemy, not with darkness, but with other Christians. Maybe I am overstating this, but I have come to believe that we Christians like to go to war against one another. We love the wind in our sails. We love to be blown about from battle to battle, guns blazing at those Calvinists or tongue speakers or those who believe in the rapture, or don't. Perhaps, it is time to aim our cannons elsewhere.

The title of this chapter may be too strong. Maybe these sermons are not the worst and not as bad as the ravings of some dark cultist or the lies of the confused atheist. But then again, eternity may show that these sermons really were the worst.

In closing out this topic, I will refer readers to a couple of examples of this type of sermon. There are many and it is not my purpose to pick on the two to which I refer you. For example, you can pick up a copy of "Why I Am a Member of the Church of Christ," by Leroy Brownlow. This book illustrates the point I am trying to make. As an alternative, you can find online the message "Concerning the Name Lutheran," by C.F.W. Walther. The gist of Mr. Walther's message is that the Lutheran Church names itself Lutheran, in spite of Luther's plea not to name the church after him, because the Lutheran Church is the one "true church" and is not like all those sects such as the Methodists, the Baptists, et cetera, which do not have the true sacraments and pure message that Luther revealed.

Walther's final conclusion is that the Lutheran Church needs its name to make it clear that the Lutheran Church is not merely Protestant, evangelical, or Christian.

Perhaps the thing that impresses me most about this message is the "logic' Mr. Walther uses to justify retaining the Lutheran name, even though Luther asked that his followers simply be called Christians, not Lutherans, and even though the apostle Paul rebuked the Corinthians for the same divisive mentality when they rallied behind the names of Apollos, Cephas, and Paul.

Here is Luther's humble but eloquent plea to his followers, which Mr. Walther talks his way around:

"I ask that my name be left silent and people not call themselves Lutheran, but rather Christians. Who is Luther? The doctrine is not mine. I have been crucified for no one. St. Paul in 1 Cor. 3:4-5 would not suffer that the Christians should call themselves of Paul or of Peter, but Christian. How should I, a poor stinking bag of worms, become so that the children of Christ are named with my unholy name? It should not be dear friends. **Let us extinguish all factious names and be called Christians whose doctrine we have.** *The pope's men rightly have a factious name because they are not satisfied with the doctrine and name of Christ and want to be with the pope, who is their master. I*

have not been and will not be a master. Along with the church I have the one general teaching of Christ who alone is our master. Matt. 23:8."

We must long for the day when believers everywhere will be content to be known only as "Christians." In the meanwhile, let us not point our finger at any one denomination for this fault. There has been no shortage of messages similar to the ones to which I have referred you. It is a common and perhaps universal reflex for churches to believe that they are the best or the true or the only. It is past time, however, that we recognized that this reflex finds it root in our carnality.

The Fractured Church – chapter 23

The Catholic challenge

(Author's note: In order to demonstrate the extent of the challenge the Catholic Church poses to Christian unity, I have set forth in this chapter some of the extra-biblical doctrines the Catholic Church espouses, as well as bold statements the Catholic Church has made regarding its leader, the pope. If this chapter comes across as anti-Catholic, that would be unfortunate. I have many Catholic friends and some of them are committed believers. However, there is simply no way to approach this issue honestly other than head on. There are serious doctrinal differences between Catholics and most Protestants; there is no avoiding that fact. Forgive me, if this part of our study is too heavy or disconcerting for you.)

The Roman Catholic Church is one of the largest churches in the world, boasting a worldwide membership approaching one billion adherents. Only God knows for sure, but there are likely millions of true believers within the ranks of Roman Catholicism. Unfortunately, when contemplating church unity, the Catholic Church poses what may be our most serious challenge.

If one were to list the essential doctrines that a person must believe to be saved, it would appear, at least on the surface, that Catholics are not all that far apart from other Christians. Catholics believe that Jesus is the Son of God, that He died for our sins and rose on the third day, and unlike churches that are clearly outside the body of Christ, Catholics mean by those words pretty much the same thing other Christians mean, though some would argue otherwise.

But here's a the larger problem: In addition to the essential doctrines of Christianity, the Catholic Church also advances other concepts that most Protestants do not and cannot accept, doctrines and practices the Catholic Church added to the Gospel without biblical authority. We are speaking of such doctrines as papal infallibility, the sinlessness of Mary, praying to Mary and deceased "saints," the existence of purgatory, the doctrine of transubstantiation, the confessional booth, mandatory celibacy for priests, the veneration of relics, and the addition of a dozen apocryphal books to the Bible.

There is also some debate regarding the role the Catholic Church affords the Old Testament law and human works in the plan of salvation. The Catholic Church does not accept the doctrine that one can be saved merely by having faith in the death and resurrection of the Son of God. In fact, the Catholic Church goes so far as to damn for eternity those who teach this doctrine,[81] which of course includes tens of millions of Protestant believers.

Here is our dilemma: There are essential doctrines a person must believe to be a Christian, and we have discussed those in some detail already. But, can a person believe those things and add to them all of the extra-biblical things the Catholic Church teaches – and still be a Christian? That determination is well above my pay-grade. Some of the more extreme Catholic teachings regarding Mary, the mother of Jesus, and the role and identity of the pope as the "vicar of Christ" border on sacrilege. How does one know whether believing these extra doctrines *crosses the line into another gospel*? This is not an easy question and the possible ramifications of any answer could be staggering.

Does the Catholic doctrine of Mary contradict Scripture?

Catholic teachings regarding the Virgin Mary are extensive and detailed. It is possible that one cannot accept those teachings and believe the Bible at the same time, at least not without applying some fairly strained interpretations to certain passages of Scripture.

For example, two passages in the Gospels seem to state clearly that Mary had other children and thus Jesus had brothers and sisters. The Catholic Church denies this and insists that Mary remained a virgin all of her life. Consider this passage in Matthew 13:

> [54] When He had come to His own country, He taught them in their synagogue, so that they were astonished and said, "Where did this *Man* get this wisdom and *these* mighty works? [55] Is this not the carpenter's son? Is not His mother called Mary? **And His brothers James, Joses, Simon, and Judas? [56] And His sisters**, are they not all with us? Where then did this *Man* get all these things?" [57] So they were offended at Him.

Matthew's Gospel does not add any qualifiers or suggest that these other children were not Mary's or were perhaps Joseph's children by a previous marriage. Writing under the inspiration of the Holy Spirit, Matthew left readers with a pretty clear impression that Mary had other children besides Jesus. Matthew named four brothers and added to his account that there were at least two sisters.

Now, Mary was a blessed woman. Her story is both beautiful and inspiring, but her place in the gospel narratives is rather limited. Nothing suggests that Mary should have the exalted role the Catholic Church affords her. Bear in mind that it did not have to be this way. There were opportunities for Jesus and the writers of the New Testament to give Mary a more prominent role, but when given those opportunities, they declined. Consider this exchange and make note of what Jesus did *not* say about Mary:

> [46] *While He was still talking to the multitudes, behold, His mother and brothers stood outside, seeking to speak with Him.* [47] *Then one said to Him, "Look, Your mother and Your brothers are standing outside, seeking to speak with You."* [48] *But He answered and said to the one who told Him, "Who is My mother and who are My brothers?"* [49] *And He stretched out His hand toward His disciples and said, "Here are My mother and My brothers!* [50] *For whoever does the will of My Father in heaven is My brother and sister and mother."*[82] *(NKJV)*

271

Jesus passed up a perfect opportunity to lift Mary to a place of prominence. He could have had her ushered in with pomp and circumstance and explained to everyone the exalted position she was to hold in the hearts of all of his followers. Instead of doing so, Jesus played down his mother's role.

There is another "Mary doctrine" that appears to contradict clear statements in Scripture. The Catholic Church teaches the "perpetual sinlessness" of Mary; not only that she remained a virgin all her life but that she, like her Son, was born of *immaculate conception*. Regarding this matter, the Catholic catechism reads:

> *#491 "...The most Blessed Virgin Mary was, **from the first moment of her conception**, by a singular grace and privilege of almighty God and by virtue of the merits of Jesus Christ, Saviour of the human race, **preserved immune from all stain of original sin**."*

To make matters worse, when the doctrine of *Mary's immaculate conception* was declared by Pope Pius IX in 1854, it was accompanied by a declaration that Christians were required to believe it or they were *shipwreck and condemned*. As you may know, the Bible teaches that *all* have sinned and come short of the glory of God,[83] and yet Pope Pius IX declared that one cannot be a Christian without believing that Mary was born sinless and never sinned during her entire life. There is also the fact that Mary herself said, "My spirit has rejoiced in God my Savior." Apparently, Mary had reason to believe that she needed a Savior.[84]

In 1950, the Catholic Church declared that Mary had been *bodily assumed* up to heaven where as the "mother of God" she reigns as the *"Queen of Heaven."* This pronouncement led to a battle even among Catholics. One prominent theologian was excommunicated for rejecting this new doctrine. Other prominent Catholics suggested at the time that Pope Pius IX was "mad" for coming up with it.

Many of the Catholic Church's teachings regarding Mary were developed at least a century after the Gospel era and most came along several centuries later. The troublesome question is, why? Why did Catholic theologians find it so important to formulate and advance doctrines for which there is no clear biblical basis? Why exalt the mother of Jesus to a place nowhere found in the Bible? Why did they consider it demeaning or somehow *defiling* for the mother of Jesus to have had an intimate relationship with her legitimate husband and bear him children? There is nothing sinful in such actions.

One might be willing to overlook some of the Mary doctrines, but the Catholic Church's decision to make these extra-biblical doctrines *essential to salvation* creates what may be an insurmountable obstacle to doctrinal unity with most Protestants. Other than some Lutheran and Anglican churches, most Protestants do not ascribe to the Catholic Church's doctrines of Mary. According to a strict interpretation of Catholic teachings, these other Protestants cannot be Christians.[85]

Perhaps Catholics and Protestants cannot work out their differences

Your first response to this entire discussion might be, "If we are going to have unity, we will just have to work these things out with the Catholics. Perhaps we can find some middle ground. Maybe Catholics can be shown, from the Scriptures, where they have gone astray." That would make sense if the Catholic Church could be persuaded by passages from the Bible, but it can't. The Catholic Church believes it has the authority to overrule the Bible and even add to it additional, infallible revelations.

Protestants, as a general rule, attempt to address doctrinal differences by appealing to the Scriptures in an attempt to determine what God has said about a subject. For most Protestant churches, the Bible is the rule book; it is the final authority and where it speaks clearly, it ends all debate.

Unfortunately, Protestants cannot simply appeal to the Bible when attempting to resolve a doctrinal dispute with the Catholic Church, because Catholics have three sources of authority, not just one. Catholics appeal to (a) the Bible, (b) the allegedly infallible utterances of Catholic popes, and (c) the long standing traditions of the church. These three are thought to be of equal authority. There are far-reaching ramifications of holding to a triumvirate system for determining right doctrine, rather than a single source of authority. If a pope speaks in his official capacity, even if there is no basis in Scripture for his words, his decrees are deemed to be equal in authority to anything the Bible says regarding the same subject, *even if the pope's words contradict the Scriptures.* Infallibility is an ongoing process for Catholics, as successive popes continue to make new, "inspired" pronunciations.

It's not hard to see why papal infallibility is a problem for Protestants, who generally believe that infallibility ended when the last book of the New Testament was completed.

The Catholic Church sees itself as incapable of error

You might ask, why does the Roman Catholic Church claim perpetual infallibility, when other churches do not? The answer lies in the way the Catholic Church sees itself. The Catholic Church sees itself as the true "bride of Christ," and as Christ's bride, the Catholic Church and only the Catholic Church possesses the authority to speak "in Christ's stead" while He is physically absent. As we shall see in a moment, it is the position of the Catholic Church that it is literally incapable of error. The very fact that it does a thing makes it "right."

Of course, Protestants hotly dispute this claim, but it is why the head of the Roman Catholic Church bears the title of the "Vicar of Christ," a title supposedly granting the pope the sole authority to speak infallibly *for Christ* (or in His place). To Catholics, when the pope speaks in his official capacity, ex cathedra, Christ speaks. In a sense, this doctrine gives the Catholic Church a blank check to say and do whatever it wishes and not be constrained, even by the words of Scripture.

The air of infallibility also encompasses Catholic traditions. To Catholics, the traditions of the Church are on par with papal infallibility. If the Catholic Church is incapable of error, as it claims, then everything it has done is right and authoritative. Most Protestants place less value on tradition. Jesus told the rulers of Judaism, *"By your traditions, you have made the word of God of no effect."*[86]

Those were strong words and suggested that the priests and scribes had added so many things to the Scriptures that they had effectively rendered the them meaningless. In spite of this warning, the Catholic Church ascribes great authority to its traditions.

So, you can see the problem. When Protestants appeal to the Bible in a dispute with the Catholic Church, the Catholic side of the discussion simply responds, *"Yes, but that's not the way we do it, and we are incapable of error."* How does one counter that position? If two sides of an argument cannot agree on the authority from which a point of contention might be resolved, how do they even begin to unravel their differences? Again, whether the issue is papal authority or the authority of church traditions, the authority issue forms what is perhaps an insurmountable wall between Catholics and Protestants.

Problems with the doctrine of papal infallibility

First, from a historical perspective the Catholic Church's claim to extra-biblical authority stands on shaky ground. No absolute or universal authority was recognized or claimed by the church at Rome or its pontiff until several hundred years after the ascension of Christ and the passing of the twelve apostles. We will have more to say about that shortly. It is also worth noting that when the apostle Paul listed the specific ministries of the church in Ephesians 4, he said nothing about the office of pope. Neither did he mention the office of cardinal or a *college of cardinals*. The Catholic Church created these offices of its own accord several centuries after the Bible had been completed.

There is also a practical problem with the papal infallibility issue: Popes have not always been the most exemplary leaders. Keep in mind that during the Middle Ages, the office of pope was at times so politically powerful that those seeking or holding the office may not have been purely motivated. In fact, at times, popes were elected and deposed like European monarchs for purely political reasons. Let me illustrate.

During one period from 1379 to 1417, there were three competing popes reigning at the same time. This embarrassing fiasco continued until the College of Cardinals finally deposed all three popes and replaced them with a fourth. If you are interested, you can perform your own research under the topic, the "Western Schism," which shows the politicization of the process of selecting popes during the period in which the French and the Italians were competing for the office.

The doctrine of papal infallibility also suffered a loss of credibility when one pope was found to be a scoundrel and was forced to resign to avoid prosecution. Another pope was widely viewed as mentally ill. But there were even more serious problems.

Blasphemy from a pope

We spoke earlier of extra-biblical Catholic doctrines that are problematic for Protestants, but there is a larger problem. Some of the historical statements popes have made about themselves and statements the Catholic Church has said about its popes make most Protestants more than a little nervous. Consider the words of Pope Boniface VIII in 1302, before he was dethroned by a French king and later died in prison.

> *"That which was spoken of Christ: 'Thou hast subdued all things under his feet' may well be verified in me, I have authority of the King of Kings. I am all in all and above all so that God Himself, and I, the vicar of God, have but one consistory and I am able to do almost all that God can do...**What therefore can you make of me BUT GOD?**"*[87]

Reading these words in context does little to soften them. Unfortunately, Boniface's statement is not an isolated perspective.

Consider the words of Gregory VII, who was elected pope in 1073:

> *"The Roman Church was founded by God alone; the Roman pope alone can with right be called universal; he alone may use the imperial insignia; his feet only shall be kissed by all princes; he may depose the emperors; he himself may be judged by no*

one; the Roman church has never erred, nor will it err in all eternity."

The pope can be judged by no man and is incapable of error? Not even the apostles of Christ claimed they were beyond correction. As we saw earlier, the apostle Paul publicly chided Peter, a fellow apostle, for blatantly hypocritical behavior. And as we know, the apostle Paul confessed that at times, *even as an apostle of Christ in the process of writing scripture,* that he was giving his own thoughts and they were not necessarily the Lord's.[88]

Ongoing animosity toward Catholicism

Over the past five centuries, many Protestant preachers have read papal proclamations regarding their unlimited authority, such as the two above, and have concluded that the Catholic pope is "the antichrist." Many Protestant teachers have called the pope the antichrist in published books and in messages that have been broadcast to millions over the airwaves.

Some of the following statements regarding popes make some Catholic defenders bristle, because they are supposedly not official Catholic doctrine. For example, Catholic Canon Law said of the Roman pontiff John XXII. ***"To believe that our Lord God the Pope has not the power to decree as he is decreed, is to be deemed heretical."***[89]

"Our Lord God the Pope?" This statement continued in Canon Law up to AD 1612 and appears to portray the pope as equal to God, if not God. The argument can be made that the Latin word *Dei* (God) was not in the official version, but appeared "in the gloss," or commentary in the margins. The problem is, the word *Dei* does appear in the text in some of the manuscripts, though not in others. Before deciding whether this lofty description of the pope represents real Catholic doctrine, it would be fair to examine other statements to see if the pope is exalted in this manner elsewhere.

(Of course, this kind of "misunderstanding" could be cleared up if the Catholic Church would simply make an official announcement that the pope is not God, is not equal to Jesus Christ, and is but a man who makes mistakes and has to seek forgiveness from time to time like all other men. After all, even the high priest in the Old Testament had to offer a sacrifice for his own sins before he dared enter the Holy of Holies.)

Whether a questionable statement about the pope was written "in the gloss" of an official Catholic proclamation or proclaimed in a formal introduction of the pope before an ecclesiastical council seems somewhat irrelevant. The issue is, who does the Catholic Church believe the pope to be? What does the Church teach its children about the pope? Rather than jump to rash conclusions, we should simply listen to what the Church itself says. Consider the following:

*"Take care that we lose not that salvation, that life and breath which thou hast given us, for thou art our shepherd, thou art our physician, thou art our governor, thou art our husbandman, thou art finally another God on earth."*⁹⁰ (Said of Pope Julius II)

"The Pope takes the place of Jesus Christ on earth...by divine right the Pope has supreme and full power in faith, in morals over each and every pastor and his flock. He is the true vicar, the head of the entire church, the father and teacher of all Christians. He is the infallible ruler, the founder of dogmas, the author of and the judge of councils; the universal ruler of truth, the arbiter of the world, the supreme judge of heaven and earth, the judge of all, being judged by no one, God himself on earth." (Quoted in the New York Catechism, this seems to be a plain spoken explanation of the identity and role of the pope, as the Catholic Church sees him. This statement also seems to contradict the New Testament teaching that Christ is the Head of the church, which is His body.)

Pope Martin V, who convened the Council of Basel in 1431, was addressed before the council as: **"The most holy and most blessed, who holds the celestial jurisdiction, who is Lord over all the earth...the anointed...the ruler of the universe, the father of kings, the Light of the World."**

During the Vatican Council, 9, in January of 1870, the statement was made of Pius IX, the longest serving pope in history (just under 32 years): **"The Pope is Christ in office, Christ in jurisdiction and power...we bow down before thy voice, O Pius, as before the** voice of Christ, the God of truth; in clinging to thee, we cling to Christ."

The following statement expresses a recurring Catholic theme, that the pope and God are of equal authority. **"Therefore the decision of the Pope and the decision of God constitute one decision....Since, therefore, an appeal is always made from an inferior judge to a superior, just as no one is greater than himself, so no appeal holds when made from the Pope to God, because there is one consistory of the Pope himself and of God Himself."**[91]

Going back to the challenge of using Scripture to challenge a Catholic doctrine, consider this claim: **"We confess that the Pope has power of changing Scripture and of adding to it, and taking from it, according to his will."**[92]

I could offer scores of additional quotations to the same effect, but these should be sufficient to make the point I must make. There are serious obstacles blocking unity between the Catholic Church and Bible-believing Protestant churches. I am persuaded that Catholics are sincere in their adoration of the pope, but it is doubtful that Protestants will ever share their enthusiasm.

The place the pope holds in the hearts and minds of devoted Catholics can be understood by considering the words inscribed in the pope's mitre, *"Vicarius Filii Dei."* This is Latin for *Vicar of the Son of God.* The practical meaning of this statement is "I, the pope of the Holy Catholic Church stand before you in the place of Jesus Christ, the Son of God, and speak infallibly on His behalf while He is not present." Catholics believe the pope speaks for God and most Protestants do not. If a Protestant believed this doctrine, he would be more a Catholic than a Protestant.

There was a time when the Bishop or Pontiff of Rome did not consider himself the head the Christian church. Consider the following statement by a Lutheran scholar, who makes the case that some Roman Pontiffs did not welcome the accolades which later Roman Pontiff's accepted:

"How glorious the name rings in the time of the Roman bishop Gregory the Great, who completely rejected the title of the universal bishop of Christianity. Gregory wrote to Eulogius, bishop of Alexandria among other things:

"You allowed a haughty designation in the title of your letter in that you grant me the title of the universal pope. I ask that hence forth you do no such thing." (L. VIII. ep. 30).

In another place this Roman bishop (who died in 604 AD) wrote that *until his time no Roman bishops had been willing to carry this title for fear that the true faith would be lost and a bishop would become the forerunner of the antichrist."*[93]

Gregory the Great is also quoted as saying to Mauricius Augustus:

"... I pray your Imperial Piety to observe that there are some frivolous things that are inoffensive, but also some others that are very hurtful. When Antichrist shall come and call himself God it will be in itself a perfectly frivolous thing, but a very pernicious one. If we only choose to consider the number of syllables in this word, we find but two [de-us]; but if we conceive the weight of iniquity of this title, we shall find it enormous. I SAY IT WITHOUT THE LEAST HESITA-TION, WHOEVER CALLS HIMSELF THE UNIVERSAL BISHOP, OR DESIRES THIS TITLE, IS, BY HIS PRIDE, THE PRECURSOR OF ANTICHRIST, because he thus attempts to raise himself above the others. The error into which he falls springs from pride equal to that of Antichrist; for as that Wicked One wished to be regarded as exalted above other men, like a god, so likewise whoever would be called sole bishop exalteth himself above others...." (Bk VII Ep 35, Eerdmans p 226 col 1 mid)

So you see, for several centuries, bishops of the Roman Church rejected the title of pope or universal bishop, *"lest the title make them a forerunner of the antichrist."* Obviously, at some point after the sixth century the bishop of Rome came to be seen as the universal and supreme head of the church, and that view has held ever since.

Consider this 1995 newspaper story regarding Pope John Paul, who was speaking on church unity:

*"Pope John Paul II said yesterday that he is willing to seek agreement with other Christian denominations on the future role of the papacy. The pope made his offer in a 115-page encyclical, 'That They All May Be One,' which is dedicated to the search for unity among Christian churches that split from each other during the past thousand years...**The pope made clear he would not accept a symbolic papacy without teeth and that Rome would have to hold the primary place among Christians. He also said a pope should have the authority to make infallible declarations regarding the basic tenets of faith.**"* [San Francisco Chronicle, 5/31/95]

In other words, Rome would like to have unity with other Christians, but that unity must be based on a recognition that the Vatican is the center of Christianity and that the pope's doctrinal declarations remain infallible. John Paul II's words could reasonably be viewed as more of an ultimatum to Protestants than an olive branch.

Submit to the pope or be lost

This is the place where attempts at unity between Catholics and Protestants usually conclude and the two sides come to a stalemate. Catholics will not abandon their doctrine of papal infallibility because that doctrine defines them and makes them the mother church and the supreme spiritual authority in all the earth. Protestants, on the other hand, cannot embrace the notion of any one man having such authority.

Sometimes, when Protestants (and even other Catholics) suggest that the Catholic view of the pope might be sacrilegious, they are accused of Catholic bashing. This is a sensitive area, so I feel compelled to offer two more statements, which appear to put the shoe on the other foot. You decide.

"Those who are obstinate toward the authority of the Roman Pontiff cannot obtain eternal salvation."[94] Pope Pius IX

No salvation unless you submit to the pope? Does that mean all Protestants are lost? If that's what the Catholic Church teaches, what does it think of all of those Protestants who believe that Jesus Christ is the Son of God, the virgin born Savior of mankind, who died on the cross to pay for our sins and then rose from the dead three days later? Apparently they are all lost souls. Weigh Pius's words in conjunction with the following statement by another pope:

"Urged by faith, we are obliged to believe and to maintain that the Church is one, holy, catholic, and also apostolic. We believe in her firmly and we confess with simplicity that outside of her there is neither salvation nor the remission of sins...There had been at the time of the deluge only one ark of Noah, prefiguring the one Church, which ark, having been finished to a single cubit, had only one pilot and guide, i.e., Noah, and we read that, outside of this ark, all that subsisted on the earth was destroyed....Furthermore, we declare, we proclaim, we define that it is absolutely necessary for salvation that every human creature be subject to the Roman Pontiff."[95] Pope Boniface VIII

These two statements, and there are many more like them, suggest that the Catholic Church places no value on the baptism and confession of faith of a non-Catholic, but condemns them forever along with all of those who reject Christ.

Some movement among the priesthood

Before we give up and walk away from the notion of any unity whatsoever with Catholics, let's explore another possibility, the possibility that some Catholics may move away from their church's hard line doctrines and its claim to exclusivity.

Lately, some Catholics priests and theologians have attempted to put a less radical spin on the more extreme Catholic positions. However, to do this they have had to ignore the actual statements which their own popes and various Catholic Church councils have made. Some are apparently willing to do that. The fact that some members of the Catholic clergy are attempting to bring Catholic teachings closer to the Christian mainstream is encouraging. It proves that there are Catholics who agree that even the Catholic Church should not contradict the Holy Scriptures, the Word of God. How many Catholic officials are of this persuasion and how far are they willing to go? Only God knows.

Vatican II, progress for Catholics?

Historically, the Catholic Church's claim that there can be no salvation outside its sphere has meant that a person was either baptized a Catholic or he or she was ultimately going to end up in hell. More recently, there has been at least the suggestion that the Church's current interpretation of this doctrine might be slightly less exclusive.

Since Vatican II, which was a Catholic Church council that ended in the mid 1960s, the Roman Catholic Church has seemed more open and respectful of non-Catholic believers.[96] The presiding pope[97] set these four purposes for the Vatican II Council:

- to more fully define the nature of the church and the role of the bishop;
- to renew the church;
- to restore unity among all Christians, *including seeking pardon for Catholic contributions to separation*;
- and to start a dialogue with the contemporary world.

The clause, *"seeking pardon for Catholic contributions to separation,"* sounds almost repentant and could represent a possible step in the right direction (depending of course on its meaning). Pay special attention to the last sentence of the following statement, which came out of Vatican II:

In its first chapter, titled *"The Mystery of the Church,"* is the famous statement that "the sole Church of Christ which in the

Creed we profess to be one, holy, catholic and apostolic, which our Saviour, after His Resurrection, commissioned Peter to shepherd, and him and the other apostles to extend and direct with authority, which He erected for all ages as 'the pillar and mainstay of the truth.' This Church, constituted and organized as a society in the present world, subsists in the Catholic Church, which is governed by the successor of Peter and by the bishops in communion with him" (Lumen Gentium, 8). The document immediately adds: **"Nevertheless, many elements of sanctification and of truth are found outside its visible confines."** (emphasis added)

From a historical perspective, that last sentence seems to be a huge step for the Catholic Church to take. It does not mean that the Catholic Church recognizes the right of other churches to exist. It is more of a recognition, of sorts, that other churches have taken things, which from the Catholic perspective, belong "inside the Catholic box," and used those things to bring grace to people *outside the box*. From the Catholic Church's perspective, Christians outside the Catholic Church belong inside the Catholic Church and should come home to the pope and recognize his exclusive authority to speak for Jesus Christ. The admission that there are "elements of sanctification and truth" outside its visible confines appears to be a break from the harder line of prior centuries.

Ongoing ramifications of the Council of Trent

However, even with Vatican II's perceived softening, there is a huge problem that cannot be easily dismissed. In response to the Protestant Reformation, the Catholic Church convened the Council of Trent in 1545, which continued for eighteen years. This was only a few decades after the Lutherans broke away, the Church of England left the fold, and John Calvin announced his new "reformed theology." With that backdrop in mind, the Council of Trent concluded with some extremely harsh pronunciations against non-Catholic or Protestant doctrines. Trent may have been a long time ago, but here's the problem: Trent's conclusions have never been rescinded and thus remain official Catholic doctrine. **In fact, every signer of Vatican II in the 1960's was required to reaffirm fully all of the findings the Council of Trent made in the sixteenth century.** This is no small matter.

Trent anathemized (cursed and condemned to hell) anyone who believes in salvation based solely on faith in Jesus Christ, anyone who believes that keeping the Old Testament law is not part of the process of salvation, anyone who says the Bible is the only source of authority, anyone who rejects the 12 apocryphal books, anyone who believes in re-baptizing adults, anyone who believes that the communion bread and wine are symbols and not the true body and blood of Jesus, and anyone who says it is a deception to pray to the saints and ask them to intercede on behalf of the one offering the prayer.

The findings of the Council of Trent are quite lengthy, but they reaffirm most of the extra-biblical Catholic doctrines that led to the Protestant Reformation, including the doctrine of indulgences (though under Trent they could no longer be sold) and the existence of purgatory. The council also cursed most of the doctrines upon which the reformation was built, and then in some detail condemned the basic tenets of Calvinism, which was a very new movement at the time. (A quick perusal of the findings of Trent makes it abundantly clear that Martin Luther and John Calvin had made Rome's "most wanted" list.)

Three possibilities

All of this background information is offered simply to demonstrate the challenge the Catholic Church poses in regard to unity and to make readers aware that the wall of separation is indeed high. All things considered, if there is going to be a solution and any unity achieved, it may boil down to three basic alternatives:

First, the Catholic Church could drop its claim to be the only true church, drop its claim to papal infallibility and all of its uniquely Catholic doctrines and practices, and in so doing open the door to a truly shared faith with other Christians. While possible, at this juncture, this is almost inconceivable.

Second, Protestants could lay down their Bibles and embrace the motherhood of the Catholic Church, the doctrine of papal infallibility, and return to the Catholic Church and embrace all of its extra-biblical doctrines. This possibility seems equally unlikely.

Third, some Catholic believers might leave the Catholic Church when they see genuine, widespread unity occurring among Protestant churches and be joined with the body of Christ as it will exist absent all of the denominational ties and labels.

Some personal experience

In the late 1960s, I attempted, as a teenager, to hold countywide, interdenominational youth meetings in my corner of the Olympic Peninsula in Washington State. This had never been done in our area, but several friends of mine liked the idea and were willing to help me give it a try. We rented an auditorium and mailed letters to pastors across the county, asking them to send their youth to a countywide worship service.

The response was excellent. Hundreds of young believers from a broad cross-section of local churches showed up to worship together and listen to the teaching of the Word. The meetings were a big success.

In response to my initial mailing, I received one reply that was not so receptive. It was from the local priest of the Roman Catholic Church. His letter stated unambiguously that this was not a Catholic meeting and thus whatever we said would be preaching *another gospel*. If I remember his words correctly, he said we were all "anathema maranatha" or accursed unto the day of the Lord.

Well, we had a series of successful meetings and many young people were blessed. Catholic youth, however, were not represented. They missed out because they were not allowed to worship the Lord with non-Catholics. Now, it is possible that someone attempting a similar project today might not receive a letter like the one I received back in the 1960s. Since Vatican II, there has been at least some movement towards limited acceptance of Protestants. Has real or substantive progress been made? Was Vatican II an olive branch or was it an ultimatum? Only time will tell.

The Charismatic Renewal opened some doors

Even though the doctrinal gap remains very wide between the two camps; it may be that unity among Protestant Christians and Catholic Christians will occur only on a person to person level, but who am I to limit God. I am of the opinion that there will be unity between those Catholics who are genuine Christians and Protestant believers, but we will have to wait to learn just how the Spirit of God will bring that to pass.

The charismatic renewal, which swept through many Catholic and Protestant churches back in the sixties, has left in its wake Catholic priests who teach their congregants to read their Bible daily, pray for an hour a day, and share the gospel with their friends and neighbors. Traditionally, these are not things Catholics have been taught to do.

Some of these new priests are teaching their parishes that (a) Christians are saved by faith and not by works; (b) that Catholics are to honor Mary, but not worship her; (c) that Christ is only sacramentally present in the Eucharist (communion bread and wine), and not physically present; and (d) that the priest can hear your confessions of sin, but only God can forgive sin. Obviously, not every Catholic priest would explain Catholic doctrines as this new breed of priests has been teaching them, but the fact that some priests are is an indication that there is hope of finding common ground with some Catholic clergy and parishioners, if not with their church. I personally know several lifelong Catholics who roll their eyes at doctrines such as papal infallibility and the sinlessness of Mary. For these Catholics, the wall of separation is not so high as for others.

As a result of the charismatic renewal, some Catholics have embraced the gifts of the Spirit, including speaking in tongues, interpreting tongues, and prophesying. While some evangelicals reject such things, many charismatic Catholics are finding common ground with Pentecostals and with charismatic Christians from most of the major denominations who share their acceptance of the charismata.

Evidence that the Catholic Church might be changing

There are other signs that the Catholic Church is changing, if not doctrinally, at least in practice. Until Vatican II, the Catholic Church required that Mass be held in Latin, even though the average Catholic parishioner did not speak or understand what was being said. Vatican II changed that, and today, Catholic congregations can actually understand what their priest is saying. This reversed centuries of incomprehensible church services for millions of Catholics.

"Official" Orthodox churches keep out the competition

We have not spent a lot of time discussing the Orthodox Church, which is really thirteen separate, self-governing churches. Each of the Orthodox churches is headed by a patriarch or metropolitan. The patriarch of Constantinople (Istanbul, Turkey) is not exactly the Orthodox Church's pope, but he is recognized or honored as the universal patriarch of all thirteen Orthodox Churches.

In countries where the Orthodox Church is powerful and maintains close ties with the government, especially in the old Soviet bloc, the Orthodox Church has routinely used the power of government to exclude evangelical churches which would preach the Gospel of salvation by faith in Christ. Orthodox churches differ greatly from Protestant Churches in their concept of salvation.

> "The doctrine of justification by faith is virtually absent from the history and theology of Orthodoxy. Rather, Orthodoxy emphasizes *theosis* (literally, 'divinization'), the gradual process by which Christians become more and more like Christ."[98]

Non-Orthodox visitors should not automatically assume that they will be allowed to partake of communion in an Orthodox Church. Some churches allow those visitors who claim to be believers to partake of the sacraments, but many do not.

Many missionaries have returned from countries where one of the national Orthodox churches is dominant and have reported that they were not allowed to build a church there or even get a remodeling permit for an existing building due to the Orthodox Church's official status and cozy relationship with the state, which cooperates with the Orthodox churches "to keep out the competition."

More could be said about the unusual relationship between Orthodoxy and the government in some Communist or former Communist countries, but that subject would require another book.

Revival or persecution?

If the premise of this book is correct, church unity will come. One way or another, it will happen. Jesus prayed for it and the Scriptures appear to demand it. The question is, will true oneness come as the Holy Spirit tears down the walls that divide true Christian believers - or will the Lord allow persecution to force us into a situation where the divisions and labels become meaningless.

These seem to be the two choices: We will either have a widespread revival of repentance, perhaps at an unprecedented level, and turn away from our divisions, or the Lord will bring unity to pass another way. History has shown that the practical circumstances of everyday life can make believers less divisive.

Unity on the frontier and in the Old West

In the early 1800s, revival broke out in the West (at that time, the West was the land west of the thirteen colonies). The revival in the frontier was part of a wider movement, which is commonly referred to as the Great Awakening or by some as the Second Great Awakening.

Life was different in the frontier. People trying to carve out a life in uncivilized territory tended to reject or ignore denominational labels. Sectarian labels and rigid church creeds were seen as divisive and impractical at a time when people needed whatever community they could find, wherever they could find it. Life on the frontier was hard and towns were usually small enough that they could only support one church anyway. In that kind of situation, how important was it whether your neighbor was a Baptist or a Presbyterian? All that mattered was that he called himself a Christian, was willing to worship God with you, and would help you when you needed it - as a good Christian of any stripe should.

The harsh life of the early frontier and later in the Old West made denominationalism pretty much irrelevant to Americans who did not live on the East Coast. A town out West was happy just to have a church, and small town preachers were generally smart enough not to preach about divisive things. If one church per town was plenty, church splits were downright impractical. Neighbors needed each other and parting ways over nonessential matters was simply not an option.

This same principle has held true in places around the world where persecution has been intense. Christians hiding out from Idi Amin during his reign of terror in Uganda, or in some other Muslim country where confessing Christ was a life threatening decision, have found that they were less concerned with denominational divisions than with survival and brotherly love. It hardly makes sense to care whether the person next to you is a Baptist or a Presbyterian, if you are hiding out in the forest or in some basement because to be known as a Christian means prison or death.

Leaders of the four major groupings of illegal house churches[99] in Communist China, which represent tens of millions of Chinese Christians, have met together and hashed out a common statement of faith, establishing the basic doctrines upon which they agree. This is something not even American churches have been able or willing to do.

Persecution is a great equalizer. It focuses the mind and spirit on necessary things and sweeps aside the petty. Persecuted Christians do not have the luxury of senseless arguments. I do not know if this is what it will take for Christians everywhere to come together and put an end to all of our senseless divisions. If that is what is in store, I pray that it will not be because we refused to repent and reverse course on our own.

I am persuaded that genuine church unity *can* happen because we choose it, as an act of obedience. Empowered by the Holy Spirit, we can resolve our differences or move past them. Unity doesn't have to happen because there is no other option. In fact, voluntary unity, unity that is motivated by love for one another and a common desire to please our Lord seems more consistent with the prayer of Jesus in John 17. Unity that springs from voluntary obedience to the Lord also seems more consistent with the unity Paul spoke of in his epistles to the early churches. I believe the Lord seeks a willing people, and I believe the Holy Spirit is able to make us willing.

As Daniel prayed a prayer of repentance for the sins of Israel, sins which he had not personally committed, so must believers everywhere begin to repent with tears for the church's divisions. We must pray prayers of repentance and prayers of faith, asking the Holy Spirit to bring unity to the body of Christ, unity like no believer alive today has ever seen.

Unity may require a mighty move of the Holy Spirit

Very few Christians alive today have seen a major revival, the powerful kind that can change the course of human history. It may be that many Christians do not believe unity is possible because they have not seen or experienced the kind of move of the Holy Spirit which leaves everything in its wake forever changed.

Following are excerpts from a few church history books chronicling revivals of the past. Some of these revivals were widespread and far reaching; others were more localized. No matter. As you read through these, you may find your soul stirred. You might even find yourself longing for a move of God like you have never seen before; not merely for the excitement of it, but for the deep sense of the presence of God that accompanies it and the lasting fruits that come from it.

Many denominations criticize feelings and experiences as if they were meaningless. They are not. Feelings and experience alone are not sufficient, nor are they a substitute for the Word of God. But, we should not forget that God made us triune creatures with a body, soul, and spirit, and He sometimes moves on us in one or all of our parts. One reading of the Psalms should persuade any serious student of the Bible that David, a man "after God's heart" sought the Lord and worshipped Him with his body and his emotions, as much as with his heart and soul.

Many of the denominations that criticize the notion that we can feel and sense God, have forgotten that in the early days of their denomination, there was a great move of the Holy Spirit and their ancestors felt and were moved mightily by His divine presence. This is true of Baptists, Methodists, Congregationalists, Presbyterians and Anglicans.

Consider the following and keep in mind that many of these events occurred as part of the Great Awakening in the 1700's and early 1800's, long before the existence of modern day Pentecostalism. Perhaps the following accounts, which take us through revivals that occurred hundreds of years ago, right up to more recent times, will give you a sense of the kind of revival that we will likely need for church unity to become a reality. God has moved powerfully in the past, many times, in fact, and there is no reason to believe that He will not do so again before the end...

Before we turn to more recent times, let's remember how it all started on the Day of Pentecost. Here's a passage from the second chapter of Acts.

When the Day of Pentecost had fully come, they were all with one accord in one place. ² And suddenly there came a sound from heaven, as of a rushing mighty wind, and it filled the whole house where they were sitting. ³ Then there appeared to them divided tongues, as of fire, and one sat upon each of them. ⁴ And they were all filled with the Holy Spirit and began to speak with other tongues, as the Spirit gave them utterance.

Note the context for this move of the Holy Spirit: One hundred and twenty disciples were gathered and they were all in one accord! The writer of the Book of Acts wanted us to know that the 120 disciples were in unity when the Holy Spirit descended upon them. Shortly after the Day of Pentecost, we have the following account from Acts 4:

[31] And when they had prayed, the place where they were assembled together was shaken; and they were all filled with the Holy Spirit, and they spoke the word of God with boldness.

The Holy Spirit moved and believers were empowered to do things they might have been afraid to do the day before. From there the revival spread to the Gentiles. Here is the account of how things unfolded at the household of a man named Cornelius:

[44] While Peter was still speaking these words, the Holy Spirit fell upon all those who heard the word. [45] And those of the circumcision who believed were astonished, as many as came with Peter, because the gift of the Holy Spirit had been poured out on the Gentiles also. [46] For they heard them speak with tongues and magnify God. Then Peter answered, [47] "Can anyone forbid water, that these should not be baptized who have received the Holy Spirit just as we have?" (Acts 10 NKJV)

Okay, that's how it all started in the early church, back before the Dark Ages. You may recall that in the chapter on church history, we looked at several accounts of the move of the Spirit during the early centuries of the church. During the ensuing centuries, such moves continued to break forth here and there as hungry believers sought the presence of the Lord outside the organized church.

Let's look now at the Great Awakening which broke forth in the 1700's and 1800's in Europe, the British Isles, the North American continent, and also among the American Indians. Congregationalist Jonathan Edwards (1703-1758), one of the most famous of Protestant preachers, relayed the following regarding revivals breaking out in the 1700's:

"There was scarcely a person in the town, old or young, left unconcerned about the great things of the eternal world. The work of conversion was carried on in a most astonishing manner, and increased more and more; souls did, as it were, come by flocks to Jesus Christ. This work of God soon made a

glorious alteration in the town...the town seemed to be full of the presence of God...."

Edwards also said:

"It was a very frequent thing to see a house full of outcries, fainting, and convulsions and such like, both with distress, and also with admiration and joy."

Jonathan Edward's wife said of the revival:

"My soul was so filled with love to Christ, and love to his people, that I fainted under the intenseness of the feeling."

Modern day Pentecostals have been criticized for "emotional manifestations," but truth be told, all major revivals have had their emotional side. It is also true that those revivals which focused primarily on the emotional and physical manifestations and ignored the preaching of the Word of God, dissipated quickly.

The Great Awakening was not confined to the United States. Evangelist George Whitefield said of the conviction of the Holy Spirit, which was falling on gatherings where he was speaking in Scotland:

"Such a commotion surely never was heard of...it far out did all that I ever saw in America. For about an hour and a half there was such a weeping, so many falling into deep distress."[100]

Church historian Charles Schmitt chronicles a gathering in Nottingham, Delaware in 1740:

"Thousands cried out under conviction, almost drowning out Whitefield's voice. Men and women dropped to the ground as though dead, then revived, then dropped again, as Whitefield continued preaching."[101]

The revival swept through New York City. Regarding Methodist Francis Asbury's meetings it was written:

"The Lord appears now to be coming down on all parts of this great city...Thousands of Christians here are praying like never before. Conversions are occurring in all parts of the city. Churches daily are crowded to overflowing, and a most fixed and solemn attention is given to the...truth."

Missionary David Brainerd said of the revival he led with the American Indians in 1745.

"The power of God seemed to descend...'like a mighty rushing wind.' And with astonishing energy bore down all before it...I never saw a day like it in all respects: it was a day wherein I am persuaded that the Lord did much to destroy the kingdom of darkness among this people."

Charles Schmitt describes the great Cane Ridge revival in Bourbon County, Kentucky in 1801, as reported by James B. Finley, who was not a professed Christian at the time. (The Revival was led by Presbyterian pastor Barton W. Stone.) Finley said of the meetings:

"The noise was like the roar of Niagara...Some of the people were singing, others praying, some crying for mercy...while others shouted...At one time I saw at least five hundred, swept down in a moment as if a battery of a thousand guns had been opened upon them...I fled for the woods."

Finley fled for the woods. I can imagine that he did. What he witnessed was too much for him. Finley returned from his flight to the woods, however. He came back. He became a Christian at that very same revival and eventually became a Methodist circuit rider. He describes one revival he later led among the Wyandot Indians of Ohio:

"After singing one of their Christian songs, only as Indians can sing, they fell simultaneously upon their knees and lifted up their faces toward heaven. While they were praying the Spirit came down on them, and the power of God was manifested in the awakening and conversion of souls. The tears and groans and shouts (were) a sign that the Great Spirit was at work upon the hearts of these sons and daughters of the forest. The whole camp was in a flame of religious excitement, the Lord having taken his own work into his own hands..."[102]

Revivals during the Great Awakening were highly effective and churches grew. Church historian Richard Riss reports that during the years these revivals were occurring Methodism grew "from only 15,000 members in 1784 to slightly less than one million in 1830. Baptists doubled in number between 1802 and 1812, and the Presbyterians grew from 18,000 in 1807 to almost 250,000 in 1835."

Meanwhile, the revival continued in the British Isles. Charles Schmitt tells of a meeting that began in a Methodist chapel during the Cornwall Revival in 1814:

"...the Holy Spirit was present in such power that the (Sunday) meeting could not be closed until the following Friday morning. People came and went but the meeting continued. During the course of that week it was claimed that thousands have professed Christ."[103]

Imagine that. If our services last more than an hour or two, we start looking for the exits. But in the Cornwall revival, the Sunday service did not let out until the following Friday morning. When the Spirit of God is moving, His work continues day and night all week long.

Presbyterian Charles Finney, a controversial figure who was said to have experienced a powerful personal conversion, began revival meetings in several eastern states. Finney describes a revival he held in New York as follows:

"An awful solemnity seemed to settle upon the people; the congregation began to fall from their seats in every direction and cry for mercy. If I had a sword in each hand, I could not have cut them down as fast as they fell. I was obliged to stop preaching."

Many modern day Christians might be surprised to read of such demonstrative and seemingly emotional accounts from a period nearly a hundred years before Pentecostalism. There are, however, hundreds of such examples, many more detailed than these, which could be included here. Churches increased two-fold, ten-fold, and even a hundred-fold as the Holy Spirit moved. Millions were brought into the Kingdom and many of those converts went out and began to preach the Gospel, just as they had received it. Growth was exponential.

In the middle 1850's, the revival was so readily apparent that newspapers began covering its progress on a daily basis, stating the conversions were numbering 50,000 in a single week. Within a two year period, it was reported that two million converts were made.[104]

One person who attended a D.L. Moody meeting in 1875, said of the meeting:

"When I got to the rooms of the Young Men's Christian Association, Victoria Halls, London, I found the meeting on fire. The young men were speaking in tongues, prophesying... Moody had addressed them that afternoon..."[105]

A Presbyterian minister said of the revivals at the time:

"If in these degenerate days a new Pentecost would restore primitive faith, worship, unity, and activity, new displays of divine power might surpass those of any previous period."

We might say the same. Does it not stand to reason that the last great revival of the age would be the greatest? I am persuaded that we must begin to yearn for that. We must pray for it and believe for it. Emotions or no emotions, we must see a move of God's Spirit.

Charles Spurgeon was a man reported to have won tens of thousands of converts to the Lord. Spurgeon said of the revivals of the mid eighteen hundreds:

"The times of refreshing from the presence of the Lord have at last dawned upon our land. A spirit of prayer is visiting our churches. The first breath of the mighty rushing wind is already discerned, while on rising evangelists the tongues of fire have already descended."

It is common for churches to assume that they know how God will move. Then, when He moves in another way or moves somewhere else, they close their hearts. We must all guard against this mistake

Spurgeon warns against putting the Spirit in a box

Charles Spurgeon described revivals during the Great Awakening as occurring in different ways, some of them demonstrative and some not. He warned Christians not to miss God because He came in ways they did not expect.

"Observe how sovereign the operations of God are...He may, in one district, work a revival and persons may be stricken down and made to cry aloud, but in another place there may be crowds and yet all may be still and quiet, as though no deep excitement existed at all...He can bless as He wills. Let us not dictate to God. Many a blessing has been lost by Christians not believing it to be a blessing because it did not come in the particular shape that they had conceived to be proper and right."

The Pentecostal movement broke forth in the early 1900's. Pentecostal meetings were not dissimilar to the very demonstrative revivals which the Methodists, Presbyterians and other denominational churches had experienced during and after the Great Awakening, but history repeated itself again and the Pentecostal revivals were widely criticized by most other denominations.

We will skip over hundreds of descriptions of those meetings, because people expect Pentecostals do get "all emotional." I'll provide just one describing the Azusa Street Revival, but keep in mind that God does what He wants where He wants and as Charles Spurgeon said; we can miss a blessing when it doesn't come in the way we thought it properly should. Here is one account as described by Frank Bartleman, a holiness journalist who was part of the movement:

"Suddenly, the Spirit would fall upon the congregation. God himself would give the altar call. Men would fall all over the house, like the slain in battle, or rush to the altar en mass to seek God...the services ran almost continuously. Seeking souls could be found under the power almost any hour, night and day...God's presence became more and more wonderful. In that old building, God took strong men and women to pieces and put them together again for His glory. It was a tremendous overhauling process. Pride and self-assertion, self-importance and self-esteem could not survive there."[106]

In the mid 1900's, something new began to stir in both the Pentecostal camps and in the evangelical camps. In 1948, a very controversial movement commonly referred to as the "Latter Rain Revival," started in Canada and then spread to the United States and eventually on to other continents. The emphasis of the Latter Rain movement were the doctrines of the laying on of hands, prophecy, and corporate worship which was referred to as the heavenly choir. (According to some church historians, the Latter Rain movement influenced the charismatic movement, which broke forth a decade or two later and was very widespread.)

At almost the exact time that the Latter Rain movement was sweeping through Pentecostal circles (circa 1948-1952), revival began to stir among the non-Pentecostal evangelicals. Out of that movement, far-reaching ministries such as evangelist Billy Graham, who preached to millions; Bill Bright, who launched Campus Crusade for Christ; and Jim Rayburn, the director of Young Life, were launched.

In 1947, there was a meeting arranged by a Presbyterian named Henrietta Mears, who is known as the founder of the modern day Sunday School movement. Bill Bright was there. Here is one account:

"They prayed on into the late hours of the night, confessing sin, asking for guidance, and seeking the reality and power of the Holy Spirit. There was much weeping and crying out to the Lord...then the fire fell....God answered their prayers with a vision. They saw before them the campuses of the world teeming with unsaved students, who held in their hands the power to change the world. The campuses of the world – they were the key to world leadership, to world revival."[107]

This sounds like the same environment in which we have seen the Lord move before: Men and women weeping and crying out to the Lord, confessing sin, and seeking the move of the Holy Spirit. That's the environment in which miracles can occur. God moves when there is genuine repentance and a hunger for more of the Lord than we have experienced before.

In conclusion, it is time to forget the old ways, the ways of dissention and division. It is time for a fresh new way of viewing the body of Christ. It is time for a new thing to spring forth; something that only God can do; a door only He can open. As the Prophet Isaiah wrote:

[18] *"Do not remember the former things, nor consider the things of old.*
[19] *Behold, I will do a new thing, now it shall spring forth; Shall you not know it?*
I will even make a road in the wilderness and rivers in the desert. (Isaiah 43)

The church of Jesus Christ can become one, but first we must recognize our condition, and with humble hearts, repent of our divisions and our complacency. As we do, we will be visited by the Holy Spirit. He will come as He has come throughout history when men and women have sought Him with hungry hearts. Lord, grant us such hearts!

I am persuaded that you can see revival and restoration occur right in your home town. Don't worry about the rest of the world or the Catholic/Protestant divide. Get together with believers from other churches in your town and ask God to visit you. Begin with repentance and move to worship and do it until you are visited with revival.

Unity by way of persecution or revival? It seems likely that the choice is ours to make.

Plain ole Christians.

For most believers, especially in the western world, denomina-tionalism defines the Christianity we see around us. It is the only world we know. Seeing churches scattered all over town, all with different names and separate doctrines, is for us the norm. The *norm*. Let's consider for a moment what it means for something to be "the norm."

Children today grow up in a highly technological world. Devices that did not even exist a few decades ago are viewed as indispensible to their lives. Our kids cannot fathom a world without cell phones, ipods, laptop computers, and the ability to pause live TV. To those of us who grew up before the invention of microwaves, these new technologies must be learned. They are not our natural environment.

Denominationalism is to all of us what cell phones, ipods, and laptops computers are to our kids. They're the norm. We don't even think about them, because they're the only world we know. When something is your norm, you don't stop to question its legitimacy, which explains why we almost never ponder the legitimacy of being surrounded by so many brand names of Christianity. As a fish is not aware that it lives in the water, so we are not aware that we live in a world of terribly divided churches.

We say almost without thinking that we are Baptists or Southern Baptists, or American, Conservative, or Free Will Baptists. We say we are Pentecostals, but to be more precise we must say we are

Assembly of God, Open Bible, United Pentecostal, or Foursquare Pentecostals. We say we are Lutherans, but to be more accurate we must identify with a particular synod of Lutheranism. Methodists or Free Methodist, Presbyterian USA or Presbyterian Church of America. Church of God Cleveland, Church of God Anderson, Church of God in Christ, or Pentecostal Church of God. On and on and on it goes. With tens of thousands of denominations in existence, it is hard to think of a name some denomination has not taken already.

We do all of this branding with a preciseness and casualness that betrays our blindness to our sin.

"Plain ole Christians" are a rare breed these days. Almost all of us wear some sort of identifying tag, even if it is "nondenominational charismatic" or "nondenominational evangelical." Even community churches that pride themselves in being autonomous and nondenominational tend to fellowship exclusively or at least primarily with other churches that are of the same structure and doctrinal school and rarely fellowship with other churches that believe almost exactly as they do, but happen to be part of an organized denomination. In some sense, our nondenominational status makes us just another division of the body of Christ.

Watching all this in action, one might conclude that there are no people on earth more cliquish than Christians. Of course, if we are pressed on the matter, most of us will admit that we all worship the same God, believe all of the same essential doctrines, and are all baptized in the same name. Even though in our hearts we know these things, we do not act as if they are true.

Often, when we have occasion to sit down for a chat or visit with a fellow believer, one who does not belong to our particular brand of Christianity, the first thing we attempt to do is ascertain what species of Christian they are, so we will know the specific areas where we disagree with one another. Are they a Calvinist or do they believe in freewill? Are they charismatic or not? Do they dunk or do they sprinkle? Do people raise their hands in their church? Do they clap? Do they believe in a rapture before the tribulation?

This is how we find out what's "wrong" with the other guy. It is as if we would rather argue and "straighten one another out" than share together the goodness of our Savior's grace. These other matters may make for more "stimulating" conversation, but debating them nonstop is the opposite of the way one would go about building unity.

The source of our problem

I have thought long about this problem and pondered it from every angle I could imagine. I have tried to identify a single factor that makes us behave as we do. I think I may have found it.

Of course, we know from Paul's first letter to the Corinthian church that divisions stem from carnality. That's the root. But carnality is a pretty broad term and includes such things as pride, self-interest, greed, lust for power, lust for influence, and a desire for personal significance. These are *all* driving factors that lead to division, but I am not sure they fully explain why we do not see in the church a fervent desire to repent of our divisions and turn from them.

It occurs to me that the primary reason we remain where we are today is ignorance. Carnality may have divided us, but to some extent it is our ignorance that keeps us where we are. Our ignorance takes two forms. First, we are ignorant because we have not seen division as God sees it, as the debilitating curse that it is. We have not turned from our divisions, because we don't realize how bad they are. Second, but no less important, we have been ignorant of our desperate need for connection to one another. This may be our most serious problem. We desperately need one another, but don't realize it.

We have failed to see our need for connection

We have heard sermons about the body of Christ and how we are all part of that body and have different functions, but somehow we have missed the parts that speak of connection. We know that we all have different roles to play and different jobs to fulfill, but we have not understood that we cannot function in those roles unless we are connected to one another. This is especially debilitating because we have seen the body of Christ as our individual churches, ignoring the fact that there was only one church per city in the New Testament. Divisions other than on a city basis were unheard of.

As we stressed earlier, our local churches are like body parts scattered all over town with no connection to one another. If there is no connection of the parts, there is absolutely no way *"every part can supply"* what it has and the rest of the body needs. Can you conceive of a way a member of the body can serve the other members, if there is no fellowship among them and no meaningful connection? Here are Paul's familiar words from I Corinthians 12:

> *[20] But now indeed there are many members, yet one body. [21] And the eye cannot say to the hand, "I have no need of you"; nor again the head to the feet, "I have no need of you." [22] No, much rather, those members of the body which seem to be weaker are necessary. [23] And those members of the body which we think to be less honorable, on these we bestow greater honor; and our unpresentable parts have greater modesty, [24] but our presentable parts have no need. But God composed the body, having given greater honor to that part which lacks it, [25] that there should be no schism in the body, but that the members should have the same care for one another. [26] And if one member suffers, all the members suffer with it; or if one member is honored, all the members rejoice with it.*

The connection the apostle describes in this passage may be far more vital than we have acknowledged. The churches in our cities have suffered because they have not been connected to one another. We have been unable to function as a body, because we are not a body. We are rather an assortment of disconnected body parts scattered around town.

There is another aspect of our disconnection, which for some may even be more compelling. The New Testament tells us that our bodies are temples for the Lord, places where the Holy Spirit dwells in our "earthen vessels." It makes this point regarding our individual bodies, but it also says this in regard to believers collectively; that together we are being built into a temple for the Lord. Here's a passage from Ephesians 2:

¹⁹ Now, therefore, you are no longer strangers and foreigners, but fellow citizens with the saints and members of the household of God, ²⁰ having been built on the foundation of the apostles and prophets, Jesus Christ Himself being the chief cornerstone, ²¹ <u>in whom the whole building, being fitted together, grows into a holy temple in the Lord, ²² in whom you also are being built together for a dwelling place of God in the Spirit.</u>

As with the "body" language from I Corinthians 12, we see again in this passage the connectivity issue. In this case, Paul says *the building is being fitted together*; that we are *being built together* for a dwelling place of God in the Spirit. Think of a brick or stone building with every piece in place. It was not a building when there were piles of stone or bricks lying in piles around the building site. It became a building or a temple when all the parts were in their place and joined to one another.

The apostle Peter said it this way:

...you also, as living stones, are being built up a spiritual house, a holy priesthood, to offer up spiritual sacrifices acceptable to God through Jesus Christ. (I Peter 2:5)

The building is made of stones, but they are alive. We are those stones. Collectively, these passages make it pretty clear that God is building a spiritual house out of living stones and that God is going to dwell in it when it is finished. Consider the ramifications of that. Neither Peter nor Paul says that this has already happened. It is described as an ongoing process that has been undertaken with an end purpose in mind, *to make a place for God to dwell*.

What happens when the temple of God is finished?

I don't want to frighten you, but this sounds very much like the Old Testament Tabernacle of Moses and Temple of Solomon. When those two structures were finished, they were a dwelling place for the presence of God. In both of those cases, building materials were gathered before construction began. In the case of the Temple of

Solomon, it took many years to gather all the materials from which the temple was to be built. The gathering of materials started with David, but it was under his son Solomon that the temple was finished.

Here is the fascinating part: When all of the materials had been fully assembled; when everything was in its place and the structures were finished, the Lord arrived. His glory came down and filled the place; so much so that the priests could not minister because of the smoke that filled the house.

These Old Testament structures were merely shadows of the New Covenant temple – the one the Lord is assembling out of living stones. Here's what happened when the Tabernacle of Moses was completed:

> *So Moses finished the work. ³⁴ Then the cloud covered the tabernacle of meeting, and the glory of the LORD filled the tabernacle. ³⁵ And Moses was not able to enter the tabernacle of meeting, because the cloud rested above it, and the glory of the LORD filled the tabernacle.* (Exodus 40:33-35)

Can you imagine that? A pile of animal skins, wooden poles, and cloth materials was assembled into a portable gathering place, which had been constructed and furnished with six articles of furniture built out of wood, brass, and gold, according to God's specific instructions. Then when it was finished, the glory of God came and filled the place so powerfully that no one could enter.

When the Temple of Solomon was completed, several hundred years later, here's what happened:

> *When Solomon had finished praying, fire came down from heaven and consumed the burnt offering and the sacrifices; and the glory of the LORD filled the temple. ² And the priests could not enter the house of the LORD, because the glory of the LORD had filled the LORD's house. ³ When all the children of Israel saw how the fire came down, and the glory of the LORD on the temple, they bowed their faces to the ground on the pave-*

ment, and worshiped and praised the Lord, saying: "For He is good, For His mercy endures forever." (II Chronicles 7:1-3)

If the glory of the Lord filled the Old Testament Tabernacle of Moses and the Temple of Solomon, when they were finished, will the completion of the spiritual temple, which is the church, not result in the presence of the Lord in a way that has never been possible before? When the building materials are no longer scattered in piles all over town, but are connected – with every living stone in its proper place, will we not be the dwelling place for the presence of God like never before? Will the glory of the spiritual temple not exceed the glory of its Old Testament shadows?

That's why I believe connection is so vitally important. It is not enough to gather the building materials into piles and stockpile them around town. They must be brought together. We have not done so because we have not understood that we cannot be complete without being connected to one another. Yes, that includes the believers in all of those denominations and independent churches whom you have never met - or even wanted to meet. They need you and you need them, and we must all come to the place where we can acknowledge that and respond accordingly.

Yes, Baptists need Pentecostals. They cannot be complete without each other. Methodist believers need Presbyterians and Lutherans. "Church of God" believers need "Church of Christ" believers, and so on. Every part must be connected and those things which keep us apart must diminish, day by day, until they disappear.

Someone has said that the true New Testament church is like a bottle of medicine that has many ingredients in it, but there is no label on the bottle. It believes in salvation by faith in Christ, but there are no Lutherans. It practices baptism, but there are no Baptists. It believes in predestination, but there are no Presbyterians or Calvinists. It believes in holiness, but there are no Methodists. It fears God, but there are no Quakers. There are bishops, but no Episcopalians. It believes in the baptism of the Holy Spirit, but there are no Pentecostals. The ingredients are all there in the one bottle, but there are no labels to identify the ingredients and fragment the church. (Source unknown)

What do we do now?

So, where do we go from here? What can we do today to change our "norm" and reverse the course we are on? These are questions I pondered deeply before writing the first chapter of this book. I am sure that there will be others who will add to what I have said here and will say it better as the Lord leads them, but here are my suggestions.

It should go without saying that the first and most important thing we can do is to pray earnestly and ask the Lord to bring His people together. Pray alone. Pray in groups. Pray as a congregation. Pray as groups of pastors and elders across denominational lines. As we all begin to pray, things will begin to change, for the effectual, fervent prayer of righteous men avails much.[108]

Remember the prayer Jesus taught us all to pray? He said that when we pray, we are to say, "Thy will be done on earth as it is in Heaven." I taught my children to pray these words when they were young, even when they were praying over a meal. They would end each prayer by saying, "Most of all, Thy will be done on earth as it is in Heaven."

Why would Jesus tell us to pray for something that could not happen? He told us to pray for God's will to be done on earth, so we should, and we should believe for it and not be double-minded and secretly expect Satan's will to be done on earth. There is unity in Heaven, so we must pray that there will be unity amongst God's people here. I submit that we should pray specifically for the church to be perfectly one, as the Father and Son are one, because Jesus prayed for this to happen. This is a godly prayer. We have every right to ask the Lord to break down the denominational walls and all the other barriers which divide His people, for when we make such a request we are praying according to His expressed will.

When you drive by a Bible-believing church of any stripe, pray for the people there; pray that they will know the Lord and be blessed by His presence. Pray that their leaders will be moved to recognize the ways in which they are contributing to division and pray that they will turn and begin to do all they can to end all unscriptural divisions between them and other churches.

When anyone asks you what kind of church you go to, refuse to use any of the labels that divide. Tell people that you are just a "plain ole Christian." When they ask again or demand more specificity, simply say, "I believe that Jesus Christ is the Son of God and that He died for my sins and rose from the dead. I have submitted my life to His lordship. That's the kind of Christian I am. Is that the kind of Christian you are?"

If you are a denominational leader, suggest to the board that it sell its headquarter facilities and contribute the money to missions, turn over all its other buildings and real estate to local congregations, and free them to join with other local churches, as the Lord leads. Free them to be autonomous and self-governing. Free them to change the name of their church and end affiliation with the denomination. Suggest that the board begin to wind down all denomination's affairs and perhaps dissolve. The example of one denomination doing this could be the spark that changes the course of human history.

If you are a local church leader, begin to meet with the leaders of other Bible-believing churches in your area to pray, to plan regular joint worship services and joint evangelistic outreaches. Discuss ways your congregations can better be joined to one another. Pray for one another with a genuine spirit of brotherhood; not as competitors, but as fellow servants, as if one's hurts or successes are the others' – for indeed they are.

Above all, begin to repent together of your divisions. Repent with godly sorrow and tears. If it helps, wash one another's feet. I have seen that practice break barriers and accomplish humility like nothing else. The Son of God did this. Are we above our Master?

When your congregation meets, pray for specific churches in your town, especially those located closest to yours. Pray that God will bless them and that souls will be saved and that there will be no walls between you. As a congregation, pray for their success, as if their success is yours – for indeed it is.

Share with your congregation the things you learned in this study or elsewhere about church unity. Impart to the people in your church the vision for church unity that you have received. Make this a topic for small group studies, so as to make unity a priority among those in your flock.

Church unity is not a goal. It is not an end in itself. Unity is the gateway to the place where God commands the blessing. It is the place where the Lord of Glory comes to dwell. It is a place of spiritual maturity; a place where the people of God are no longer tossed to and fro by winds of doctrine. Unity is the place at which we must arrive for the world to know that Jesus Christ really was sent by God.

We mentioned earlier that many priceless truths were lost during the Dark Ages and most of those truths have been restored over the past 500 years. We talked about our denominations, to a large extent, being memorials to things that the Lord has done in the past.

A few days ago, my teenage daughter had a friend over from her church youth group. She told the boy that her dad was writing a book; so of course he was curious and asked what kind of book I was writing. I told him I was writing a book on church unity and the end of denominationalism. He immediately responded with these words, which he said he had heard someone say, but he couldn't remember who or where.

He said to me, "Telling me the name of your denomination doesn't tell me where you stand with God; it tells me where you stopped." I smiled. He was just a teenager, but he understood. The saying he shared there in our kitchen describes all of us, not just those *other* Christians.

We have forgotten that we are on a journey, and because we have forgotten, we have put down permanent stakes. We have remained camped when it was time to move on. All of us have stopped somewhere, at least at times. But we must remember ancient Israel in the wilderness and the cloud of God's presence they followed. Where the cloud moved, they moved. They picked up camp, took everything they possessed, and set out. It didn't matter how comfortable they were where they were camped. They moved when God moved, or they were left behind.

I believe the cloud is stirring again. It is time for God's people to get restless, shake off their complacency, and prepare to break camp.

It's time to become dissatisfied with where we stand. It's time to see the Promised Land up ahead, a land of *perfect unity*, precisely the kind of unity Jesus asked his Father to give us.

Epilogue

W hen I set out to write this book, I had in mind to talk about
the prayer of Jesus in John 17 and the passage in Ephesians
4 about the church growing to the full measure of the stature of the
fullness of Christ. In the course of my research, I came upon an
excellent book, which I have referenced several times here, "Floods
Upon the Dry Ground," by Charles P. Schmitt. With the permission
of the author, I will close this study with the Epilogue from his book.
If I had written my own, this is what I too would have said:

"When we look at what actually exists at present…we see a
church that has come a long way in recovery since the Dark
Ages. But we see a church that is still very immature and very
much divided (if not in love, then surely in faith). That which
is yet on the horizon for this generation is clearly that final forward push towards 'the measure of the stature of the fullness of
Christ,' that we may '*all* attain to the unity of the faith, and of the
knowledge of the Son of God, to a mature man…' Thus the fervent prophetic prayer of our Lord Jesus in His final hours for the
oneness of His church will be answered visibly upon the earth--
'that they all may be one, even as Thou, Father, art in Me, and I
in Thee, that they also may be in Us; that the world may believe
that thou didst send Me.'…The most important thing for us in
this generation is that we simply walk very tenderly and softly
before the Lord, so as not to second-guess how exactly He shall
consummate all things in His church and bring in everlasting

righteousness…In every generation He has wrought a brand-new thing. And we are truly on the threshold of a further brand-new working of God that is destined to bring *all* true believers together…that all the world might know and see that He has sent His Son, Jesus, to be the Savior of the world! Hallelujah!"

Amen, Pastor Schmitt! May all those who love the Truth and are called by the name of Jesus Christ be one. May all of God's people be hungry for a fresh move of the Spirit, the kind that changes the course of human history and lets the whole world know in an undeniable way that Jesus was sent to us by the Father. Let us all believe for this!

I leave you with this one final thought: Don't ask yourself if what you have read about church unity in this book is possible or even likely; ask rather if it's *biblical.* If it's biblical, then it's not only possible, but inevitable. Recall to mind the prayer that was uttered by the Son of God, in John 17, that we would all be one as He and the Father are one. Remember who said those words. It shall be with that prayer, which came forth from the mouth of God, precisely as the Lord spoke through the prophet Isaiah, saying,

"So shall My word be that goes forth from My mouth;
It shall not return to Me void,
But it shall accomplish what I please,
And it shall prosper *in the thing* **for which I sent it."**
(Isaiah 55:11)

####################

Watch for Book II, "The Un-Fractured Church," coming next. Join with us as we return with the apostle Paul to the fictional Corinth of chapter 5, where the apostle will meet with the elders of the divided churches there and tell them what they should do to end their denominational divisions.

We have a program available on our website, www.fractured-church.com, for you to have a copy of "The Fractured Church" mailed as a gift to someone you think should read it. Also avail-

able on the website are "Fractured Church Study Guides" and other useful aids to further the work of church unity.

We provide on the website regular updates regarding cities that are taking steps to establish church unity, crossing denominational and even charismatic/non-charismatic lines. You will be blessed and encouraged to learn of the progress others are making and please tell us of yours. May the Lord bless you and empower you as you seek to do His will.

End Notes

[1] Acts 8:9-24

[2] Mathew 16:8

[3] The designation of "sainthood" reserved only for special deceased Christians is foreign to Scripture

[4] *Epistle of Clement to the Corinthians* 22:14 and 19:5-6

[5] Charles P. Schmitt, *Floods Upon the Dry Ground*, (Revival Press 1992), 18

[6] Philip Schaff, *History of the Christian Church*, Vol. 1 (New York: Charles Scribner's Sons, 1882), 491-498

[7] Lars P. Qualben, *A History of the Christian Church*, (New York, Thomas Nelson & Sons, 1933), 86, 96

[8] Charles P. Schmitt, *Floods Upon the Dry Ground*, (Revival Press 1992), 16

[9] Acts 12:23

[10] Matthew 19:28

[11] Revelations 21:14

[12] Mark 16:17-18

[13] The Book of the Revelation 2:2

[14] Signs that could be proven in a court of law

[15] Acts 20:23

[16] There may be in Scripture a marked difference between the spirit of prophecy, the gift of prophecy, and the office of a prophet

[17] I Thessalonians 5:19-21

[18] *Readers interested in delving further into this issue might wish to review "Why Apostles Now," by Ernest Gentile and "Apostles, the Fathering Servants" by Bill Scheidler. These studies will at least stimulate further thought.*

[19] Lars P. Qualben, *A History of the Christian Church*, (New York, Thomas Nelson & Sons, 1933), 98

[20] II John 1:7 and I John 4:3

[21] Charles P. Schmitt, *Floods Upon the Dry Ground*, (Revival Press 1992), 45

[22] Items of clothing, personal possessions, and even body parts of the apostles and deceased saints

[23] Justin Martyr, *Dialogue with Trypho*, in Vol. 1 of the Ante-Nicene Christian Fathers, eds. Alexander Roberts and James Donaldson (Peabody, MA: Hendrickson Publishers, Inc. 1994), 240, 243

[24] Irenaeus, *Against Heresies*, in Vol. 1 of the *Ante-Nicene Christian Fathers*, eds. Alexander Roberts and James Donaldson (Edinburgh: T&T Clark, 1874), 409, 531

[25] Tertullian, *Against Marcion*, in Vol. 3 of the Ante-Nicene Christian Fathers

[26] Novatian, *The Trinity*

[27] John W. Kennedy, *The Torch of the Testimony* (Gospel Literature Service, 1965; Goleta, CA: Christian Books, reprint), 122

[28] "Johann Tetzel" *Encyclopedia Britannica* 2007

[29] Charles P. Schmitt, *Floods Upon the Dry Ground*, (Revival Press 1992), 87

[30] Florenumdus Raemundus, *"History of the Origin etc. of the Heresies of the 16th Century"*

[31] John H. Armstrong, *Your Church Is Too Small*, (Zondervan 2010), 131

[32] John 6:27-29

[33] John Calvin, who came shortly after Luther, also believed in the perpetual virginity of Mary.

[34] Murray, Stuart (2010). *The Naked Anabaptist: The Bare Essentials of a Radical Faith*. Herald Press

[35] Many contend that were actually three awakenings, including the Pentecostal movement and charismatic renewal

[36] Richard Riss, *Latter Rain – The Latter Rain movement of 1948 and the Mid-Twentieth Century Evangelical Awakening*

[37] Jennifer LeClaire, *Charisma News, Pentecostals Growing with Church Plants, April 4, 2012*

[38] Patterson, Eric; Rybarczyk, Edmund (editors) (2007). *The Future of Pentecostalism in the United States*. New York: Lexington Books. p. 158

[39] Acts chapter 4

[40] Matthew 15:26-28

[41] Acts 11:18

[42] James 1:5

[43] John chapter 1

[44] II Peter 1:21

[45] Isaiah 28:10-13

[46] Exodus 25:31-40

[47] Daniel 4:19-37

[48] A.W. Tozer, *The Pursuit of God*, (Camp Hill, PA, Christian Publications, Inc., 1993)

[49] *Books by "non-rapture" authors such as Kenneth L. Gentry, Jr., Gary DeMar, and David Chilton offer readers an entirely different perspective than many have heard. One of my favorite books addressing the end times is, "The Final Triumph," by Ernest Gentile. This book lists every verse in the Old and New Testa-*

ments regarding the coming of the Lord. Seeing all of those verses together, back to back, is highly enlightening and "perspective changing."

[50] II Timothy 3:16

[51] Luke 18:8

[52] Deuteronomy 6:4

[53] *Pentecostal Evangel* 1950

[54] Hebrew 8:1-13 and Galatians 3:24

[55] A.W. Tozer, *The Pursuit of God*, (Camp Hill, PA, Christian Publications, Inc., 1993)

[56] David Platt, *Radical: taking back your faith from the American dream*, (Colorado Springs, CO Multnomah Books 2010)

[57] Francis Schaeffer, *The Mark of a Christian*, (Downers Grove, IL, Inter Varsity Press 1970)

[58] Francis Schaeffer, *The Mark of a Christian*, (Downers Grove, IL, Inter Varsity Press 1970)

[59] Ephesians 4

[60] II Timothy 3:16.

[61] Matthew 10:34

[62] Francis Schaeffer, *The Mark of a Christian*, (Downers Grove, IL, Inter Varsity Press 1970)

[63] Acts 20:29 and Matthew 7:15

[64] II Corinthians 11:14

[65] John 14:6

[66] John 3:36

[67] Acts 4:11-13

[68] Hebrews 1:6

[69] Watchtower publications rarely state the doctrinal positions of the Jehovah's Witnesses. They appear quite mainstream on the surface.

[70] *Discourses of Brigham Young, Pg.53-54*

[71] John A. Widtsoe, *Evidences and Reconciliations, Pg.209*

[72] National churches often maintain very large numbers due to their status as the "official" church of a nation. One should not infer from those numbers that everyone, or even a majority of those who are members of national churches, believe the Gospel and are indeed Christians. That is a matter for God to sort out.

[73] James 3:17

[74] Matthew 10:33-35

[75] Revelation 5:12-13

[76] II Timothy 3:7

[77] Colossians 2:3

[78] I Corinthians 13

[79] Ephesians 4:2

[80] I John 4:20

[81] The anathemas of the Council of Trent

[82] Matthew 12

[83] Romans 3:23

[84] Luke 1:47-48

[85] Eastern Orthodox Churches also embrace most of the Mary doctrines

[86] Mark 7:13, Matthew 15:6, Colossians 2:7

[87] *The Catholic Encyclopedia*, (New York, Encyclopedia Press, Inc. 1917)

[88] I Corinthians 7:6-12 and verse 25

[89] in the Gloss on the Extravaganza of John XXII, (AD 1316-1334)

[90] Christopher Marcellus in Oration addressing Pope Julius II, in Fifth Lateran Council, Session IV (1512), Council Edition. Colm. Agrip. 1618, (Sacrorum Conciliorum, J.D. Mansi (ed.), Vol. 32, col. 761)

[91] Augustinus Triumphus, in Summa de Potestate Ecclesiastica, 1483, questio 6. Latin.

[92] *Roman Catholic Confessions for Protestants Oath, Article XI, (Confessio Romano-Catholica in Hungaria Evangelicis publice praescripta te proposita, editi a Streitwolf)*

[93] C.F.W. Walther, *Concerning the Name "Lutheran"* Der Lutheraner v. 1, pp. 2-4, 5-7, 9-12. translated by Mark Nispel 1994

[94] *Quanto Conficiamur Moerore, DNZ:1677, (quoted in Apostolic Digest, by Michael Malone, Book 5: "The Book of Obedience", Chapter 1: "There is No Salvation Without Personal Submission to the Pope")*

[95] Unam Sanctam, Bull promulgated on November 18, 1302

[96] Unlike Vatican I, held nearly a century earlier, non-Catholics were actually invited to attend Vatican II as observers. In fact, seventeen Protestant and Orthodox observers attended.

[97] Pope John XXIII began the council at Paul VI presided at its end

[98] Daniel B. Clendenin, *Eastern Orthodox Christianity: A Western Perspective* (Grand Rapids, MI: Baker Books, 1994)

[99] In some parts of China, officials ignore house churches and in other parts, leaders are imprisoned and beaten, if caught.

[100] Colin C. Whittaker, *Great Revivals*, (Springfield, MO: Radiant Books, 1984)

[101] Charles P. Schmitt, *Floods Upon the Dry Ground*, (Revival Press 1992),

[102] James B. Finley, *Sketches of Western Methodism* (1854)

[103] Charles P. Schmitt, *Floods Upon the Dry Ground*, (Revival Press 1992),

[104] Charles P. Schmitt, *Floods Upon the Dry Ground*, (Revival Press 1992), 153

[105] Baptist minister R. Boyd, as quoted by Charles Schmitt

[106] Bartleman, as quoted by Richard Riss and Tim Peterson

[107] Ethel May Baldwin and David B. Benson, *Henrietta Mears and How She Did It!* (Glendale, CA: Gospel Lighthouse Publications, 1966) 232

[108] James 5:16